AMERICAN
BISHOP
AT THE
VATICAN
COUNCIL

AMERICAN BISHOP AT THE VATICAN COUNCIL

Recollections and Projections by

BISHOP ROBERT E. TRACY

McGraw-Hill Book Company
New York · Toronto · London · Sydney

AMERICAN BISHOP AT THE VATICAN COUNCIL

Library of Congress Catalog Card Number: 66-26583

65131

Preface *c./*

One of the most surprising aspects of my experience at Vatican Council II was my own reporting of it.

This reporting, which eventually covered all four sessions, first began on a private scale and was made to a limited circle of persons. Later, unexpectedly, it developed a public aspect by way of a brief weekly account, during the fourth session, to *America* magazine. My present attempt to write a book on the Council, however, represents the most surprising reportorial development of all.

My initial interest in reporting the Council stemmed from a pastoral impulse to provide the priests, religious and laity of my diocese with a clear and warm account of everything of interest that was about to transpire at Rome as the Council opened in 1962. In addition, I decided to send my report also to relatives, friends and former students of mine to whom I write at least once a year, especially at Christmas time.

Thus, over the four-year period, I produced 24 eight-page "Rome Letters" which were mailed out to some 2,500 people. Our diocesan newspaper *The Catholic Commentator* also published portions of the letters as they appeared. At first the letters were written every two weeks, but toward the end of the Council they were coming out every single week.

These "Rome Letters" reached people quickly. I always tried to send them air mail, special delivery, from the main post office

of Rome, in the Piazza San Silvestro, no later than 5:30 P.M. on
Friday so that they would be at the chancery in Baton Rouge
on the following Monday morning.

When my envelope reached our chancery, the transcribing
and mailing of my current "Rome Letter" was given a priority.
Cynthia Duhon and Susan Schwab, my secretaries, would immediately type the text for the duplimat; and Jay Acaldo, our
printer, would run it through the accumulated traffic of various
printing jobs waiting in his office, like an ambulance going
through stop lights. John J. Kennedy, head of our data processing
division, organized the addressing, stamping and sorting of the
envelopes in advance, by the crew who run our IBM machines.
Therefore, my "Rome Letters" were normally in the main post
office of Baton Rouge by 5:00 P.M. on the same day they arrived. Thus my news from Rome was fairly fresh when it was
received.

At the start of the fourth session, Father Thurston N. David,
S.J., editor-in-chief of the national Jesuit weekly *America,* asked
me to send him a report on the Council each week. I was thrilled
by the invitation. I had no idea that a national publication like
America would have any interest in the rather informally written material I was mailing home. Besides, the prospect of writing
each week for *America* had certain attractive angles: This would
be my first regular paying job as a writer; it would force me to
become more alert, to work harder and to study more thoroughly
matters and developments at the Council; and it would mean
very little extra work since I was already writing each week
for the home folks. I had only to mail Father Davis a carbon of
my regular "Rome Letter" and let him select whatever he wished
from it for publication in *America.*

My next surprise was to receive in Rome a letter from David
H. Scott, then of the McGraw-Hill Book Company, asking that
I write a book on the Council for publication as soon as possible
after its closing! Father Walter M. Abbott, S.J., of the *America*
staff, it seems, had been kind enough to show him some of my
letters.

Mr. Scott wrote that, although there was no lack of books

about the Council, I was perhaps in a position to make a unique contribution to the field of Council literature. He pointed out that nearly all volumes on the Council which had appeared so far fell mainly into two categories: either they were written by *experts*—that is, professional theologians, historians, etc.—or they were written by *journalists* who had no votes in the proceedings. Mine could perhaps be the first volume written by an American bishop in the role of simply a *pastor*. He felt that my account would have a certain authenticity, pastoral character and personal quality not found in any of the other Council books thus far published.

I was certainly willing to try. Again, I felt it would be a good thing for me to do, for it would compel me to undertake a further amount of reading, as well as a round-up of all matters connected with the Council. It would also give me an opportunity to play a small role, perhaps, in helping people to make contact with the mind of the Council. Besides, it would be exciting, I felt, to be working on a book for the first time in my life.

After consultation with knowledgeable people, it gradually became clear to me what I should strive after in my book. And my objectives are now the following:

First of all, the basic point-of-view, the central approach and the tone of the book is one of pastoral concern.

My specific aim is to help clarify the Council and its work for the average layman. Many of my good friends have said, in ways that made me believe them, that my Rome letters made them feel that they were "right here at the Council" and that my letters gave them information they did not find in newspaper accounts.

Clarifying the Council for the average layman, I feel, means avoiding the matters which are too involved and technical, as well as matters which are hardly calculated to hold his interest. My account therefore does not aim at completeness in its reporting; yet I hope that I have not overlooked anything essential to the story of the Council, as I have proposed to tell it.

My approach involves a certain amount of chronicle and also

some interpretation as to *how* various important developments came about. It includes, in addition, accounts of my impressions, experiences, conversations, reading and action at the Council.

I also attempt, here and there, to sketch vignettes of notable personalities; for the Council made it possible for us to come into contact with some of the outstanding church people of our time.

Expectations and predictions about the effect of the Council on the life of the average Catholic, its impact on Americans generally, and the problems of the future bring my story to a close. But not, I hope, before I have done my own small bit in helping to make the Council better understood by the "everyday" Catholic.

The Council was to me a priceless opportunity to become educated in those things so utterly important to the life of the Church and to the world in our times. If I can help, even in a minor way, others who have not had my own good fortune to be present and active at the Council to understand it better and, especially, to imbibe something of its renewed, vigorous and open new spirit, I shall be more than happy and feel wonderfully repaid.

I wish to acknowledge with gratitude the editorial services of David and Kitty Scott, as well as those of Monsignor Patrick Gillespie, Father C.J. McNaspy, S.J., and Father Walter Abbott, S.J., the research services of Miss Regina Schmidt and Miss Jacqueline Hatrel, and the secretarial services of Mrs. Cynthia Duhon and Mrs. Evelyn Roubique.

Contents

AMERICAN
BISHOP
AT THE
VATICAN
COUNCIL

Chapter 1

My Preparation for the Council

It was on August 16, 1959, that a letter from the Vatican, signed by "D. Card. Tardini," arrived on my desk in the rectory at Abbeville, Louisiana, where I was pastor of the parish of St. Mary Magdalen and Auxiliary Bishop of the Diocese of Lafayette. The letter was dated two months earlier—June 18—and requested "the transmission (to His Eminence) as soon as possible, and not later than September 1, 1959, of my opinions, sentiments, convictions and requests as one of the Fathers to be called by law to the forthcoming Ecumenical Council." That gave me—a newly appointed Auxiliary Bishop—exactly two weeks to comply. The late arrival of my letter was probably due to the fact it took a little time for the Cardinal's office to get word that I had become a bishop. In fact, I had been consecrated only three months earlier.

In reply to Cardinal Tardini's letter, I wrote to say that I wished to be excused from submitting my opinions and ideas. I was "a new boy at school"; I had received the request only two weeks before the deadline; and, in view of these considerations, I wished simply to endorse whatever recommendations my superior, Bishop Maurice Schexnayder of Lafayette, Louisiana, may have entered, etc., etc.

But perhaps my story about the Council really begins earlier in 1959, on January 25. This was the ever-famous day on which Pope John XXIII revealed privately, to the seventeen cardinals who attended him at the feast-day Mass at St. Paul-outside-the-Walls at Rome, his intention to call the first ecumenical council of the Church since 1870. According to reports, the cardinals were completely taken by surprise.

My own introduction to the Council was also, in its own way, mildly dramatic.

On the same Sunday evening, January 25, 1959, I arrived in Chicago by plane from New Orleans, en route to a national meeting of Newman Club chaplains at Notre Dame University. At the time, I was charged with the care of the 4,000 Catholic students enrolled at Louisiana State University in Baton Rouge.

Wearily, I walked toward my room at the Conrad Hilton Hotel, but hardly had I inserted my key into the lock of my door than I overheard an excited voice which gave me my first intimation of that great event which was destined to affect so profoundly my own life as well as the life of the Church.

The voice was that of a young man farther down the corridor, walking beside his wife, and casually looking at an opened newspaper as he walked along. Something in the newspaper suddenly caught his eye, for he stopped and called out excitedly to his wife:

"Say, will you look at this!"

"Look at what?"

"This news about the Pope in this evening's paper. It says here that he is going to call a council."

"A council? What's that?"

I waited to hear no more, but turned back to the elevator with as much speed as I could summon to buy a paper. Never has an elevator dragged or stopped at so many floors as this one did. Meanwhile my thoughts were doing rapid flashbacks, hurriedly digging out of my memory whatever material had been stored there about Church councils.

I remembered, quickly enough, that there were different levels of councils, for I could recall the ancient *local* councils of Carthage and Hippo (from the Bible classes I was teaching at the time at LSU) and also the *plenary* councils of Baltimore, as well as the four *provincial* councils of New Orleans. However, this

council of Pope John's was to be a *general* council of the whole
Church.

"Well, let's see," I pondered, "among the general councils of
the Church there were: Nicaea . . . Ephesus . . . Florence . . .
Trent . . . and, of course, the Vatican Council of 1870. Hmm
. . . Now which were some of the others?"

"Main floor—lobby!"

This announcement by the elevator boy snapped me back into
the twentieth century. I dashed from the elevator to pick up the
first newspaper available at the stand, almost forgetting to pay for
it in my preoccupation.

There it was, all right, in black and white:

VATICAN CITY (AP)—Pope John XXIII Sunday summoned
an ecumenical council of the Roman Catholic Church aimed at unit-
ing the Christian forces of the world. His action was historic
and unexpected.

The 77-year-old pontiff made the announcement on the anniversary of the conversion of St. Paul, the Roman Jew, who, according to Christian belief, saw a vision of Christ while on his way to
Damascus to persecute Christians. After his conversion he preached
the gospel of Christ to the gentiles.

The wording of the Vatican statement indicated that Christian
churches outside the Roman Catholic Church may be invited to
participate in the council, at least as observers. Ecumenical means
worldwide.

There has not been an ecumenical council for nearly a century.
Such a council brings together cardinals, archbishops and bishops
of the Church from all over the world. . . .

Thus did the Second Ecumenical Council of the Vatican enter
my life and my consciousness for the first time. But at the moment I had no reason to suspect that I might ever become personally involved in its action. Hence it did not occur to me that I
might possibly attend the Council, speak there as one of the Fathers, or, most fantastic of all, one day write a book about it!

At the time I was Right Reverend Monsignor Tracy and, as I
have said, chaplain-in-charge at the Catholic Student Center,

LSU. The very fact that I feel it necessary to explain how I became qualified to become a responsible participant in the Council suggests that I might also appropriately add here something brief, by way of introduction, regarding my identity and personal history.

I was born on September 14, 1909, in New Orleans, Louisiana. Indeed, I claim to be the first native-born New Orleanian to become a bishop in all the 248-year history of that venerable city. This claim is politely contested by Monsignor Henry C. Bezou of New Orleans who, in the course of the discussion of this point, at the time of my consecration, cited, in the interest of accuracy, the following unusual happening as evidence to the contrary:

It seems that in the early days of the city a certain English sea captain put his ship into port at New Orleans and immediately brought his wife, who was about to give birth to a child, to the city's hospital where, so the account goes, she presented him with a son who later went on to become a bishop somewhere in England.

I will leave it to you, dear reader, to judge whether or not such a fleeting contact with my native city really does make this rival of mine an authentic "native New Orleanian." Or perhaps it is better that we leave this momentous dispute of whether or not I am the first "Nouvelle-Orléannais" to reach the episcopacy to a later day when, as my namesake, Robert Emmet, the great Irish patriot, said in the dock, "Other men and other times can do justice to my memory."

As you may have guessed, I was born of Irish parentage, or more precisely, Irish ancestry. It was my great-grandfathers—one on each side of the family—who first came to New Orleans during the 1840's when the famine in Ireland sent so many immigrants to the shores of the United States.

The Irish who came to New Orleans, in the early days, nearly all settled in a strip of the city located roughly between Magazine Street and the river and between Canal Street and Louisiana Avenue. This was "uptown" New Orleans, and American—as distinguished from "downtown" New Orleans which was French. "Uptown" was on one side of the great main boulevard called Canal Street, the widest in the United States, and "downtown" on the other. Seldom did people cross from one section of the city to the other. My first and only appointment as a curate was to St. Leo's in downtown New Orleans; and to tell the truth, I hardly knew how to reach my assignment, so seldom had I visited this "other city."

For one hundred years New Orleans had but one parish church, that of St. Louis, the ancestor of the present basilica in Jackson Square. But with the coming of Irish immigrations, a second church was built, the celebrated St. Patrick's on Camp Street in "uptown" New Orleans, in the heart of what came to be known as "the Irish Channel," or simply "the Channel" as everyone calls it even to this day.

All my family on both sides came from the Channel, and our life there revolved about the parish served by the Redemptorist Fathers for more than a hundred years.

After parochial elementary school in New Orleans, I studied under the Benedictine Fathers at St. Joseph Seminary and Abbey at St. Benedict, Louisiana, between the years 1921 and 1926.

Today, the Abbey church and refectory are famous for their colorful murals by Dom Gregory De Witt, O.S.B. Even the barbershop has been ornamented by the hand of the artist. This monastery barbershop is decorated with a unique portrayal of the scene of the home at Nazareth done with a few delightful anachronistic touches. St. Joseph is in the process of cutting the hair of the Child Jesus who is sitting on a high stool in the kitchen. St. Joseph is wearing spectacles and the Blessed Mother is seated nearby, knitting, in a rocking chair. There is a Catholic calendar on the wall and a tiny angel is sweeping up the golden locks of the Baby Jesus as they are cut and fall to the floor. St. Joseph is wearing his halo and so is the Blessed Mother; but the halo of the Child Jesus is hung on a nail in the wall while he gets his hair cut. The final touch to the picture is the inscription beneath it:

> Not a hair falls from your head
> Without the will of your Father
> Who is in Heaven.

In September, 1926, I entered Notre Dame Seminary in New Orleans to begin studies in philosophy and theology. There, after six years under the tutelage of the good Marist Fathers, I was graduated and ordained a priest on June 12, 1932.

I wish now that I had paid better attention during my classes in church history in which I sat for five years! Had I done so, perhaps I could have stored up all sorts of data on general councils. But how could I have known, then, that I would become involved so intimately in a general council one day?

However, a number of difficult but very helpful experiences, early in my priesthood, aided me in rounding out my education —informally, but not at all ineffectively. I was hardly ordained, at the age of 22, and appointed a curate at St. Leo the Great Church in New Orleans, than my pastor, Father Vincent Prats, was stricken permanently with arthritis. Then, before it was possible to appoint an administrator of the parish to assume the pastor's responsibilities, the Archbishop of New Orleans, John William Shaw, died. Thus, because of unusual circumstances, I acted for two years and a half as administrator, without any assistance, in a large city parish, in the very depths of the great depression years—that is, during the early 1930's.

The parish had a debt of $150,000 which, in those times, was quite a crusher. Thousands of people were out of work and, single-handed, I had to conduct nine parish novena services every Tuesday, each service jammed to the guards with people praying for a way out of their distress.

In May, 1935, the new Archbishop, Joseph Francis Rummel, arrived in New Orleans, and he lost no time in sending the present pastor, Monsignor James J. Gillespie, to St. Leo's to take charge, while I remained on as curate. By this time I had aged considerably—I was then all of 25 years of age and a real veteran in parish administration!

The thirty months of my administratorship were a sobering experience for me. But they were also a good education in practical, pastoral science.

I soon had another opportunity for informal education (unwittingly in preparation for the distant council) with my appointment as director of the Confraternity of Christian Doctrine for the Archdiocese of New Orleans in 1938. This assignment required me to do a great deal of teaching of religion to hundreds of lay catechists and religious sisters and a certain amount of study on my own, over a period of nine years. I was forced to read and consult professional theologians merely to keep my head above water.

My next opportunity for "do-it-yourself" education came in 1941 when I was asked to go over to Tulane University and its affiliate Newcomb College in New Orleans, both 25 per cent Catholic in enrollment, and work out a CCD program for the Catholic students there. The Catholic student leaders, many of whom I correspond with even to this day, were looking for study groups and lectures in philosophy and religion. This forced me to go back once more to the books and also to explore volumes on subjects I had never even studied before—subjects like anthropology, genetics, and experimental psychology.

When the present Bishop of Lafayette, Maurice Schexnayder, was advanced to the largest parish in the Archdiocese of New Orleans, that of St. Francis de Sales in Houma, Louisiana (a burgeoning oil center down near the Gulf of Mexico), on May 15, 1946, I was called upon to succeed him as head chaplain of the Catholic students at Louisiana State University. This appointment came, I have always thought, because at the time I was perhaps the only other priest in the archdiocese engaged in Newman work; and of course, my appointment quickly solved a difficult problem for Archbishop Rummel—that of staffing a Catholic student center on a secular campus.

At LSU, for more than 40 years, there has existed a religious council which has brought the campus religious leaders together, once a month, for a luncheon with top university officials, in a spirit of what we would now, in Council language, call "ecumenism." The administrators of LSU were actively ecumenical as far back as 1929, to my knowledge, and perhaps even farther back than that. As a result, particularly because of the interest shown in the past by General Troy H. Middleton, as president, by Dr. Paul M. Hebert, K.S.G., as acting president, by Major Fred C.

Frey, as dean of the university, and by Arden O. French, as dean of men, an excellent foundation has already been laid in our diocese. I was able to go to the Council already well-conditioned to the ecumenical approach, due to my training in it received at LSU.

At LSU I was deeply involved, of course, in religious education. This has bearing on the Council, too. For one of the areas in which I took special interest at Rome was the discussion of the conciliar schema on Christian Education.

In 1954 I was chosen to serve as national chaplain of the Newman Club Federation and as chairman of the National Newman Chaplains' Association. In the former post, I was national chaplain to all the Catholic students enrolled at non-Catholic colleges in the entire United States. In the latter capacity, I chaired the regular meetings of all the priests assigned to serve as their chaplains. We used to meet—students and chaplains—three times a year at all the long holidays (Christmas, Easter and during the summer) at colleges across the country. During the two years of my tenure, 1954–1956, I flew 50,000 miles a year on campus visits.

Newman work was coming into its own. It was beginning to gain recognition as a positive apostolate of the Church and not just a life line thrown out to Catholic students on the secular campus in order to "save their faith."

My immediate predecessor as national chaplain, Paul J. Hallinan, was a man in the same positive tradition as the founder of the Newman Club in 1893, Father John Keough, and that aggressive Newman leader of the 'twenties, Father John O'Brien. Paul Hallinan was a man strongly committed to an educational program, not just a pastoral one. He had written a fresh "Newman Club Manual," which to this day remains the Magna Carta of the modern Newman movement. I agreed to succeed him in the national office mainly because I wanted to make sure that his forward-looking program for the Catholic youth on non-Catholic campuses would be continued.

Paul Hallinan will appear often in the story I have to tell about the Council. Today he is the Archbishop of Atlanta and is to be found among the seven or eight American prelates constantly mentioned in the news as a possible candidate for the red hat of a cardinal.

On March 18, 1959, I received word that I was to become an auxiliary bishop in the diocese of Lafayette, Louisiana, assistant to Bishop Maurice Schexnayder.

I remained on the LSU campus, still acting as chaplain, until July 1, 1959, when I departed to take up my duties in the Lafayette Diocese—a period of three months and a half during which the students referred to me (behind my back) as "His Grace, Trace." My consecration as a bishop had taken place on May 19, 1959, in St. Louis Cathedral in New Orleans with the present Apostolic Delegate, Archbishop Egidio Vagnozzi, as principal consecrator. It was his first episcopal consecration in the United States.

I was pastor of St. Mary Magdalen Parish in Abbeville, Louisiana, from July 1, 1959, to January 1, 1960—exactly six months. I was then assigned by Bishop Schexnayder to Our Lady of Fatima Parish, in Lafayette.

In August, 1961, I was appointed by the Holy See to Baton Rouge, this time as Ordinary of a new diocese comprising twelve civil counties, cut off from the Archdiocese of New Orleans. On November 8, 1961, I was installed as Bishop of Baton Rouge, a diocese composed of 44,000 Catholic homes and 160,000 souls, in an area of 5,600 square miles on either side of the Mississippi River. Baton Rouge, the capital of the state of Louisiana, was founded in 1722, and its cathedral and its historical records are some of the oldest in the United States.

With this introduction to myself, I trust that you have gained an image of the kind of American bishop to whom Cardinal Tardini directed his letter. Let me, then, begin my narrative of that extraordinary experience which came to me when I traveled to Rome to participate in the Second Ecumenical Council of the Vatican.

Chapter 2

The Year of the Great Council

Domenico Cardinal Tardini, who opened my account with a letter addressed to me in 1959, must also open this chapter in his role as chief conciliar executive for Pope John XXIII in the months that followed. Tardini's letter was the first official document I received about the Council. And I was very happy to get it, for I was not sure until then whether "mere auxiliaries" would be invited. Here at least was a ticket to the ball game. I especially liked having Tardini refer to me as a *"futurus Concilii Pater"*—a future Father of the Council. With that phrase—auxiliary or not—I was "in." After that, I could hardly wait for the Council to open.

Cardinal Tardini had been appointed by Pope John to head what was known as the Ante-Preparatory Commission of the Council. Tardini, in turn, chose Archbishop Pericle Felici as his secretary general. In this post, Felici became prominent at the Council meetings in St. Peter's and will be mentioned frequently in this account. But Tardini, unfortunately, died before the Council even opened. Though I never knew him except by reputation—which was awesome—his death was a great loss.

Tardini was a remarkable man, and many of the plans and blueprints of the Council, regrettably, went to the grave with him, for he kept many things connected with the Council in his head. Pope John had great confidence in him, and since he was highly capable, energetic—and conciliatory to boot—Tardini, had he lived, could have rendered immense service in ordering and smoothing over many Council matters as they came up for attention. He had familiarized himself so well with the ante-preparatory and preparatory phases of the Council and, at the same time, was so close to Pope John and knew his mind so well, that no one else could possibly have gone back and recovered all the fine resources which Tardini had developed. So when Tardini died, Pope John, one might say, lost his right-hand man, and the Council got off to a rockier start than it otherwise might have done.

It may be well to clarify, here, how preparation for the Council was organized under Tardini and Felici, as I learned about it in Abbeville and Lafayette. First, there were to be "ante-preparatory" and the "preparatory" phases, entailing mainly three things:

Ante-preparatory: (1) The requesting and cataloguing of the "opinions, sentiments, convictions and requests" of the 2,600 bishops of the world of whom more than 2,000 replied; (2) The setting up and organizing of the "preparatory commissions and secretariats" which were to *process* this material.

Preparatory: (3) The actual casting of this material into "schemas" or documents to be debated when the Council opened.

Once the Council opened, there were to be two more phases of Council work: (1) The debate, refinement and voting in connection with the subject matter submitted in the various schemas; and (2) the approval and promulgation of the conciliar documents by the Holy Father.

Twelve preparatory commissions and three secretariats were established by the Pope, bringing together what seemed to be the flower of the Church's resources—hundreds of expert bishops, writers and scholars. These men labored for three years on the initial schemas, yet it is interesting to note how different were the final conciliar texts on most subjects, after they had been debated and voted on by all the bishops of the world. The impact of the Council commission members, elected by the bishops themselves (as will be described later), would also become quite evident.

It is perhaps important to recall that Pope John had the benefit of a kind of "trial run" or, in military terms, maneuvers, in preparation for the Council. He had called a synod or local council of the diocese of Rome—and with Tardini's help he had carried it out, watching, pad in hand, every phase of the organization of the gathering as it unfolded. This must have been of great help in working out preparations for the Council; still it could not provide all the experience needed. Only the actual processes of the Council in action could do that. For never before in history had anyone ever witnessed a world congress with 2,600 members, all of whom had a right to the microphone!

One cannot help but give deserved credit to the office of the secretary general on whom fell most of the burden of organization, for the Council and during the Council. And with the loss of Tardini, the preparatory work must have been doubly difficult.

In time, seven out of the seventy schemas arrived by mail in July, and others were distributed to us later in Rome. Two I especially recall receiving in Louisiana were those on the liturgy and divine revelation. These were two of the first subjects to come up for debate after the Council began. The schemas were thick booklets, paper-bound, measuring 8½ x 12½ inches, with gray covers, and printed on good quality, heavy paper.

I went to work reading the schemas immediately, and was at once impressed by the care and erudition with which they were composed. Apparently no pains had been spared by the preparatory scholars in producing well-chiseled statements, amply supported by documentation.

However, since I was not a professional scholar, the import of much of the material escaped me, as well as most of the controversy lurking in the theological and related corners, until I reached the Council where I received an unexpected education.

During the summer of 1962 I tried to read as much as I could about councils. My principal reading was as follows:

The Church in Crisis by Monsignor Philip Hughes, whom I had visited earlier at his home at Notre Dame University, and whom I was surprised to find doing the manuscript for this history of ecumenical councils, as he did all his books, in longhand, with a quill pen!

Council Reform and Reunion by Father Hans Kung, whom I

had met at the Catholic Student Center at Oxford University in England, just before the Council, during the summer of 1962. Father Kung told me that I was the first American bishop he had ever met; and he inquired anxiously (as well he might!) about the reception of his controversial volume in America. Later I came to know Father Kung well, and he included my intervention at the second session in his published collection of Council addresses.

The Vatican Council 1869–1870 by Dom Cuthbert Butler, author also of *The Council and Papal Infallibility*. He was a Benedictine Abbot of Downside Abbey in England who, in 1850, became Bishop of Birmingham. (Vatican II also had its Butler— Dom Christopher Butler, likewise Abbot of Downside, who became a very prominent speaker.) Cuthbert Butler's book was based on letters from Vatican I, written by the English bishop William Bernard Ullathorne.

One of the most helpful pieces of reading which I undertook in preparation for the Council was not a book at all, but a small pamphlet entitled *The A B C of the Council* by Herbert Keldany, published in England.

After reading and pondering the contents of these books, and with the day of my departure drawing near, I felt that I owed it to the people of my diocese to share with them some of the things I had learned about Vatican Council II, and to help prepare them for what was to come by giving them a perspective on it. Accordingly, drawing heavily on Keldany's booklet, I penned a pastoral letter, formal in style, to my priests, religious and laity. Following the custom of papal letters, I employed an opening phrase that would serve as a name for the document itself:

THE YEAR OF THE GREAT COUNCIL, The Second General Council of the Vatican, summoned by His Holiness, Pope John XXIII, to convene on October 11, 1962, will almost certainly go down as a year to remember.

I provided for the administration of the diocese in my absence, and then explained how the Council started. Highlighted early in the letter was Pope John's own statement of the purpose of the Council:

First, there must be a Council to reform the Church and revive the spirit of the Gospel; then we shall be able to understand our separated brethren and they will understand us.

After dealing with some of the seemingly certain issues of the Council, such as unity and reform, and describing how the decrees would be prepared, discussed and promulgated, I asked the priests, religious and laity of my diocese to view their responsibility to the Council in this light:

Let us, then, place our firm trust in Divine Providence and particularly in the guidance of the Holy Spirit of God. But let us also endeavor to assume to ourselves some of the responsibility of the Council. It is true that the responsibility of the layman is not to sit in the Council and enact decrees. That is a function which Christ Himself has reserved to the Apostles and their successors. But each Catholic still has his own role and an important role at that. He has the opportunity to reflect the spirit of the Council in his own life. For our separated brethren will observe not only the humility and religious spirit with which the Council works. They will observe, even more immediately, the conduct and loving spirit of their Catholic neighbors.

With this parting message, I departed from Baton Rouge on September 29, accompanied by Monsignor Patrick Gillespie, Vicar General, and headed out for the Council. I traveled to Rome, for the first time in my life, with a heart full of anticipation and excitement. The Council was so clearly the work of God, it seemed to me, that one could not help being awed at the prospect of participating in it. 1962 was going to be a great year—a wonderful year; it was going to be The Year of the Great Council!

Chapter 3

The Council Opens

Monsignor Gillespie and I visited Ireland in the interest of recruiting vocations for our diocese, on our way to the Council, but had little success. Later on, however, we did succeed in having four students sign up for the diocese of Baton Rouge in various Irish seminaries.

On October 5, I boarded an Irish Airlines plane in Dublin, leaving Monsignor Pat behind in Ireland with his family, after planning to meet him in Rome within a few days. The same Friday evening at 10 P.M., I landed in Fumicino, at the Leonardo da Vinci Airport, and, after a 16-mile drive, arrived in Rome.

The hotel of my choice, the Michelangelo, is near St. Peter's and caters mainly to American tourists. It is not a luxury hotel by any means, as a magazine at the time stated, probably because it was new and air-conditioned. Indeed, I found it suitable for a brief tourist-stay, but rather confining for a two-months sojourn. And so Archbishop Hallinan and I soon transferred to the Residence Palace Hotel near the Villa Borghese, in the Parioli or "American" section of Rome. We were well pleased with the Residence Palace, but after the new Hilton opened, during the second session, a year later, so many bishops left the Residence Palace that I found myself missing my contacts with them. Worst of all, I had to ride a daily bus which stopped at so many places that it required a full hour to get back to our hotel from St. Peter's each day. So, midway in the second session, I too succumbed, and went over to the Hilton where more than sixty bishops, nearly all Americans, were registered, and where one could depend on getting back to the hotel from St. Peter's within ten minutes.

The other American bishops resided in various hotels, religious houses and *pensiones* (Roman-style boardinghouses) in various parts of the city. Rome has been the center of pilgrimages, congresses and tours for many, many centuries. The city is prepared, therefore, to house and feed large numbers of visitors without strain. Even the two-month stay of 10,000 Council visitors, including bishops, experts and attendants, did not touch off any housing, feeding or transportation crisis.

On Saturday, the day after my arrival, I went to work enthusiastically on the job of getting prepared for the opening of the Council. This was to take place on the following Thursday, October 11. First, I made contact at a little nearby parish church called Santa Maria alle Fornaci, and there I made arrangements to say Mass each day until I could set up a portable altar in my studio-type hotel room.

On Sunday I took the noonday parish Mass at Santa Maria. It was quite an experience. Italian people are just naturally demonstrative, and they show it especially in the way they approach their religious devotions. While I celebrated Mass at the high altar, there were at least three or four different other programs in progress in the church—a Novena to Our Lady of the Holy Rosary aloud (it was her feast), as well as various blessings and private devotions and even the taking of photographs of the parish priest with families of the parish in a side chapel. But if one is "simpatico" it is possible to understand how cold and unfeeling our former rigid process of silent, dignified assistance of Mass must have seemed to these warm and sentimental folk. At any rate, the church was filled with people and their thoughts were certainly on things divine. To the Italian, the church is His Father's house and he cannot help but feel very much at home in it. Children will never stay put; they must scamper about and return to their parents to ask questions about the articles and adornments and other marvels of the sacred edifice. It sometimes comes as a surprise to American travelers that the Holy Father is greeted on his formal entrances into St. Peter's by a roar of "Viva, il Papa!" and a thunder of handclaps that re-echo throughout the great church building. But one must understand that these people could no more stand by silently on such an occasion than could the cheering section of LSU when the Tigers have the ball on an opponent's one-yard line!

Fortunately for me, Bishop Ryan of Hamilton, Ontario, a fellow-resident of the Michelangelo who had been a student in Rome and knew the ropes, took me under his wing and guided me around on my first day to all the necessary places for registering and making other arrangements: the Central Office where the bishops get their passports to the Council and their *tessera* (tickets) assigning them to a numbered seat in St. Peter's; the NCWC "Rome Office" which offered a variety of services to U. S. bishops—from secretarial aid to changing American money; and the American USO where you may find a variety of U.S. newspapers and where, later on, the U.S. press panel would be held almost daily. All of these offices were on the Via della Conciliazione, the wide avenue developed by Mussolini which leads up to St. Peter's Square, and which was solemnly opened at the consummation of the Lateran Treaty establishing peace between the Vatican and the Italian state—hence, "The Street of the Great Accord."

Failing to locate Archbishop Cody of New Orleans, and finding that two of my students at the North American College were on retreat until Sunday, I returned to the hotel and there enjoyed a reunion with Bishop Schexnayder and Bishop Boudreaux of the Diocese of Lafayette. Shortly Archbishop Cody telephoned and invited me to have supper with him at Alfredo's, that world-renowned restaurant of Rome where the proprietor himself serves every order of *fettuccine* (Italian noodles), mixing them while he does a kind of "twist." Alfredo's had a photograph taken of our group which still adorns his walls after four years. It is unlikely to come down in the near future since Archbishop Cody is now referred to in Rome as *Il Cardinale prossimo* (the next cardinal).

On the following day, the Sunday afternoon before the Council opened, Archbishop Cody invited me to accompany his party out to Tivoli, about a half-hour's drive away, where I witnessed a real Roman Sunday afternoon. Thousands of families had come out to enjoy the golden autumn weather and to walk in the fabulous Villa D'Este (there is no charge on Sundays) with its hundreds of fountains (where the movie "Three Coins in a Fountain" was partly filmed). Briefly, the Villa D'Este is the estate of the Renaissance Cardinal D'Este, son of Lucretia Borgia, created by him during his retirement after his fall from favor at the Vatican court and his loss of the influential post of Papal Ambassador to France. There is a river high on a mountain on the estate which courses along hundreds of feet above the valley; and D'Este ingeniously employed the pull of gravity to send the water spouting through hundreds of fountains and also, on occasion, cascading down the mountain on top of hostile armies approaching from below.

About five o'clock we reached a beautiful old Roman restaurant named La Sibilla away up in the Alban Hills. There you can look down from a rocky eminence upon a most enchanting countryside that is immediately reminiscent of familiar Italian landscape paintings of the Renaissance. The restaurant is named after a certain sibyl (or fortuneteller) who lived there long before the Christian era and who is credited with foretelling the birth of Christ.

Two associations came to me: First, the *"Teste David cum Sibylla"* (testified to by David and the ancient sibyl) which is sung in the Latin of the Requiem Mass; and, secondly, the Sixth Eclogue of Virgil, the Latin poet, which we had to learn by heart as boys at St. Benedict as the Christmas season drew near. The lines are beautiful and touching:

> Jam redit et virgo
> Redeunt Saturnia regna
> Jam nova progenies caelo dimittur alto.

> Then shall the virgin return;
> And the glorious reign of Saturn.

>Then shall a new generation
>Descend to earth from heaven on high.

In the light of the new and broader understanding provided by the Council, it becomes even more believable that the ancient pagan poet may have received from on high the inspiration to announce, in this way, the coming mystery of the Incarnation a hundred years before it took place.

Monday was devoted to "getting things organized" for the Council. One thing needed, I was told, was Roman garb. There is a certain "good form" that one observes in Rome. When a cleric goes abroad in public, he always wears an ankle-length coat over his cassock; and the proper hat to go with this outfit is a black broad-brimmed "capello." A bishop, in the evening, wears under his long coat a simple black cassock together with his pectoral cross and ring. And, at the first session of the Council, this form was, to some extent, observed. After all, when in Rome, use Roman candles! But by the time the fourth session had rolled around, *borghese* attire, that is, civilian dress, was in evidence everywhere in the evening. I was never too keen about this "good form" because I felt it set the clergy off too much from the people. But the hats were fun.

The pectoral cross and ring were status symbols of considerable practical value. They opened all sorts of doors. Italians in Rome are sensitive to titles and they make no mistake by always giving you a title a notch higher than the one you actually have. Thus "Excellenza" easily becomes "Eminenza."

Our taxi driver was once simply outraged that we were halted at a certain gate. "Io ho due Cardinali qui!" ("Look, I have two Cardinals here!") he shouted. But the Roman is given to flattery anyway. You go to get a suit and the tailor steps back to admire your "wonderful build"; you go to a dentist and he is impressed to find that you have teeth *"com'un Romano Antico"* (like an ancient Roman).

A typewriter (electric) and a portable altar put me in business. *Newsweek* reported my next action, but, thank heaven, without mentioning my name: I mailed to every family in my diocese

40,000 Christmas cards from the Council! The new Diocese of Baton Rouge had a "Foundation Fund Program" just getting off the ground, and I thought the cards would be a superior public-relations gesture. So I found a Vatican postal employee named Pivato Bruno, and he and his wife and all his *bambini* stayed up nights licking 40,000 stamps for two months before Christmas, earning a little extra holiday money.

On Wednesday morning, Archbishop Cody took me into St. Peter's for my first visit to the interior of the great basilica. What I saw there made me feel that it was simply impossible that things could be ready for the solemn opening of the Council the next day. Cables were strung out all over the floor; seamstresses were sewing like mad on various cloths and tapestries; and, above all, the *Sampietrini,* the renowned hereditary workers of the basilica, were in the course of giving the most exciting aerial performance I have ever seen in my life.

These ecclesiastical acrobats were swinging on ropes from one side of St. Peter's vast arches to the other, hanging the magnificent red draperies which form the background for the long strings of crystal chandeliers with which St. Peter's is decorated on great occasions. Both drapes and chandeliers stretch down in great lengths to the floor, far below, from the great Corinthian capitals at the top of the pilasters around the rotunda and central altar.

When the *Sampietrini* had finished hanging one of the drapes, they would swing out into open space on their ropes, then when their feet hit the wall, quickly climb hand-over-hand up to the capitals above. On reaching them, another swing out into open space was required and a leap of extra power was necessary to vault over the capitals onto the ledge above. Sometimes they did not make it on first try; but nearly always a second or third attempt brought success.

In spite of what looked to me like complete confusion in St. Peter's on Wednesday, everything was in perfect and beautiful order and ready for the solemn opening of the Council the next morning.

Also on Wednesday, I had occasion to try out a seat at the

Council "for size." I found it roomy and comfortable and cleverly arranged. It was something like a seat on an airplane, constructed of very fine wood, foam rubber cushions, and green plastic upholstery. Each bishop had a seat with arms, a kneeler, an adjustable shelf which served as a desk, and a magnetic pencil to record one's presence and one's vote on IBM cards, which would then be processed by automatic computers.

That night I walked around St. Peter's Square alone and tried simply to absorb the magnitude and the magnificence of the scene. It requires a good deal of time and reflection to do this. The most appropriate historical associations and literary allusions do not come to you all at once, and esthetic reaction develops only gradually. All sorts of random recollections and impressions make themselves felt at first impact. For example, I could visualize Pope Pius VII coming out of the same front door of St. Peter's and getting into his springless carriage which was to take him to Paris and his crowning of Napoleon. And I could not help asking myself what kind of a man was *Paulus Borgesius Romanus*, who inscribed his own name in huge letters across the center of the façade of St. Peter's, while relegating to one side the starting words of the inscription *"In Honorem S. Petri, Principis Apostolorum."* Again, one could not but ponder the inspiration and sweep of the artistic imagination, as well as the engineering skill, of the men who had the daring to attempt an enterprise like St. Peter's, which no succeeding age has since been able even to approach either in size or grandeur.

The lights in *il studio di Santo Padre* burned brightly, high up on the top floor of the Apostolic Palace overlooking St. Peter's Square. But, at length, they went out, one by one, as Pope John called it a day after a demanding schedule in which he had seen visitors from around the globe.

Shortly before the Council opened the Holy Father made his celebrated trip to Assisi and Loretto. Even after the "Great Accord" of the Lateran Treaty, popes were still uneasy about treading the soil of their former oppressors. Journeys like Pope John's, however, were opening up a new era which were to set the stage for the epoch-making peregrinations of Pope Paul VI to the

Holy Land, to India and eventually to the U.N. and the shores of the U.S.A. At the time, Pope John's visit to Assisi and Loretto was considered quite revolutionary and symbolic of a new order to come.

On the same day, the Wednesday before the Council opened, we drove down to Fumicino, to the airport, to welcome to Rome Archbishop Joseph Francis Rummel of New Orleans, who had been my Ordinary for twenty-four years. Archbishop Cody, in 1962, was Apostolic Administrator of the archdiocese. Archbishop Rummel came in on an Alitalia jet to attend the opening of the Council after twelve hours of continuous flying from New Orleans, via New York, but he was fresh as a daisy in appearance, although on the eve of his eighty-sixth birthday. He was chatty, gay, giving directions about luggage, and generally conducting himself like a man who had been in similar situations many times before and who knew exactly what to do. Once a flashbulb popped and a microphone was placed in his hand, years meant nothing to this great man who was able to rise to every occasion almost to his dying day.

Only a few years before, already in his eighties, Archbishop Rummel had taken a serious fall which had put him in the hospital for over a year. At the time, it was predicted that he would never walk again. Now, walking very well, Fumicino seemed to him to be just one more airport. But it wasn't. It represented the unbelievable triumph of a man, almost blind and in advanced years, over a crippling accident. "Made in Germany of prewar material" is a way the Archbishop was once described. Before departing again from Fumicino some weeks later, Archbishop Rummel would have received in Rome one of the most remarkable tributes ever accorded a bishop anywhere in the world. He would be applauded by many a bishop as he entered the Second Vatican Council because of his celebrated courageous leadership in publicly condemning racial segregation as "morally wrong and sinful" long before the U.S. Supreme Court decision of 1954. He would be the first U.S. prelate to see Pope John in private audience during the first session of Vatican II; he would be tendered a birthday dinner with four American cardinals attending; and he would receive a standing ovation from every cardinal, archbishop and bishop from the United States as he attended the first meeting of the American bishops at the Council.

As the Council opening drew near, most of the bishops were worried about how to get into St. Peter's. There were no passports or *tessera* issued even up to noon on Wednesday. One Council official replied, when I began to urge some action on the matter: "Now, bishop, please relax. After all, you can expect that there will be *'un podi de confusione'* (just a mite of confusion) at the time of the opening of the Council." That sounded to me like the understatement of the twentieth century. Yet, when the time came, it all somehow worked out. We never did get tickets and a definite seat number before the opening, but this was an advantage as far as I was concerned, for it enabled me to occupy a seat far closer to the Bernini altar than the date of my consecration (which established seniority) would otherwise have entitled me to have. However, we did get our passports, late Wednesday night, and everything was set at last.

On that final Wednesday night before the opening, the weather was extremely bad. By this time, ten thousand Council Persons had descended on this teeming city of the Romans, and the streets were full of them. Rain poured from the heavens all night, and everyone was expecting that there would be no outdoor procession next day to solemnly open the Council. This would be a great disappointment, for no one living had ever seen the entire hierarchy of the Catholic world, including the Holy Father, moving in solemn procession together, and the sight would certainly be most impressive.

Thursday, the day of the grand opening, at last arrived. The moment I awakened, I jumped from bed immediately and made straight for the window to have a look at the weather. It was not raining, but great accumulations of clouds hung overhead in a most threatening manner. After a private Mass I boarded a special bus which was to take the bishops residing at the Michelangelo to the Vatican Museum where they were to vest in white cope and white mitre for the ceremony. The procession was scheduled to begin at 8:30 A.M.

Up a tremendous winding staircase we went, around and around, almost endlessly, and then on and on, through the interminable halls of the Vatican Museum, filled with masterpieces of art ranging from the earliest Greek and Roman eras to the present day. Finally we came to a huge corridor just crowded with bishops getting into their vestments. Beside me were a bishop from East Berlin, another from the Argentine and three other bishops with lay attendants. A bishop near me whispered that they were bishops from Iron Curtain countries, with three guards appointed by their Communist governments to guard them.

As we awaited the signal to start, right on time, the sun suddenly broke through the clouds, an omen of the perfection with which the entire ceremony was to be conducted. Now the weather quickly cleared and the outdoor procession began.

The procession was a moving sight. Across St. Peter's Square almost all the bishops of the Catholic world began marching, eight abreast, toward the great front doors of St. Peter's.

The crowd assembled in the square was by far the largest I have ever seen, overflowing the piazza and spilling out into the Via della Conciliazione, while windows and rooftops provided special vantage points for thousands of other onlookers. A Vatican choir of splendid voices began to intone, over a faultless public-address system, familiar Catholic hymns and songs in which all the bishops and many a person in the great crowd joined: the Third Credo, the *"Ubi Caritas"* ("Where Love Is, There God Is Present") and many others.

Monsignor Pat had arrived in Rome on schedule and had departed early to get a good place in St. Peter's. As a matter of fact, he did much better than I did. With no seat numbers to worry about, I was able to locate a place about halfway up the central nave of the basilica. But Monsignor Pat found one in the gallery or tribune just over the cardinals' seats and therefore close to the Pope's chair. However, the amplification in St. Peter's is the best

I have ever heard, and so I kept up with the speaking reasonably well, while a powerful pair of field glasses provided close-ups of everything that transpired at the altar.

Then came my first sight of Pope John.

With a blast of silver trumpets, the tremendous center doors swung open and in came the papal procession. Pope John was seated on his *sedia gestatoria,* a chair borne on the shoulders of eight bearers so that the Pope might be seen easily by everyone, since the crowd always strains for a good glimpse of the Pope as he passes by. Before, around, and behind the Pope came a most brilliant entourage of cardinals, papal nobility, Palatine Guards and the knights of various orders.

Although the *sedia gestatoria* is a practical measure—like a notable visitor sitting on the back of a convertible in order to be seen by the crowds which line the streets—still, the device does project the image of an oriental prince, especially when the huge *flabella,* the great fans made of ostrich feathers, are carried on either side of the portable throne. Simple Pope John was known to be embarrassed at having to use these props, required by long-standing protocol at the Vatican. And one bishop near me commented:

"You know, I think he's right. They ought to send those things back to the Cleopatra movie set!"

But Pope John is said to have also found his ride up the nave on the *sedia gestatoria,* between the ranks of the bishops, out of keeping with his feelings. He is reported to have said to his attendants: "That's enough. Put me down so that I may walk the rest of the way among my brother bishops." Whether this is true or not, I do know that the portable throne was put down, in fact, right in front of me, just halfway up the aisle, and Pope John did, indeed, walk the rest of the way to the Bernini altar.

This first sight of good Pope John was a moving experience for me. He had already sent me a message, in French, some time before, through Monsignor Lohmann, then Rector of our Cathedral, during an audience the Monsignor had with him. Asking Monsignor the name of the diocese he belonged to, the Pope was told that it was Baton Rouge. Pope John immediately picked up the French name and replied jokingly in French, "Well, tell your good bishop not to go using that '*bâton*' on the people!"

As I gazed at Pope John through my field glasses, I could look at those kindly features and immediately sense, somehow, that here was a man of God. Pope John's very presence breathed the supernatural. It is my view that if canonizations by acclamation were in order today, as they once were, Pope John would be acclaimed a saint just as readily as was St. Francis of Assisi. Pope John was obviously used by Divine Providence to achieve a major renewal of the Church in our times, and a universal cult already exists in his cause. Nevertheless, in keeping with modern procedures, a regular process will be instituted, in his favor as well as that of Pope Pius XII, according to Pope Paul's announcement at the last session of the Council.

Truly, anyone who saw Pope John could immediately sense, even at a distance, the warmth of his personality. I can never forget my feelings as I stood in the crowd, that same evening, and heard the Pope speak to the torch-lit crowd that massed in the piazza below his window. He ended his remarks by speaking to all the fathers present, asking them to go home and to bend over the cribs of their babies and to give them a kiss sent to them by their Holy Father in Christ himself. Pope John could do a thing like this without making the gesture seem in the least "corny." The genuineness of his feelings simply got through to you at once.

Again, on a cold, bright-blue day, toward the end of the first session, I paused, on leaving St. Peter's at noon, after a morning's meeting, to say the "Angelus" along with Pope John and an immense crowd of people in the square. After prayer, the Pope gave a brief talk in simple, homelike terms. He revealed that he had been very ill and that, in fact, before his recovery, some thought that he was surely going to die. Later on, he said, someone asked him: "Were you afraid to die?" Pope John told us that his reply was: "Not at all. When you think of it, any day is a good day to be born, isn't it? And so any day, also, is a good day to die. After all, there is Someone who watches over us and cares for us." Before he was through, there were tears all over the piazza. Pope John, even when he was high up at his window, far removed from his hearers and speaking over a public-address system, had a strange power to move the hearts of his hearers.

So as Pope John came up the great nave of St. Peter's to open the Second Vatican Council, one could not help but feel: "Here is my Father," and I think this feeling was experienced by the non-Catholic observers also, for no Pope in history had opened his heart more fully to our brethren of other faiths or received them more kindly.

Cardinal Tisserant said the opening Council Mass, in the presence of the Pope, and then there was placed before us the great Pre-Reformation Bible, a symbol of our interest in Christian unity and of the spirit of love for all men in which we were called to meet.

It was a deeply impressive thing, then, to witness the Pope humbly kneel down before us and make his Profession of Faith, in the very same words spoken by adults whom we receive into the Church, just before their baptism—a profession which we all repeated after the Pope.

And when it comes to a dialogue Mass, surely there was never any like this one, with 2,600 bishops answering the prayers of the celebrant in the presence of the Holy Father himself. After four years of regular and constant meetings with the Pope at various functions, the Council Fathers—all of us—perhaps tend, rather naturally, to take such meetings a little for granted. At least the novelty of the experience cannot endure, although one never fails to be moved, always, in the presence of the Vicar of Christ. But my notes remind me of what my feelings were that day when I saw a living Pope for the first time in my life—and that Pope happened to be Pope John!

At length, Pope John sat down on his throne before the great altar and spoke to us in earnest words which will live forever in the memory of the Church. You might say that these words actually ushered in a new era in Christian life—that they served to signalize and point up the great renewal the Holy Spirit was about to set in motion among us.

For Pope John's address was filled with a spirit of startling renewal and with phrases that no Pope had ever used before. It must have been heartening to many of those present to hear the Holy Father state so uncompromisingly the aims of the Council. This celebrated address of Pope John's has been analyzed over and over again by the experts. There is no point in striving to be complete by reporting it here. Yet there may be some value in simply listing, briefly, some of its more striking thoughts, as a reminder:

There was his framed reference to "the prophets of doom," those men about him who "though burning with zeal," are not endowed with "very much sense of direction or measure." Pope John was referring here to those among his advisers who wanted to simply freeze the position of the Church as it had been described at Vatican I and at the Council of Trent, and who felt that the Church must not go out in friendship to a world full of "prevarication and ruin." There is hardly a Council document which would have escaped disaster had this position of "the prophets of doom" prevailed.

"It is imperative for the Church to bring herself up to date, where required, in order to spread her message to all men throughout the world"; and the Church, further, must open new avenues to the Catholic apostolate, while never departing from "the sacred patrimony of truth received from the Fathers."

"The substance of the ancient doctrine of the deposit of faith is one thing, the way in which it is expressed is another." This means that new and continually improved means of expressing Catholic truth are constantly being developed and we must use them.

"Nowadays, the bride of Christ [the Church] prefers to make use of the medicine of mercy rather than that of severity." In other words, we want no condemnations to come out of the Council, even of obvious and dangerous errors such as the error of communism. Rather will the Council eventually reach out even to the atheist, regarding him as one who, unwittingly, is actually seeking contact with His Creator.

"The entire Christian family has not yet fully attained the visible unity in truth" desired by Christ. This is a serious problem on which we must confer and pray with other Christians of good will. Thus, was the ecumenical movement officially born in the Church.

This, although not a complete summary of what Pope John had to say, does put into a few clear words the main thoughts he placed before us as the first session began. Any subsequent action at the Council could, I think, be placed under one of the above five headings.

Pope John summed it up in his own way:

> You might say that heaven and earth are united in the celebration of the Council—the Saints of heaven to protect our work, the faithful on earth persevering in prayer to the Lord for us, and you, seconding the inspiration of the Holy Spirit of God, in order that the work of all may correspond to the modern expectations and needs of the various peoples of the world.

After that first appearance, Pope John did not again attend the Council until the day before the first session adjourned. However, he did follow the proceedings with deep interest over closed-circuit television, and he kept a revolving door going at the Vatican receiving non-Catholic visitors with courtesy and tact. On occasion this required him to dispense with various incrustations of Vatican protocol, such as the time that he picked up his chair and sat down on the same level as his non-Catholic visitors, instead of on an elevation of at least one step, as required by the rule.

Observers from non-Catholic communions were present in impressive numbers, although the absence of representatives of the Greek Orthodox communion was a disappointment, and the unexpected appearance of the delegates from Moscow a sensation.

Seventeen international bodies of separated Christians were represented by observers at the first session. There were also "special guests" invited by the Secretariat for Christian Unity, men who had distinguished themselves in the cause of Christian unity but who did not officially represent any group. It must have required the utmost tact on the part of the Secretariat to complete all the arrangements for the attendance of the various Observers and guests, and to the utmost satisfaction of the non-Catholic bodies involved. Indeed, Observers frequently expressed their surprise at the important but unexpected role they found themselves playing at the Council. Officially, their function was to observe and report the Council to their own communions. Unofficially, they frequently found themselves called upon to indicate the probable non-Catholic reaction to this or that pronouncement or wording of a conciliar document. The tone of the Council was to be pastoral and ecumenical. But how could any Catholic tell whether this phrase or that was truly "ecumenical" unless you asked some knowledgeable non-Catholic about it? The only realistic thing to do, under the circumstances, was to find out how it sounded to them!

Bishop Fred Corson, the Methodist bishop from Philadelphia, flew to Rome on a plane with thirty-five Catholic bishops. He was received early by Pope John—the first time in history that any official contact had taken place between the Holy See and a representative of the Methodist Church. I came to know Bishop Corson well. I also became well acquainted with a number of other Observers, largely through the Paulist Fathers at Santa Susanna, the "American" church in Rome which used to have a regular Sunday-evening supper for the Observers from the United States and for the American bishops who were especially interested in meeting them.

With some of the Observers I became especially friendly: Dr. Albert Outler of Southern Methodist University (Methodist); Dr. Douglas Horton, former dean of Harvard Divinity School (Congregationalist); Dr. Robert McAfee Brown of Stanford University (Presbyterian); Dr. Fred Lindbeck of Yale Divinity School (Lutheran); Dr. Warren Quanbeck of Luther Theological Seminary, St. Paul (Lutheran); Canon Bernard Pawley of Ely Cathedral, England (Anglican); Dr. James H. Nichols of Princeton Theological Seminary (Presbyterian); Dr. George Caird of Oxford University, England (Anglican).

At the beginning of the Council, we Americans were posed with a number of problems connected with living in Rome. One of these was language. I had never studied Italian, and the same was true of some other bishops, though most American bishops had, at some point, studied in Rome and could, therefore, speak Italian with varying degrees of competence. All the Italian I knew came from tours I had organized for students at LSU to the performances of grand opera—mostly in Italian—in New Orleans. Now in Rome, when I did not know the Italian word for something, I simply inserted the Latin word for it, so much so that it was a by-word among the Roman taxicab drivers who knew me that I spoke "mezzo Italiano, mezzo Latino." I was always able to handle the essentials for survival—to get something to eat and to haggle with the taxicab men.

Then, there was the problem of traffic. The traffic in the streets of Rome is a phenomenon worth mentioning. Everyone, of course, drives only small cars of the Volkswagen type: they are more maneuverable, cost less, and burn less gas (in Rome gas is 80¢ a gallon). But everybody drives with what seems to be the utmost recklessness. The traffic is not so dangerous as it may appear, because the cars are small and maneuverable and do not actually get up much speed on the crowded and twisted streets. To cross a street, the trick is to simply step out boldly in front of any oncoming traffic, no matter how fast-moving or how congested, and look over your shoulder at the drivers with unconcealed scorn. As long as you are on "the zebra" (black-and-white-stripes) you can stop them in their tracks, although most of the time they will dart expertly around you. Maintenance of insurance premiums is, nevertheless, highly commended to the Rome visitor.

The traffic cops (the *vigili*), who wear white gloves and help to develop traffic snarls, are men worth watching. If a disappointed driver lets go with an insult, all traffic must be halted until the *vigile* has had equal opportunity to make answer. Horns may blow and tempers may rise, but the insult must be avenged. While Italians lay down a wonderful barrage of imprecations, they almost never get around to slugging each other. There is much fist-shaking but few fisticuffs.

The first daily meeting of the Council lasted only about fifteen minutes! Then the meeting was adjourned until the following Tuesday, and immediately the bishops came streaming out of St. Peter's. Apparently Pope John was caught napping. He was not at his closed-circuit TV, thinking, perhaps, that the first daily meeting, taken up with voting for commission members, would be rather routine and tiresome. At any rate, when the Pope heard the noise of many voices out in St. Peter's Square, he dashed to his window to look down upon what appeared to be a flood of purple flowers as though a vast garden of azaleas had suddenly blossomed in the piazza!

"*Cosa c'e?*" he turned and asked a visitor to his apartment, in utter dismay. What, indeed, could possibly have happened to terminate the first meeting of the Council inside of fifteen minutes after all the carefully laid preparations?

The Council witnessed many exciting moments and many significant happenings during its four years of meeting. But if I had to cite a moment that was particularly stirring, an event that was especially important, I think I would choose the gambit that sent us out of St. Peter's and back to our hotels fifteen minutes after the start of the very first daily congregation.

The gambit was instigated by the French Cardinal Liénart who wished to have the voting on the Council Commission members delayed by three days in order to give the Fathers of the Council more time to consult among themselves as to the merits of candidates from various countries before making a choice.

Cardinal Liénart's move was of lasting and signal importance. There was some danger, as the Council opened, that the commissions would be dominated by the officials and experts of the regular governmental bureaus of the Vatican. These men, however good and dedicated, had not, on the whole, been very enthusiastic about the proposed reforms—perhaps understandably so. They were convinced that Church affairs would be impaired if taken out of the hands of experienced and trained Vatican experts and placed in the hands of persons unfamiliar with the delicate system of central Church government—persons, moreover, whom they regarded as unduly influenced by the advice of radical advisers and half-baked reformers. They sincerely felt this to be a great danger to the safety and good of the Church and they had acted accordingly. For example, the developing notion of collegiality among the bishops had got short shrift in its Preparatory Commission, while the text on "Revelation" came out of its preparatory stage couched in language which gave little indication that Pius XII had ever lived or that his great encyclical *"Divino Afflante Spiritu"* (up-dating biblical research) had ever been written. In short, because of the heavy representation of the Vatican officials on the Preparatory Commissions, many of the initial schemas reflected a highly conservative flavor, not at all in harmony with the sentiment of the Council Fathers as a whole. And danger hung over the Council that, if the influential leaders in the Vatican departments were to succeed in getting men of their views on the new Council Commissions in sufficient numbers, it would be much more difficult for the sentiment of the Fathers as a whole to find successful expression. Catching the Roman conservatives off guard (or maybe they simply thought the proposal would fail!) Liénart's motion, which was instantly seconded and passed, was basic to the cause of securing wide and genuine representation of the views of the Fathers in commission meetings.

Such representation on the various commissions was extremely important, for it was in the commissions that proposals to be voted on were worded and, as we learned, a proposal could be arranged in such a way as to favor a certain position. For example, we were asked at times to vote only on whether we were willing to support a given commission in the way it had handled a certain matter, instead of being asked to vote on the substance of the question itself. Thus, one had to vote "no confidence" in the commission if one wanted the matter treated differently. This, I felt, was stacking the deck just a little! Normally, bishops are disposed to go along with commissions comprised of other bishops, and only in rare instances and in matters of extreme seriousness would they fail to give any commission a vote of confidence. So when the Liturgy Commission proposed to retain the collect of the Mass in Latin, we could only vote on whether or not we still had confidence in the commission. There was no direct voting on whether we wanted the collect in the vernacular or not! Not unnaturally the Fathers voted to support the commission "in the way it had handled the matter," although subsequent events have shown that the bishops of the world overwhelmingly wanted the privilege of having the collect, as well as other parts of the Mass, in the vernacular.

So the move to give the bishops of the world time to work up slates of candidates for commissions was truly representative of the thinking of the Fathers. It was a move of prime importance which affected everything else that happened thereafter at the Council.

The development also had tremendous significance for the individual bishops. Personally, I came to the Council not at all sure that I would have very much of an active part to play in it. I was not a professional theologian, canonist or Scripture scholar. Moreover, I had been brought up to regard with awe officials highly placed in the government of the Church. As an ordinary administrative bishop, I would not have been surprised to find that, at the Council, the Vatican experts would simply tuck the ball under their arms and run with it. This is the way the only other Church council I had ever attended, the Sixth Diocesan Synod of New Orleans, had been run. The clergy, in general, simply came in and dutifully agreed with the Archbishop's decisions. There were advisory committees in advance, but they did not decide anything. And so, I felt, that the subject matter of the Council had been fairly well settled in the Preparatory Commissions, over the past three years, and that we were called to Rome simply to exhibit our solidarity with the "approved authors" and with the Holy See.

The move of Cardinal Liénart and its quick adoption by the Council gave me a brand-new view of the Council: apparently every bishop who was interested could plan an active role in the proceedings. And Paul Hallinan and I were definitely interested. Exhilarated by this new openness, we immediately went to work contacting leaders of various countries to ask whom they had to offer as candidates for the Council Commissions, while we, in turn, expressed our own views about the possible American candidates. Other U.S. bishops were doing the same thing, and, by the time a meeting of American bishops was called on Monday, a fair consensus had been reached among us, independently of each other, as to the make-up of an international slate of candidates for each commission.

When the Council opened, the Preparatory Commissions went out of existence, their work finished. Now there had to be set up ten new commissions which would be "Council Commissions," each with twenty-four members. Of these the Holy Father had directly appointed eight and we were to vote for sixteen others. This meant that we had to put down 160 names on our ballots; and, with 2,600 ballots to be counted, there were more than 400,000 names to be processed—by hand, since the ballots were not on IBM cards as the usual votes at the Council were. So we voted on Tuesday and then recessed while the vote-counting took place.

The ten Conciliar Commissions and one Secretariat, and their Cardinal-Presidents, were as follows:

Theological (Faith and Morals)	Cardinal Ottaviani
Bishops and the Government of Dioceses	Cardinal Marella
Oriental Churches	Cardinal A. Cicognani
Discipline of the Sacraments	Cardinal Masella
Discipline of the Clergy and the Christian People	Cardinal Ciriaci
Religious	Cardinal Valeri
Missions	Cardinal Agagianian
Sacred Liturgy	Cardinal Larraona
Studies, Seminaries and Catholic Schools	Cardinal Pizzardo

Apostolate of the Laity for the
  Press and Entertainment   Cardinal Cento
Secretariat for Promoting Unity
  (Given status of Commission
  on October 19, 1962)   Cardinal Bea

The Pope named the Cardinal-President of each commission and the President, in turn, named two vice-presidents from among commission members and one secretary from among the experts of the Council.

The function of these commissions was this: to receive the interventions of the Council Fathers, whether spoken on the floor of St. Peter's or written; to assign them to sub-committees so that the original text of the schema could be reworked in the light of these interventions, with a view to winning a two-thirds favorable vote for the revised text from the Fathers when it was next presented to them. Commission and sub-commission meetings were usually held in the afternoons at 3:30 P.M. The president of a commission and the chairman of a sub-commission had no special parliamentary rules to follow other than those he chose to make himself as he went along. This caused dismay at some points, but it also got things moving at other times. For example, the president of a commission could let a whole week go by without calling a meeting, even though the majority of the commission could be demanding daily sessions! On the other hand, once Pope Paul sent down a request for action, the presidents usually turned out the work in short order. This procedure must have been hard, at first, on commission members unused to this style of running a railroad, but in the end it worked out very well. The truth is that cooking a schema in Rome is very much like cooking a "gumbo" in Louisiana—there is just no way of doing it fast, it has to simmer!

At the first session there were ten Council "Presidents" who took turns chairing the daily meetings in St. Peter's and who also acted as the top administrative body of the Council. Under them (although this jurisdictional arrangement was not too clear) was the "Coordinating Commission" which served as a clearing house to send material to this or that commission for consideration. Sometimes a matter had to go to two commissions, say those on Liturgy and Theology. In some instances questions were directed to "mixed commissions," set up by the Pope or by the Coordinating Commission, from the membership of a number of interested commissions. At the start of the second session, Pope Paul appointed four "Moderators" to chair the meetings and to speed things up, and the Presidents were increased to twelve. All Presidents, Coordinators and Moderators were of the rank of Cardinal. The General Secretariat of the Council was the fourth major administrative body of the Council.

It would be too tedious here to spell out the details of procedure for speaking in the aula or "Council Hall" of St. Peter's, that is, the great nave in which our seats had been set up. However, it was briefly this:

If a Council Father wished to speak, he first went up to one of the four sub-secretaries with a written request, accompanied by an outline of what he wished to say. The Moderators would go over the list of those entering such requests each day and assign them a certain priority. If the speaker were a Cardinal or if he spoke for a large number of bishops, he would be advanced on the list. Next, the speaker would check with the sub-secretaries each day to learn how far he had advanced on the priority list, as the speaking went on. Sometimes cloture was invoked before his turn came. That happened to me on my first attempt to make an intervention. I had been assigned to be speaker No. 53 during the Liturgy debate on the Divine Office, but cloture was invoked after the 46th speaker had been heard. In such a case, the speaker would simply hand in his speech as a written intervention. It would thus receive equal attention from the commission, but it would not have the same impact on the Fathers assembled as a spoken intervention might have, unless a copy were given to the press.

The General Secretary would announce first that a certain Father would now speak and that a second Father would advance to the microphone to speak next. There was a small open space at the bottom of each section of 66 bishops equipped with a small clear plastic rostrum, a microphone, a light, a telephone and a chair.

Speakers were given ten minutes in which to address the Council, and the Moderators were generally prompt in halting a speaker who had exceeded his time. This led to many an amusing incident. Some speakers, when admonished, would quickly run through the rest of their speech before the Moderator could cut them off the air. Others would panic at the sound of the Moderator's voice (coming out of nowhere), stop abruptly, sort of stunned, then quickly say "Dixi" and sit down without completing their remarks. "Dixi" (the Latin for "I have completed my remarks") was the agreed signal with the Moderators that the speaker had concluded his speech.

Procedure also required that a speaker submit the full text of what he had said. A secretary would receive this and deliver it to the Secretary General. In addition, two tapes were made of the talk while the speaker was at the microphone. Later young student priests, transcriptors, would compare the records and produce an accurate copy of what was said for the office of the Secretary General. Vatican II will certainly be the best recorded Council in the history of the Church!

Archbishop Hallinan was elected the only U.S. member of the Council Commission on the Liturgy. His election was additional evidence that the Council was a more open affair than I had anticipated, for Hallinan is well-known for his independence of thought as well as for his progressive attitudes. His election also gave me an opportunity to learn just how the Council Commissions operated and how the inside workings of the Council were carried out, for I was able to watch him work at firsthand and sit in on many of his conferences with the experts.

Liturgy was chosen as the first topic for debate, I have thought, primarily, because this was one subject on which the experts of the world had reached, over the years, something of a consensus. Hence, one could expect the Liturgy Commission to move ahead with its work more smoothly than other commissions—more smoothly than, for example, the Theological Commission, on which there was so much difference of opinion among the experts that, for a time, it was almost useless to call a meeting. Moreover, the Liturgy represented an area in which the Church could immediately touch the life of the everyday Catholic, an area in which the individual member of the Church would quickly sense the Council reforms, as the familiar rite of his daily or at least Sunday life-time pattern of worship was renewed.

More thoughtful writers have also suggested deeper doctrinal reasons for advancing the Liturgy to the head of the list, namely, that the treatment of the Liturgy, in the Council Constitution, takes dogmatic stances on a number of subjects, like the Church, which would be fully developed only later on in other documents of the Council. The Liturgy document was perhaps used to pave the way for the others!

There was another advantage, too, in taking up the Liturgy first, and perhaps Pope John had this in mind also. Liturgy is a subject concrete and familiar enough to be debated by the average administrative bishop. For a bishop need not be a professional theologian to discuss the reforms required in the daily worship of God, as he senses the need for renewal in his own diocese. Debate on the Liturgy enabled the Council to open a subject on which the bishops at large would feel competent to speak freely. This went far in making for a more "open" Council, and the bishops on this subject, at least, did not hesitate to express themselves.

From this early point on, I felt that I had a real part to play in the Council.

On the Friday evening of that first working-week of the Council, a little group of us gathered for supper at the well-known Roman restaurant *La Cisterna* ("The Magic Cistern"). Let me say that, while Archbishop Hallinan was busy at Liturgy Commission meetings, I agreed to take care of certain business we had in common. One of the items of this business was the arranging of evening meals with various groups we wanted to become acquainted with. And so from time to time I set up a dinner with the Observers; then I would set up a "French" dinner, an "Irish" dinner, a dinner with the young newspaper correspondents and journalists, a dinner with Council experts, and the like. Our gathering at *La Cisterna* that first Friday was composed of assorted Council people, mostly Americans.

The restaurant features a group of very obliging musicians. That night they made a special effort to render such unfamiliar American tunes as "Hold That Tiger!" and other outlandish requests. All they asked was that you hum the melody for them, once or twice, and they were ready to go with great enthusiasm into a most unlikely Italian-style version of your requested number. Their "Dixie" was particularly hilarious. It started off as "El Rancho Grande" which midway became "Oh, Susannah!" It was enough to topple General Robert E. Lee from his perch at Lee Circle in New Orleans. It was only later that I discovered that this version of "Dixie" had been hummed to the musicians by a Yankee, Bishop McDevitt of Philadelphia!

At one point in the evening we were discussing Pope John's health and his age. One of the group asked a waiter jokingly: "Should Pope John die, whom at this table would you pick as the best man to succeed him?" Without hesitating, the waiter pointed immediately to the clerical-collared Bishop Fred Corson, the Methodist from Philadelphia!

We had been talking and reading about the Liturgy for several days, but the debate on the subject had not yet begun. On Friday of the first week, the Council Fathers had issued a "Message to All Men" as a preliminary statement of their intent. This was unprecedented at Ecumenical Councils, which formerly always addressed themselves exclusively to the members of the Catholic Church. With this message now promulgated to the world and a new tone of "openness" set, everyone was anxious and ready for the discussion to begin on Monday on the Sacred Liturgy.

Chapter 4

The Sacred Liturgy

The great debate on the Liturgy began in St. Peter's on October 22 with twenty-one Fathers rising to speak at the fourth General Congregation or daily meeting. The Liturgy remained the subject of addresses until the eighteenth General Congregation on November 13. This debate set a tone and laid down certain general principles which had an effect on all the debates to follow. My notes say that, in the first twelve daily meetings, we listened to more than 250 bishops. Most of these talks were really first-rate. After all, anyone who rises to speak before all the assembled bishops of the Catholic world will surely make an effort to give the very best speech of which he is capable. And the quality of Council interventions was ordinarily high. What made the speeches tiresome, at times, was not their lack of quality but the repetition of the same thoughts by a long succession of speakers.

The thoughts expressed concerning the "tone" of the Liturgy schema and the "principles" laid down gave the Fathers of the Council plenty to think about.

The very first question to be considered, of course, was: "Just why does the Sacred Liturgy need renewal at all?" It cannot be denied that there were many present, in the beginning, who felt that the Liturgy was generally very good the way it was; further, if there were to be any improvements, they felt the Sacred Congregation of Rites was the agency properly suited to make those improvements. In addition, there was the feeling among many bishops that certain independent writers and professors, who did not share the responsibility of either the Sacred Congregation of Rites or of the bishops, were urging certain reforms—imaginative and even dangerous—which represented a radical departure from the regular traditional approach to divine worship.

Actually, most of the reforms proposed were not unrealistic or fly-by-night proposals at all. They were the fruit of profound thought, study and discussion by the finest students of Liturgy around the world, and they were based on the soundest scholarship, as well as on a genuine interest in the cause of sacred worship. The fruits of this scholarship and this interest had been reported to the world for more than thirty years at frequent meetings on the Liturgy, culminating in the great international congress at Assisi in September, 1956. In 1958, even the Sacred Congregation itself had issued a decree calling for a number of reforms: participation by the people, the use of community singing and of lay commentators, and a number of other like measures.

The reason why the Liturgy needed renewal was, briefly, this: that the *spirit* of divine worship offered by human beings needs to be refreshed from time to time: while essentials cannot change, of course, such things as certain *external rites*—the use of gestures, vestments, processions, prayers, singing and so on—not only *can* change, but *must* change in order to have divine worship remain meaningful to those who are worshiping.

Through history, in the face of new historical developments, liturgical emphasis had often changed in order to meet a crisis, but sometimes it has failed to shift back again after the crisis has passed. These crises have a way of giving character to a whole epoch, so that attention is drawn strongly to one single phase of the period in question. Cardinal Suhard of Paris pointed out in his postwar writings that it is facile enough to single out certain "moments" in the Church's existence: the moment of *martyrdom* (Early Church), of *sovereignty* (beginning with the crowning of Charlemagne, of *royal patronage* (in the Middle Ages), the moment of *siege* (the moment of withdrawal from the world and of negative insistence on the condemnation of errors beginning with those of the Reformers and ending with those of the Modernists), and so on.

All of these "moments" obscure the nature of the Church as she exists in all her fullness and richness of truth and grace, because they concentrate entirely too much on *the crisis* of each "moment."

And so the "siege moment" (especially the latter half of the nineteenth and first half of the twentieth century), in which all living Catholics have found themselves, was preoccupied with meeting attacks on reason and authority. The withdrawal of the Church from the human arena had a good effect, in one way, for it repaired the damage which the Church had sustained within her own fold, and this was necessary at the time. However, too much and too prolonged a concentration on her own defense left the Church in large measure irrelevant to the needs and opportunities of the pulsing new society without.

The new marvels of science and the problems of hunger, war and world poverty were now raising questions everywhere. There Christ's Church should surely share the world's concern and even join hands with all humane and compassionate forces to face and meet the crises confronting the modern man—not exclusively the crises confronting the modern *Catholic* man.

Pope John, himself, was deeply concerned; and he wanted the Church as a whole to share that concern and to send its great dynamism into action. The Church could not do this effectively by always sticking to the strictly logical definitions found in the catechism and taught by rote, even to tiny youngsters. For example, the logical definition (which we all learned): "The Church is the congregation of all those who profess the faith of Christ, participate in the same Sacraments. . . ." Christ, on the other hand, had called the Church "a light on a mountain top," a "net cast into the sea," a "sheepfold." And writers like Yves Congar were describing the Church as "The People of God, advancing to destiny, servants and witnesses to life and growth in Christ."

By comparison, how cold, legalistic and uninspiring the old academic definitions now seem! These definitions did serve their purpose in the days when the Church was worried about the need of defining her position against attack. Now it was becoming evident that we had failed to worry about something much more important, namely, *the meaningfulness* of the Church's teaching to all hearers of the Gospel in their personal lives; their understanding of their own position and role in the Church; and their dedication to a life of dynamic apostolic action.

Above all, it had become evident that the modern Catholic must be helped to attain a realization of the Presence of Christ in the Church and in himself—not just in static, inactive fashion—merely to be visited, adored and spoken to—but in a dynamic projection of His work into the agonized society of our times. Central is the realization that Christ is present for action—to get His work done; that He is present in His *Word*, the Scriptures; supremely in His *Sacrifice*, the Mass; in His *Sacraments;* in His *Ministers*, the Pope, bishops and priests; and also in His *Laity*. The laity, through Baptism and the Holy Eucharist, are appointed and equipped to do the work of Christ on earth in their own special capacity, which, although different, is no less necessary as a vital part of the entire life of the Church.

Nowhere did the "siege mentality" affect the Catholic so much as in his public, liturgical worship. There his role had become static. The layman was to simply observe and carry out assignments given him by the clergy. He was not allowed to worship in his own tongue (he must be protected from possible "disunity"); he was not allowed to read aloud or make comment at Mass (he must be protected from the insidious idea of a "priesthood of the laity"); he must let trained altar boys and a trained choir represent and act for him (to protect him from making embarrassing liturgical mistakes)!

Attendance at Mass was carried out in the same spirit as a private visit to the Blessed Sacrament—one was occupied with good, religious thoughts, indeed very appropriate ones—but even in a full church, the worshiper was alone in the crowd, preoccupied with his own personal devotion and rather unaware of the essential community spirit, called for even by the very text of the Mass itself. This text the layman was urged to read to himself in

English while the priest read the same thing *to himself* from *his* missal in Latin.

The way the Council eventually expressed itself about the aims of the Council, which were also reasons for the reform of the Liturgy, was as follows:

> To give vigor to the Christian life of the faithful.
>
> To adapt what is changeable to the needs of the day.
>
> To promote union among all who believe in Christ.
>
> To strengthen the Church's mission to all mankind.

Hence, there were also ecumenical reasons for reforming the Sacred Liturgy. It was not good to have the Church seem so strange, so foreign, so withdrawn to outsiders. Nor was it a good thing to have non-Catholics, who frequently attended Catholic services, especially weddings and funerals, find the services, to a large extent, meaningless, although perhaps mysteriously impressive.

These considerations had been familiar for years to many a participant in the world-wide liturgical movement; and, in the Decree of 1958, they began to receive some recognition even from the Sacred Congregation of Rites. Still, such thoughts represented a view which many bishops were not enthusiastic about at the start of the Council, but to which they became educated as the spirit of the Council developed.

In addition to this need for general reform of the Liturgy, there were also many specific irritations. In the interests of safety of the faith and of proper worship, rigid control of worship all over the world from Rome was thought to be essential. But the worship imposed was a worship developed centuries ago, a Roman-style worship which centered about the celebrant as though he were a temporal prince or a grandee of some kind, who depended on ribbons and jewelry to assert and underline his position. Worship was also largely designed along either courtly or monastic rather than parochial lines. This caused considerable difficulty, especially in mission lands, where the image of the priest must be that of a father and where prince-images evoked only the unpleasant overtones of colonialism. It also caused some real problems, for example, in Africa where the color for a wedding ceremony or any joyful event is black, since white is the color of mourning; or in Japan where a genuflection means nothing, but where a graceful and profound bow is the current language of courtesy and diplomacy.

The use of Latin, instead of a language understood by the people, was particularly a great barrier and also a great nuisance. The plea for the use of Latin was its value as a symbol and as a bond of unity. One bishop agreed that it was indeed a unifying force, because, no matter where you go in the whole world, it is equally unintelligible!

One of the most impressive interventions on behalf of a wider use of the vernacular in the liturgy came from Maximus IV Saigh, Melchite Patriarch of Antioch. The patriarch at the time of the first session was already 84 years of age, but one could always count on him, when he rose to speak, to give the liveliest possible performance. For example, he made it a great issue that a patriarch should have ceremonial precedence over a cardinal ("After all, the Pope is a patriarch!"). Hence, when he rose to speak at the Council, he addressed the patriarchs before he addressed the cardinals.

Ultimately, a measure of diplomacy and compromise eased the situation on all sides. The patriarchs were given a special place in the aula, facing, but not below the cardinals, and on an elevation. Then a number of patriarchs were appointed as members of the Oriental Congregation, an appointment which had gone previously only to cardinals. And, finally, Maximus and two other patriarchs, Stephanos I. Sidarouss, C.M., and Paul Meouchi, were offered the cardinalate itself by the Pope which, this time, they courteously accepted, as long as they would not have to give up the ceremonial dress of a patriarch. (Maximus, by report, had refused previous invitations, from Pius XII and John XXIII, to accept the red hat.)

There was plenty of spark in the aged Maximus and this was evident to all whenever he made his spirited and humorous addresses in St. Peter's. Most of the bishops, I thought, felt that

Maximus greatly exaggerated the importance of the patriarchate in today's world in a loyal effort to revive a situation which had gone with the wind many centuries ago. But they admired his spirit and his spunk and they greatly enjoyed his wit and shrewdness. These qualities show through in his very first intervention made on October 23. It was the last speech of the day and it favored the wider use of vernacular in the Liturgy. Maximus made the following points:

He did not like the basic idea of giving Latin an almost *absolute value*. Christ and the Apostles would never have thought of speaking to the people or of conducting the Lord's Supper in anything but language their hearers understood;

Then he cleverly introduced a quotation from St. Paul (1 Cor. 14: 16–19): "If thou dost pronounce a blessing in this spiritual fashion [that is to say, speaking an incomprehensible language] how can one who takes his place among the uninstructed say Amen to thy thanksgiving? He cannot tell what thou art saying. Thou, true enough, art duly giving thanks, but the other's faith is not strengthened. . . . In the church, I would rather speak five words which my mind utters for your instruction, than ten thousand in a strange tongue."

Latin became the single universal language of the Roman empire only in the *Middle Ages;*

Every language is liturgical and no language should be untouchable;

Let *episcopal conferences* decide upon the language to be used in the Liturgy!

Many bishops followed Maximus with assaults on the current use of Latin in the Liturgy and with pleas for the wider use of vernacular. Bishop Rau of Argentina was an especially impassioned speaker who vowed that he would be true to death to the Roman Church but not to the Latin language! The Polish bishops could point to the actual use of the vernacular in their liturgy over the past fifteen years as a prime means of saving the faith in their country. Then, Archbishop Hallinan, I think, startled the Fathers somewhat when he urged the ecumenical reasons for using the vernacular, citing his American see of Atlanta as only two percent Catholic! Finally, Pope John, himself, gave an indirect assist to the cause of the vernacular at the observance of the anniversary of his coronation as Pope of November 4. He began his address in Latin and then quickly switched to Italian "because it is better understood by the crowds of faithful who have come here to celebrate the anniversary of their Pastor and Father."

Lively interventions were also heard on the subjects of communion under both species, concelebration of Mass by a number of priests, evening Masses, and the placing of St. Joseph's name in the Canon of the Mass. Objections were made that concelebration was a spectacular innovation which deprived the Church of graces, reducing many Masses to one Mass; while modern-day hygiene, the use of lipstick and the danger of spilling the chalice, especially on ladies' dresses, made communion under two species impractical!

However, the larger considerations of the public and communal character of the Mass and the explicitness of Holy Scripture on having the faithful "eat this bread and drink this chalice" did prevail, especially in view of the fact that none of the objections seemed to hold water in the Eastern rites where the practices had always been common. Then, Pope John took a shortcut by simply placing St. Joseph in the Canon of the Mass, at his own decision, without waiting for Conciliar action.

With debate on the Liturgy underway, the Fathers settled down to a steady daily routine. My own schedule called for the celebration of private Mass each morning at about seven o'clock at the hotel. My window at the Michelangelo was only a few feet away from the windows of the apartment house next door and each day a considerable number of apartment-dwellers watched my celebration of Mass from across the alley. I used to give them a sign of recognition, at the end of Mass, by reaching far out of my window to impart the final blessing. Later I wondered whether this was not invading the Papal privilege—to impart a blessing from a window right in the Pope's back yard! At the time this did not occur to me, and I don't think Pope John would have minded anyway!

Our daily bus arrived at 8:30 A.M. and brought us to St. Peter's where bus after bus rolled into the square delivering Council Fathers from all over the world. At the Residence Place, pupils from the Parioli International School, mostly American children, used to line up outside the hotel, with the bishops, as they awaited the bus to take them to school. One day as our bus arrived first and the bishops with their 'school bags' proceeded to get aboard, one boy yelled: "Yeah, Council!" to which a few of us, out of courtesy, could not help replying in kind: "Yeah, Parioli!"

The daily Mass at the Council began at 9 A.M. It was usually a low Mass with participation. However, most of the singing was done by a polyphonic Vatican choir of boys and men, instead of by the bishops themselves, which would have been more normal. Listening to that polished choir day after day was like eating ice cream for breakfast, dinner and supper. As they say here in Louisiana: "Too much sugar for a nickel!" At the last session, this procedure was corrected somewhat and a new Mass book issued to the Fathers more in harmony with the Constitution on the Liturgy. It did seem strange for the Fathers to work up so magnificent a statement on the Liturgy as the Constitution was, and then seem to ignore its spirit among themselves in, of all places, the very hall of the Council!

On some days there would be Masses in the various other rites of the Church around the world. It was both interesting and delightful to listen to their ancient liturgical harmonies carried by such beautiful and well-trained voices. And I could not but wonder what ever became of candidates for the priesthood in rites, say, like the Byzantine, when it was discovered that the candidate was tone-deaf! For every oriental-rite priest and bishop seemed to have excellent vocal equipment, compared generally with the celebrants of our Latin Masses. A Latin American bishop, hearing the singing of an Oriental Mass for the first time, said to me, in English: "Good, eh? How you say in English—*much throat!* O.K.?"

After Mass the great book of the Gospels was brought in while all the bishops sang: "Christus vincit, Christus regnat, Christus imperat!" A bearded bishop behind me sang this always with a great deal of spirit, and he was usually about a half-beat ahead of the rest of us. His rendition came rolling out with immense gusto: "Chr-r-r-istus vincit, Chr-r-r-istus regnat. . . ." Then the Secretary General proclaimed each day: "*Exeant Omnes!*" and the Swiss Guards and all others not entitled to be present at the daily meeting had to depart. Immediately, the Fathers got down to the business of the day, with our daily prayer "*Adsumus*" ("Lord, we are here!")—a prayer which has been recited before daily council meetings for many a century.

My row of six bishops at the first session of the Council, like many another row, in this immense stadium for 2,600 bishops, was highly cosmopolitan in its make-up ("S" stands for "Sinistra", left side; the opposite tier was marked "D" meaning "Dextera", right.):

S. 917—Bishop Juan y Soliman, Santo Domingo
S. 918—Bishop Robert E. Tracy, Baton Rouge, U.S.A.
S. 919—Bishop Paul Piché, Mackenzie, Northwest Canada
S. 920—Bishop Joseph Denning, Brooklyn, U.S.A.
S. 921—Bishop Jean Karroum, Syria (Oriental rite)
S. 922—Bishop Anthony Nwedo, Nigeria

Each row held six bishops, and the whole section consisted of eleven rows. To each section was assigned a young priest-student who acted as secretary-assistant to sixty-six bishops. This secretary issued and collected the IBM cards, carried messages, and distributed booklets and other materials.

Fascinating is the word to describe the variety of dress used by bishops from around the world. There were Franciscan bishops in gray outfits with red cuffs, looking like Confederate generals. Then there were the Oriental bishops, entering in groups, and looking from the back, to an American, like a bevy of mothers superior. And there were the Dominican bishops in white, the Capuchins in brown and still other bishops, from the desert lands, in striking sheiklike robes carrying brilliant ornamentation. But the spirit of unity ran strong among them, gathered as they were around their Father, Pope John, the Vicar of Christ on earth, to work together with him and with each other for the renewal of Christian life throughout the world.

One bishop near me was most attentive and intense. He always reacted visibly to all that was said—either favorably or unfavorably. If he did not approve of a thing, you knew it at once—he turned his back and waved down the speaker. But if he agreed, he would emit a low whistle of approval while slowly drawing a circle, formed by his thumb and forefinger, down from eye-level to the bottom of his beard.

For those who needed a stretch and a break after a long spell of listening, there was the Coffee Stand, which came to be known as Bar Jonah, set up under magnificent sculpture in a corridor connecting the sacristy with the Canons' chapel. Here democracy held sway. Late in the morning you had to work your way up to the stand for your *cappuccino* (café-au-lait) through a solid mass of cardinals, patriarchs, archbishops, bishops and observers, all of whom moved forward in the utmost good humor and in every-man-for-himself style. Indeed, before long coffee became one of the finest signs of unity among us!

All the Fathers of the Council were bound to *secrecy* on official matters discussed or transpiring at the Council. At first this applied to debates in the aula, but this restriction was relaxed to permit a speaker to be quoted by name. The reason given for secrecy was that the Fathers might hold back in their remarks if they knew they could be quoted publicly. The rule was also founded on the somewhat naïve notion that secrecy in so large a gathering could, somehow, be maintained. Actually, today, secrets travel faster than anything else! Besides, the concept of secrecy is understood differently in different countries. In the U.S. "classified information" is taken seriously, whereas a French newspaper I used to read, *La Croix*, prided itself on printing every "secret" it found as fast as it could discover it. Similarly, in America a No Admittance sign means that you cannot get in. But

in Italy, an official told me that one of my priests could not—
under any circumstances—get into a certain ceremony without a
ticket. "However," he added, "if he comes in his monsignor's outfit, we are certainly not going to be rude enough to turn him
away!" And so it is with secrecy: "Not a word! However, if you
see that it will do more harm than good to observe secrecy, then
use your own prudent judgment!"

Actually, it was a bit visionary to imagine that anyone could
tell secrets to some 2,600 human beings and not have these secrets
somehow leak to the press. Personally, from the beginning, I
found the whole secrecy policy at the Council somewhat in-
equitable. Many bishops did observe secrecy strictly, while others
took a relaxed view of it. Hence, some newspapers published fairly
complete accounts while others, with fewer contacts, carried far
less complete information. Perhaps it was due in some measure to
the unrealistic restrictions of "secrecy" that the one thousand
correspondents who had assembled at Rome for the opening of
the Council slowly began to fade away until only a few hundred
were left.

It was hard on the officials to handle so huge and unfamiliar a
congress as an Ecumenical Council, and it was not surprising that,
at first, press relations were not of the best. But our U.S. correspondents eventually received excellent assistance in writing their
stories: they received a mimeographed release about the morning's session about 3 P.M. from the office of Father Edward L.
Heston, C.S.C. Then, at 3:30 P.M. the newsmen could go to the
USO and question a panel of priests who were experts in such
fields as liturgy, theology and history. It was my impression that
this panel provided the reporters a valuable avenue to an accurate
interpretation of Council reports, and that the newsmen were
well pleased with it. Actually, the U.S., in the end, was the only
country at the Council to provide comparable service to the
press.

It may seem strange—now that the Fathers have adopted the
Constitution on the Liturgy so overwhelmingly—but on November 6, 1962, I made the following notation in my book of Council

Notes: "Some reporters have it that few changes will take place in the area of public worship; but other observers foresee very deep and significant reforms in the Liturgy. However, the majority, I would say, expect to see many realistic changes all along the line." The point is that, as little as four years ago, it was not at all clear, even to the Fathers of the Council, that there would be promulgated a document as forward-looking as the Constitution on the Sacred Liturgy. However, by the time the final congregation of the second session was reached on December 4, 1963, a great change had come about: the Fathers were almost unanimously in favor of the final text. Indeed, when the final landslide vote was announced (2,147 votes in favor, and only 4 votes opposed), one bishop near me jokingly exclaimed: "Who do you suppose those four *non-placets* are—the mental cases?"

However, before that near-unanimous vote was taken on December 4, 1963, there had been some anxious moments during the voting on the Liturgy in the course of the second session. The vote on the whole schema had been taken on November 22, 1963, and came off: For—2,158; Against—19; Invalid—1; yet, prior to that, there had been a large number of amendments entered and voted on. Some of these were interesting; it was somewhat frustrating not to be allowed to vote on all of them directly:

1. The Liturgy Commission, when the vote on Chapter II as a whole failed to get a two-thirds vote, agreed that the form of the Sacraments should be in English. So we got to vote on "Whether it pleases the Fathers to have the vernacular used more widely in the Sacraments?" The vote, of course, was "placet" and the chapter was saved.

2. However, the Commission did not favor having the collects of the Mass in the vernacular (these are, properly, the prayer of the priest, although said aloud). So we did not get to vote on whether we wanted the collects in the vernacular or not; we only got to vote on whether we were willing to endorse the Commission in turning the proposal down. We would have been forced to vote "no confidence" in the Commission to get the collects in the vernacular and Fathers were unwilling to publicly repudiate the work of the Commission in such a matter, even though they may have

wanted the collects in the vernacular. The Commission was sustained.

3. "Do you approve of the Commission's action in refusing Communion under both species to bride and groom?" was the substance of the next proposition; and, of course, the Fathers again sustained the Commission.

4. Fortunately, the Commission *favored* giving the local bishop the right to regulate the concelebration of Mass in his diocese. Hence, we got to vote directly on this one, and it naturally won a "placet" vote.

The collects of the Mass and a great deal more besides are now possible in the vernacular, due to later relaxations by the Holy See, and so is reception of Holy Communion under both species by bride and groom. But the rule on vernacular for the priest's daily recitation of the Divine Office, established at the Council, remains unchanged: it may be conceded to an individual priest by his bishop but only when the use of Latin is "an obstacle to his devout recitation of the Breviary."

The Constitution on the Sacred Liturgy also specifies that no one—not even a priest—may take it upon himself to introduce any changes in the Liturgy until there has been the necessary promulgation of such changes and their application, by the required juridical steps:

1. The Pope must approve and promulgate any change;

2. In the case of using vernacular, the territorial body of bishops must approve the translation to be used in a diocese and then have that decree approved by Rome;

3. After this, the local bishop may approve the use of vernacular, according to the decree, in his own diocese;

4. Any change in the rites themselves, however, must be undertaken by a postconciliar commission with the aid of experts from around the world. This commission is now meeting under Cardinal Lercaro and Archbishop Hallinan is a member of it.

There has been some interest in the matter of experimentation with rite changes, especially of the Mass. The view has been advanced that the present rite is still more "pontifical" and "monastic" than pastoral; further, whatever reform of the Liturgy was realized at Vatican II came not from the top, that is, not from the Sacred Congregation of Rites, but from the grass roots, that is, from students of the liturgy and other interested persons not in official positions but closer to the people and the scene. Therefore, these latter should now be the pioneers in further experimentation.

However, the Church is clear on how experimentation is to be carried out. The students of liturgy are surely expected to continue to advance their ideas about healthy reform, in writings and addresses, as they have always done. Over the years the most effective advocates of liturgical reform have proposed reform in this manner, while always adhering strictly to the laws of the Church, which alone has the right to regulate the sacred public worship of God. Today it is possible to have priests authorized to work out particular experimentation with the approval of the postconciliar commission, the Sacred Congregation of Rites and his own bishop, under very definite regulations. However, no one—not even a priest—may attempt experimentation on his own.

As the debate on the Sacred Liturgy began, it became clear that many a bishop had already received a quick education in the liturgical needs of the day by simply reading the schema. Many bishops who were not especially students of the liturgy and who had not, until then, read very much about the reforms discussed by liturgy groups over the years, once the facts were pointed out to them, found the proposed renewal entirely reasonable. Moreover, they were encouraged by the position taken in the course of the debate by such men as Cardinals Frings, Lercaro, Montini and Doepfner. These cardinals led off at the Council by stating that the schema was well adapted to the needs of the day since it was written in the spirit called for by Pope John—namely, with emphasis on the pastoral, practical and ecumenical aspects of the Church's mission to the world. They also found the schema to be composed with a view to the great value of Holy Scripture in the liturgy and with a truly Christ-centered approach.

Perceiving the importance of renewal of the Liturgy to the entire work of the Council, the typical non-specialist bishop began to do collateral reading on the subject and to attend some of the lectures which were being given by world-renowned writers and professors almost every afternoon. As a result, a vast amount of self-education began taking place.

Important lectures and press conferences were being given by experts in various fields from around the world; for example:

Father Jean Danielou: on the episcopate;

Bishop Henri Jenny, Auxiliary of Cambrai: on the Liturgy;

Father Hermann Schmidt, S.J., Gregorian University: on the Liturgy;

Father Henri de Lubac: general conference;

Father Gustave Thils: on the theology of the episcopate;

Dr. Hans Kung: general conference;

Professor Oscar Cullmann: press conference on behalf of the observers.

Moreover, it was possible, in the course of the morning at St. Peter's, to arrange to speak, privately or in a small group, to many an expert on the liturgy. One could find the *periti* up in one of the tribunes or galleries hung overhead between the great arches of the central nave. Monsignor Pat went up to one of the galleries one morning but could recognize no one in the group by sight. Undaunted, and confident that before him was many an author whose books he had read, he took out a pad and pencil and passed it around, requesting signatures. When the pad came back to him it was filled with the names of well-known authors which he immediately recognized:

A. G. Martimort

Frederick R. McManus

Robert Trisco

Yves Congar, O.P.

John E. Steinmueller

Bernard Haring, C.Ss.R.

P. Charles Boyer, S.J.

Barnabas M. Ahern, C.P.
Eugene H. Maly
George Higgins
Gregory Baum, O.S.A.
George W. Shea
Rudolphus J. Bandas
Joseph A. Jungmann, S.J.
Sacerio Parenti
C. B. Daly

Some of the newspapers contained valuable educational material as well. *La Croix*, the Catholic French daily, for example, ran two full pages of report and commentary every day.

Thus when Pope Paul, receiving the American and Canadian bishops in audience a few days before the close of the Council, reminded us that we had had unusual opportunities for education at the Council, he was pointing up one of the most important of what I have often called "the hidden gains of the Council." Personally, I found these avenues to education so varied and so rich that, at first, I hardly knew where to begin or which of them to avail myself of. Basically, I kept in close touch with the great work Archbishop Hallinan was doing as a member of the Liturgy Commission, and I went to many a conference and many an evening meal with him at which he thrashed out things with the scholars.

Hallinan was less than an expert liturgist when he was elected the only member of the U.S. hierarchy to sit on the Council Commission on the Liturgy. But he had a lively interest in the subject, had read extensively on it, and had introduced the new liturgical reforms of 1958 into his diocese at Charleston with marked success. Once he found himself on the commission, he went to work with that drive and originality which are so characteristic of him. Today, he possesses a superb background on the subject and indeed has produced a booklet entitled *How to Understand the Liturgy*. He has also been appointed by the Pope to the Postconciliar International Concilium on the Liturgy which is headed by Cardinal Lercaro. Archbishop Hallinan is also the representative of the U.S. bishops on what we jokingly call "The Common Market"—the group of English-speaking bishops who are exploring the possibility of a common international English text for liturgical functions. My association with him was a further source of education for me—probably the very best I had, for it stimulated me to make better use of all the other sources.

In addition to lectures, conferences, and reading on the Liturgy, I also conducted a "lab" during the third session of the Council: namely, the renovation of my cathedral in Baton Rouge, according to the principles laid down by the Constitution on the Sacred Liturgy. In this experiment I took advantage of my contacts with experts from all over the world to organize a blueprint for the renewal of the building. At home, I invited a committee from almost all parts of the U.S., composed of thirty experts in various fields: architecture, art, liturgy, engineering, vestment-making, music, landscaping, etc., to advise me. I also flew to Mexico with advisers to inspect the liturgical renewal already put into effect there by Bishop Mendez-Arceo in his cathedral building at Cuernavaca.

The renewal which is now under way in my cathedral, and which will cost $300,000, consists mainly in emphasizing those elements in the building which are fundamental and necessary to the worship of God and to the Christian life, and the lifting of emphasis from those elements which are merely optional or accidental. For example, the altar, the bishop's throne, the presbytery, the organ and choir, and other such items are all arranged with a view to full, conscious and active participation by everyone present. Next, the Sacraments are given special emphasis: the baptismal font is located at the entrance, so that each person who enters the church must pass it and recall that it is through Baptism that we are given the right and the power to offer Mass; there are "stations" which are inlaid bronze markers in the floor where the Sacraments of Confirmation, Matrimony and Holy Orders are received, and there are "communion stations" which indicate the location at which the Eucharist is received by the faithful. The Holy Oils are kept, not in what often appears to be a fuse box in the wall, relegated out of sight of the people, but in three separate, adorned containers. These are in full view of the faithful. Before each a tiny lamp burns as a mark of respect. The Holy Books are also given a special place of honor in view of the congregation. Only those statues of saints are retained which have some good reason for being in this particular building; and no candles burn except those which have some connection with the liturgy.

Our cathedral is 113 years old and built in Gothic style. It cannot, therefore, be completely oriented, as a new church might be, to the new liturgical order, but it certainly can be vastly improved—indeed, it does lend itself in many respects to liturgical renewal. At any rate, a running discussion of the proposed reforms which appeared regularly along with sketches in the newspaper *The Catholic Commentator* served not only as an exercise in the study of liturgy for me but also for the faithful at large.

One of the basic considerations in the debate on the Liturgy at the Council was that of authority. Who should properly regulate the Sacred Liturgy, the Holy See alone—or also others, acting with the approval of the Holy See? Those who generally favored as little change as possible in the liturgy, it seemed, favored regulation by the Apostolic See alone. On the other hand, those who argued for renewal wherever it was needed, also as a rule asked that the local bishop and territorial bodies of bishops be given some measure of legislative power with approval required only from the Holy See. However, these generalities do not describe the position of *every* bishop. Cardinal McIntyre of Los Angeles, for example, did not favor legislation by territorial bodies of bishops at all, whereas Cardinal Meyer of Chicago favored legislation only in those areas cited by the Holy See. Perhaps Cardinal Meyer felt, as I know some other bishops did, that it would be better to have church laws come out of Rome than out of Washington meetings, even though in the latter case opportunity would be provided for participation in the making of the laws when the bishops assembled at Washington. The cardinal felt that once there was a Conciliar Constitution to appeal to, a local bishop could work more efficiently directly under the Holy See. Full legislative power in hands of the national body of bishops, besides, might limit the freedom of a local bishop too much, by giving him not one but two bosses—one in Rome and another in Washington.

Nor did the Holy See, in the past, favor placing legislative power in the hands of national bodies of bishops. In fact, it had required that the name of the National Catholic Welfare *Council* be changed to *Conference*, because the word "council" carried overtones of authority. Personally, I was for legislation at the national level in which I would have a say and a vote. But one of my friends among the bishops thought I was working against my own best interests in taking this stance. He explained that a national body of bishops might make a law in connection with racial matters that I would find virtually impossible to carry out in our circumstances in the South. But I remained willing to take my chances since, in a wholly impossible situation, I could always appeal to the Holy See.

So there was some vigorous opposition to the proposal of having laws governing the Sacred Liturgy made by anyone but the Apostolic See. And it is true that, in some respects, the Sacred Congregation of Rites would have more resources to draw on in framing legislation. On the other hand, the Sacred Congregation of Rites had certain drawbacks. Among these was its past record of being out of contact with the local scene in many ways: its rigidity and inflexibility in liturgical matters, as evidenced by its attitude on the use of the vernacular; and, above all, the failure of many of its officials to grasp and appreciate the need and value of reform as the Council would eventually spell it out. Indeed, these were the very reasons why Pope John had called a Council instead of simply calling in the heads of his various Roman Congregations to reform the Church. Too many of them did not understand his concept of reform, and too many of them simply did not want to buy his brand of it.

The Pope had a very delicate task to perform. He had to

continue to depend on the Sacred Congregation of Rites for daily advice and for the daily discharge of the Church's business. Moreover, he could not overlook the competence and dedication of the trained officials who staffed it, nor could he seem to belittle their role. On the other hand, he had to move ahead with reforms to which they were lukewarm or even opposed. Thus, even after the Council, when Pope Paul had appointed a Postconciliar Concilium, under Cardinal Lercaro, charged with directing the implementation of the Council's decrees on the Liturgy, the documents of the concilium still carry the name of Cardinal Larraona, Prefect of the Sacred Congregation of Rites, in the top spot—with Cardinal Lercaro taking second billing. This represents a typical example of the prudent compromise you often find in Church government: the concilium is in charge of the implementation, but not at the cost of loss of prestige to the Congregation.

It is unfortunate that certain writers, apparently for purposes of dramatizing the Council, have inflamed the imagination of the public by painting the members of the Curia, on the whole, simply as the bad guys, the villains of the piece, who were out to get the good guys, the outright champions of liturgical and other reforms. By contrast, Pope Paul, in announcing the reforms of the Curia, was completely balanced about the matter: the members of the Curia were not selfish, delinquent officials; they were dedicated men who, however, needed to be put more in touch with things. For example, Archbishop Dino Staffa, Secretary of the Congregation of Seminaries, a learned, able and dedicated man, stated in an intervention in St. Peter's that nobody but the Holy See had any *right* to regulate either doctrine or worship, and that national conferences of bishops with legislative power were completely out of order—a view solidly rejected by the Council. Staffa also did extensive research and wrote a very able treatise attempting to prove that collegiality of the bishops was a mistaken idea which could not avoid infringement on rightful Papal authority. This treatise was an honest effort, undertaken with great zeal for the Church's welfare. Still, the Council rejected its basic contention and now the concept of collegiality is clearly established in Catholic doctrine and practice.

In addition to well-argued presentations of conservative position, there was also a certain measure, at times, of what may be called overzeal, or what St. Paul has termed "a zeal but not according to knowledge" (in other words, according to *emotion*). This overzeal at times led protagonists of a certain position to indulge in tactics which some of us found unworthy of the work in which we were engaged. For example, efforts were made to stall off meetings or the taking of a vote when it appeared that sentiment would probably go against a given position. This was done in the hope that, given time, the opposition could be brought to see the light, or that the Papal authority could be persuaded to intervene in the matter before it was brought to a conclusion.

On learning about such tactics, some journalists and American readers expressed their shock in the discovery that there was a certain amount of politics in the Council. I would like to disagree with this reaction. The use of such tactics did not stem at all from the obsession to have one's own view or the view of one's group prevail. Rather, their moves were motivated by their sincere desire to save the Church from pitfalls or possible disaster. Further, when it was clear that a consensus of the Fathers had been obtained, there was acquiescence, as the almost unanimous vote on the Liturgy Constitution clearly exhibited. Politics, as the word is used among Americans in a derogatory sense, would imply using unworthy tactics simply to advance a measure favorable to one's own private interests as contrasted with the common good. This was not the spirit that prevailed at the Council or even showed itself in any noticeable way.

And it is unfortunate that certain writers never seemed able to get over their surprise that Council Fathers and Vatican officials are, after all, human beings. It seems to me that the wonderment of many journalists could have been much better directed to the phenomenon that such human beings could, under the guidance of the Holy Spirit, achieve such honest and healthy decisions in connection with the reform and renewal of the Church. This concept of the happenings would have been just as dramatic and a lot more constructive than the good-guys-and-bad-guys slant.

Although voting on the Liturgy would continue all through the first and second sessions of the Council, on and off, as the Commission on the Liturgy got material prepared and as the material was presented to us, still I find it better to continue with my remarks on the Liturgy here and bring them to a conclusion in this chapter. This will perhaps make for a more understandable story.

The debate on the Liturgy, then, centered around a few main considerations: (1) Should all decisions about the liturgy be made in Rome, with national bodies of bishops merely *proposing* changes, or should these territorial bodies have *legislative power* with the Holy See approving? (2) Should the *vernacular* be permitted in the Latin Rite and, if so, to what extent? (3) Did the Latin liturgy, generally, need to be *renewed all along the line*, or was it satisfactory, on the whole, as it was? (4) Was there a need for *active participation* by the people in prayer and song in the liturgy, or was this only a distraction? (5) Was there need for greater use of *Holy Scripture* and more emphasis on *Preaching* in the liturgy or not? (6) Should the laity and religious on certain occasions be permitted to receive communion under *both species?* (7) Should *concelebration* of Mass by a number of priests be permitted more widely?

It soon became clear which way the tide was running. While there was no lack of Fathers to plead for retaining the old forms as much as possible and for keeping things centralized in Rome, there was even stronger leadership which spoke up for renewal. My recollection is that those who favored the renewal set forth in the schema were worried at first whether the schema would receive sufficient support. The schema was "in possession." This meant that a one-third vote plus one could send it back to the Commission for reworking—a distinct possibility, it seemed to me at the time. I felt that the bishops from countries like Italy, Spain and Ireland would be conservative about the liturgy right down the line and would generally oppose the changes. I was surprised to learn that the bishops of these countries felt the same way about the American bishops. Cardinal Spellman was known to favor keeping the Mass rite as it was and against using the vernacular, and after all, wasn't he the Voice of America?

Those of us who favored the reforms of the schema had to depend, time and again, on the services of Cardinal Ritter of St. Louis, who gladly supported the schema. It was necessary to have a cardinal take the lead in the matter to make it clear to the Fathers as a whole that the leadership among the U.S. bishops was not all in one camp. And Cardinal Ritter did an excellent job. It was said that the Cardinal was at first a little uneasy about taking the lead in anything at the Council since he was not familiar enough with Roman procedure. However, after his maiden speech on the Liturgy, he was so widely acclaimed and congratulated by bishops from the U.S. and other countries that he continued to speak up regularly thereafter during all four sessions of the Council and, along with Cardinal Meyer, made regular major contributions to what may be termed the "progressive" movement at the Council.

A great deal has been written about the use of the terms "progressive" and "conservative" in connection with the Council and, as many have pointed out, these terms are not completely satisfactory for the simple reason that a bishop could be progressive on one question and conservative on another. Cardinal Spellman, for example, wanted the vernacular for the Divine Office, certainly a stand for change and progress in reforming the existing regulations; however, he did not favor the use of vernacular at Mass and spoke against any change in this area. Incidentally, his position puzzled bishops from other countries, and they would ask: "Why does the Cardinal want English for the priests but Latin for the people?" Again, the Italian Archbishops Parente (Holy Office) and Florit (Florence) both favored "Collegiality" but opposed "Religious Liberty." So, in a sense, one could not label the bishops absolutely progressive and conservative. Still, there were some bishops who were, for the most part, strongly against change as a general stance; and there were others who were, mainly, in favor of reform. So when one speaks of such bishops as being conservative and progressive I think everyone easily understands exactly what he means, even though the tags are not always appropriate in every detail.

During the first skirmishes of the Council, which were centered about the question of the Liturgy, the bishops from the U.S.A. gradually began to speak up. However, comparatively few U.S. bishops were prepared in advance to participate in the debate. In a number of other countries, there had been meetings of the bishops before the Council in order to map out a plan for their participation. The German and Dutch bishops were well prepared from the start. However, I was given the impression during the early days of the Council that the Holy Father did not favor regular meetings of national bodies of bishops lest such bodies tend to vote as a block, in the interest of swinging their weight for or against certain proposals. This, it was said, would detract from the free expression of the individual bishops and heavily stack the proceedings.

The proposal of Cardinal Liénart, however, and its enthusiastic reception by the bishops served to establish the validity of the role which meetings of national bodies were to play all through the Council, and indeed it seems highly unlikely that the sentiment against them really did come from the Pope. Actually, once the rule of territorial bodies of bishops had been determined, there were repeated requests from the Secretary General that each territory organize a body of bishops and meet at once in order to take up certain questions which the Pope had referred to them.

Meanwhile, the days went by and soon it was Thanksgiving time.

As the American holiday drew near, a group of U.S. bishops got together behind a great idea: to have a real, honest-to-goodness Thanksgiving Day dinner for the American hierarchy, with turkey and all the trimmings. Roman food is fine, but on Thanksgiving Day it would be only appropriate to have something more in the American style. Besides, after almost two months of nothing but Italian food, turkey, stuffing and cranberry sauce sounded very appealing.

Archbishop Martin O'Connor, the Rector, graciously invited the bishops to hold the dinner at the North American College, and the services of a Roman caterer were engaged to do the cooking and serving. The caterer was full of enthusiasm and he was carefully briefed on all the mysteries connected with such unheard-of items as mincemeat and pumpkin pie. After receiving detailed instruction on every item, he went to work and produced a masterpiece. Never was there a Thanksgiving Day dinner like this one. The cook threw his heart into it—along with a good measure of salami, garlic, olive oil and pasta. The "turkey" came on festooned with artichokes (you know—like Mother used to always fix at home). The bird was actually a turkey skin stuffed with salami that you sliced like a piece of bologna sausage. The spumone and cassata were obviously right from Plymouth Rock. And what would Thanksgiving Day be like anyhow without a *cappuccino* at the end? It was a real over-the-Tiber-and-through-the-woods Thanksgiving Day, and we all enjoyed it immensely.

The debate and voting on the schema on the Sacred Liturgy continued all through the second session of the Council, and the Constitution was approved and promulgated, on December 4, 1963, at a public congregation of the Council. Pope John had died before the second session had opened, and hence, it was Pope Paul who proclaimed the first official document of the Council, completing the work that Pope John had begun, as he was destined to do so effectively, until the labors of the Council were at last concluded.

Many persons ask: "How long will it take for the reforms proposed in the Constitution on the Sacred Liturgy to be put into effect?" Relying on my own imperfect knowledge and experience, I feel that perhaps in five years the reform, if not entirely completed, will have been very far advanced. The Postconciliar Concilium is working steadily now on the implementation of the constitution, as is each territorial body of bishops. But there is an immense amount of work to be done as the above highlights clearly indicate. For example, the Mass rite must be carefully revised. This will include stripping away or revising many elements which do not contribute very well to the meaningfulness of the rite: for example, at the present time, there are too many unnecessary genuflections and signs of the cross in the Mass rite and not enough variety and selectivity in the passages from Holy Scripture. To correct this alone will require a good bit of time.

But over and above the reform of the Mass rite itself there is the entire reform of the rites for the administration of the Sacraments, the rites for other services and the form of the Divine Office for private recitation.

What had been and further will be the impact of the renewal of the Sacred Liturgy on our Catholic people?

This is a mighty question which the experts on the Liturgy have attempted to answer in many excellent books. A good example is the latest such volume, *Our Changing Liturgy,* by Father C. J. McNaspy, S.J. Let me, then, make only a few brief observations here from the pastoral point of view.

I was fortunate to have come in contact with a rewarding experience twenty years ago which served to arouse my interest in a more meaningful liturgy. When I came to LSU in 1946, I found, in the campus chapel, a participated Mass already in full swing, although naturally in Latin. My predecessor as chaplain, Maurice Schexnayder, now Bishop of Lafayette, had for years trained hundreds of students to make all the Latin responses together in a vigorous voice that shook the chapel. When we traveled to Newman conventions all over the U.S. by automobile, 30 or 40 of us, we took our participated Mass with us.

Later on, as pastor, I worked hard at putting the Decree of 1958 into effect in my parishes with gratifying success, so much so that Fr. Amos Vincent, Vice-Chancellor of the Lafayette Diocese, once remarked to me the day after Palm Sunday six years ago: "Say, I hear you had a real wild one over at Fatima yesterday!"

At Baton Rouge, now, I feel that the liturgy in our parishes is developing nicely, thanks to the zeal of our priests in the matter.

Even before the Council, from the beginning of the Diocese five years ago, I have always celebrated Mass myself at clergy gatherings with all my priests participating, and I think this has a good effect, namely, that the priests felt more at ease directing their own parish liturgy once they were familiar with the procedure from their personal participation in it. In other words, they could draw on their own personal experience, and did not have to start exclusively from books in vitalizing divine worship in their parish churches.

Their people, as a result, are now also discovering a new meaningfulness in their public worship of God.

They are beginning to understand that the Sacred Liturgy of the Church provides them with the supreme opportunity to carry out their mission as children of God. Unto this were they baptized that they might actively offer their great gift, the crucified Body and Blood of the Lord, in union with their priest, to God the Father. But to be conscious of this activity of theirs at Mass, they must be active! And the readings and commentary by laymen and the community singing of hymns and the presentation of the gifts at the offertory are all serving their purpose of fastening the importance and the dynamics of their role at Mass in the consciousness of our people.

Now they are vastly more aware than formerly of the "Presence" of Christ in their worship—not just statically, but in full motion: teaching in His Word, giving life by His Sacrifice and His reception in Holy Communion, and imparting impulses to live the Christian life by His preaching. That Christ carries out all this through the ministry of His priests—and the ministry of His laymen—at Holy Mass has made the laity much more aware of the Presence of Christ in themselves in a dynamic way, namely, that Christ *does* act through them by their service. If this estimate of progress be true, and I think it is, then we are on our way to a new and more vitalized Church at the parish level.

The impact of the new liturgy is also to be found in the opportunities for our lay leaders to sit on diocesan and parish committees on the Liturgy, Sacred Music and Sacred Art and exercise a real hand in fashioning the policy to be followed in these fields.

Already there are hundreds of ways in which the use of the vernacular and the renewed liturgy are making divine things more clearly immediate to our people: the Confirmation ceremony is now a delightful one-hour service totally in English. People take part in it and come away from it truly elevated in mind and heart. At funeral parlors, it is no longer the practice to say interminable rosaries all night long—now there is one service at each hour for four hours: the Rosary, the Office for the Dead, a Bible Vigil and a Prayer Service, each only ten minutes in length. On New Year's Day I had the joy of concelebrating Mass, with a priest-visitor, in the front parlor of my family's home with all the clan assembled around me. At First Masses and Silver Jubilees I can now join my priests at the altar and offer the Holy Sacrifice with them. The dedication of the new cathedral of my friend Bishop James V. Casey, at Lincoln, Nebraska, was a model of a meaningful solemn ceremony, not unduly long, with a vast assembly of people fully participating and understanding everything every step of the way.

The impact of all this on the daily life of our people I find is tremendous. I feel that, in time, it will teach them not to be so static about living their faith, not so mechanical. They will be encouraged to be more relaxed, more apostolic, more involved in works of virtue, since they are beginning to understand now more fully the Presence of Christ in their lives through their baptism, confirmation and especially the Holy Eucharist.

I feel that the renewal of the liturgy will teach them to be more widely committed to good—that is, not merely to Catholic causes, but to all good causes, in a united effort with all men of good will. For what else can they get out of the parable of the Good Samaritan when they hear it at Mass, in the light of the Church's teaching on ecumenism?

But I do not think that all this will happen at once. It will happen gradually. But the fact is that it is already in motion, and this is greatly encouraging.

The new liturgy will have an impact too, I hope and pray, on our separated brethren. They will see our new spirit of sincere reform of ourselves and our willingness to acknowledge our mistakes. They will see us putting more emphasis on the Bible and borrowing their very fine, singable hymns. They will be able to understand us and we them, when we pray together and when they have occasion to visit our churches and we theirs. They will see their churches respected by us and their ministers received with courtesy and given a place of honor in our sanctuaries. And, although it would serve no purpose to attempt participation, on either side, in those services which express most profoundly our deepest religious convictions, still it will be clear that this is not due to any aloofness or disdain, but only to a recognition of the inappropriateness of invading so personal and intimate a religious area with a worship of God which is charged with anything less than full and total conviction.

There are problems, of course, ahead. The greatest of these is the problem of educating our people to this new spirit. But I am most interested of all in the future of our little children. A baby who is now two years old will be ten years old within eight short years. That child will never have known the old silent Latin Mass. That child will have a recollection only of the new full, active and conscious participation in the Sacred Liturgy. All the services of the Church will have been meaningful to that child from the start, and further the child will have been trained in religion classes to a dynamic understanding of his mission in life to project the Presence of Christ into his community.

Is that child going to be any better than his ancestors were? Who can say? But one thing is sure: thanks to the Council, he is going to have many more *opportunities* for meaningful religion than they ever had!

Chapter 5

Revelation · Communications · The Orthodox

Throughout the initial debate on the Liturgy the Council had been lively, interesting and fruitful. In spite of the fact that procedure had to be experimental, the discussion had moved forward. In a month's time the schema on the Liturgy had been reworked and a successful vote taken to accept it as a basis for a final text. In retrospect this was good progress; but at the time there were moments, here and there, which were heavy with repetitious, monotonous debate, so much so that the famous limerick-writing bishop of the Council (of whom everyone has heard) was prompted to complain:

> We are three thousand Fathers in session
> And we feel a great weight of oppression.
> What with cardinals talking
> And lesser lights squawking
> No wonder the bar's so refreshin'!

None of us present, however, could have anticipated the degree of tenseness or the high excitement which was to mark the discussion of the next schema, that entitled "On the Sources of Revelation." Everyone expected conflict, of course, because the very title of the schema was provocative: the "two source" mentality had penetrated even the wording of the title! So opposition to the schema was anticipated, but not the dramatic course of events which ensued. After seven days of sharp exchanges, a curiously mixed-up vote, and then a dramatic move on the part of Pope John, the schema on Revelation was completely derailed!

The story of the discussion of "The Sources of Revelation" has to begin back in history. For four hundred years a school of doctrinal thought on Divine Revelation, tracing its origins back to [the Council of Trent (1545–1563)], had dominated seminary teaching on this subject. Because the Protestant reformers had appealed from the Pope to the Bible, and the Bible alone, the reacting Fathers of Trent had placed tremendous emphasis on the Church as interpreter of the Bible and on tradition as a separate "source" of Revelation. Tradition, they stated, contained certain truths not necessarily written down in the Scriptures but preserved and handed down in non-inspired but historically reliable records called Sacred Tradition.

This traditional approach to the Bible had, however, been modified in the forty years preceding Vatican Council II, by two important developments. First, new and startling advances had been made in the field of archaeology which had great impact on biblical research. Archaeology had unearthed a vastly expanded store of evidence about the Bible which led to a much clearer and more accurate understanding of the meaning of biblical passages and of whole books of the Bible. Cities had been dug up and their life and culture exposed to view. Important new finds of written documents had been made, such as the discovery of the Dead Sea Scrolls (which gave the world a Hebrew text of parts of the Bible 1,000 years older than any yet at hand). Important new techniques of exegesis (the disciplined study and explanation of Bible passages) had been developed which resulted from better knowledge of the literary "forms" in which the sacred writers communicated with their readers and of the historical context in which the separate books had been written. All of these advances now had to be taken into account in teaching and, indeed, had already been given recognition by Pope Pius XII in his 1943 encyclical, entitled *Divino Afflante Spiritu*, on the study of Holy Scripture.

In addition, many teachers of theology and Sacred Scripture had begun to take a new, better, and more comprehensive look at the whole field of biblical study and had begun moving away from the concept of two separate sources of Divine Revelation to the concept of a single source, namely the teaching of Christ, expressed in two modes, one written and the other unwritten. This new view actually represented a return to the older view which had prevailed everywhere in the Church prior to the Council of Trent.

In the face of these developments many professors and Vatican officials became alarmed. Traditionally, the emphasis in teaching these matters had been upon security rather than upon the development of doctrine. The notion that doctrine could constantly be more and more fully probed and comprehended, the traditionalists held, jeopardized security, and security was maintained by sticking absolutely to the approach and even to the very wording of the Fathers at Trent.

Ironically enough, while the two schools of thought within the Church (the "development" school and the "security" school) grew farther and farther apart, the Catholic biblical scholar and the non-Catholic biblical scholar were coming to closer and closer agreement.

With the advantage of hindsight we can see how necessary it was to have a General Council. Biblical study, and theology too, badly needed to be updated from the time of Trent. An essential consideration here was that the necessary updating and renewal required of the Council, even in the field of doctrine, need not (and, of course, could not) mean any essential change in Catholic dogma. Inability to understand or to accept this principle and the consequent failure of this principle to prevail in the Preparatory Commission were at the bottom of all the defects in the schema on Revelation.

When Father Yves Congar, O.P., said: "There is not a single dogma which the Church holds by scripture alone, not a single dogma which it holds by tradition alone," he was stating something quite different from what I had been taught in the seminary. I had been taught—and I in turn for years had taught my students at LSU and in CCD classes—that there were a number of important truths which could be found, to any useful extent, only in tradition: Sunday as the Lord's Day, the Assumption of

Mary, and even the canon of inspired books itself. Now a view was asserting itself on this question in the most respectable theological circles, and at first I didn't like it. Later I came to realize that I was being too defensive. But it was the Council which really opened my eyes by contrasting the old and the new positions so sharply and so clearly. A truth could be contained *more explicitly* in one mode rather than the other, but all Revelation is contained in *some way* in both; and, at any rate, neither is *source*. There is but one source, the living teaching of the Lord.

This position, of course, made possible a whole new avenue of dialogue with our Protestant brethren who had been saying, all along, that all Revelation was in the Bible. Now we were granting that they were correct in this, an admission which would be highly conducive, in turn, to having them approach the question of tradition in the same open-minded way. And, indeed, many a Protestant theologian had already been doing just that. The treatment of Revelation at the Council, then, was of the highest importance to the Church both in her own internal theological life and in her relationship with our separated brethren.

Debate on Revelation opened, then, on November 14, 1962, on the basis of a schema written entirely from the point of view of one theological school, namely that which stuck absolutely to the approach and the language of Trent.

The schema was "in possession," that is, it could be rejected under the rules only by a two-thirds vote of the Fathers against it. This would be very difficult to achieve at the beginning of the Council. (Later on, when more familiar with procedure and more relaxed, the Fathers were bolder about rejecting schemas they found unacceptable.) But at the start, the Fathers were generally less critical and more disposed to go along with the work of the Preparatory Commission. This made it very difficult to assemble the 1,473 votes necessary to have the schema rejected, no matter what its defects. In addition, most of the bishops, like me, had been reared in the old tradition of Trent and found security in it. Again, the bishops were also, for the most part, elderly men not given to radical departures from the stances of a lifetime.

To have so many Fathers vote to reject the schema came as another major surprise to me, and I could sense at last the real trend of the Council: It was not only going to be an "open" Council, it was also going to be amazingly progressive under impulses of the Holy Spirit. This had already been indicated by the vote on accepting the Liturgy schema, with all its advances, as a basis for a final text. But here in the vote on Revelation was unexpected confirmation that this openness would extend all along the line.

As the debate began, the supporters of the schema on Revelation put their case before the Council with great spirit and with admirable ability. This is what they said: "The Council has been directed to speak in a pastoral tone. But the pastoral approach must be based on safe doctrine; and safe doctrine is traditional doctrine. This schema has been composed by the scholarly and experienced men on the Preparatory Commission and later reviewed and approved by other wise and eminent men on the Central Commission." (Implicitly this could mean that to attack the schema is to attack these men, an argument that had weight in view of the fact that so many bishops had been educated in Rome under these very men.) "Further, the Holy Father has given this subject-matter, Revelation, to the Council for discussion and it would be discourteous to him to simply reject it instead of simply amending it." (This appeal on behalf of the feelings of Pope John was more than a little amusing since it was he who ultimately scuttled the schema with his own hand!)

Other arguments for the schema were that, whatever its defects, there was simply no time in which to have it completely rewritten. If the Fathers started that kind of treatment of the schemas, we would all be here longer than the eighteen years the Fathers spent at Trent! Again, they argued, any schema on Revelation worthy of its salt is going to lead off with a strong confirmation of the Church's condemnation of Modernism which, in the minds of some very conservative bishops, took in any kind of development of doctrine, especially current advances in Scripture study.

Finally the proponents argued that the schema holds fast to a number of solid, everlasting things: the "two source" concept which is part of the Church's doctrinal patrimony; the spirit of the teachings of Aquinas, Trent, Vatican I, Leo XIII and Pius XII; and the scholastic approach which is one of our greatest safeguards against loose thinking and loose theological expression.

The main speakers for this position were Cardinals Ottaviani, Ruffini, Siri and Browne. There were very few bishops speaking on any subject in the early stages of the Council, since the cardinals had precedence at the microphone and were ready and willing to talk. Later on, this leveled off considerably as many cardinals began to use their privilege with more moderation.

The opponents of the schema leaped to the attack when their turn came and their denunciation was so forceful and so dramatic that few bishops left their places, even after two hours, to go to the coffee-bar. I myself was completely fascinated, especially by Bishop De Smedt of Bruges, Belgium, who always spoke to a full house.

The attack on the schema was pretty rough. And the eminent names that came over the public-address system as speakers were impressive: Doepfner of Germany, Liénart of France, Frings of Germany, Léger of Canada, Koenig of Austria, Alfrink of Holland, Suenens of Belgium, Ritter of the U.S.A., Bea of the Curia (all cardinals); Maximos of Antioch, Silva Henriquez of Chile, Dom Butler of England, Hakim of Palestine and De Smedt of Belgium.

Their general argument went as follows: There never had been two sources of Revelation. The idea of two sources was not at all traditional. The schema was not pastoral—it had a cold, un-ecumenical, scholastic approach which could not be corrected by amendments or changes. The whole thing simply had to be re-written. As it stands, it is also harmful to liberty in Biblical studies and, actually, is just a re-hash of what you can find in any theology textbook. Further, it is pessimistic, negative, full of condemnations and suspicions. It takes a tedious and unrealistic attitude toward the Word of God; it is too long, too obscure, too given to patristic and theological argument. It is quarrelsome, filled with the spirit of the Counter-Reformation. It is a museum-piece, a retread of the condemnation of Modernism of almost 60 years ago. It ignores the Eastern approach to tradition and represents only one Western school of theological thought which has not bothered to keep itself up-to-date. And so forth. . . .

On my own, I had much earlier—already in seminary days—discovered with shock that the text of the moral theology books of two eminent writers in the field, Noldin and Tanquerey, was identical—word for word. And, while at LSU I encountered, in a volume called *College Reading and Religion,* a polite but dry reference to the fact that the same condition existed in the case of many Catholic books in philosophy. Now we were running into practically the same duplication even in a council schema, if not word for word, at least idea for idea.

The greatest charges against the schema, then, were these: it was not up-to-date; it represented only one school of theological thought and it did not encourage dialogue with our separated brethren.

At last a vote was taken on whether or not to reject it. Again the supporters of the schema were pretty confident of themselves, and with reason, as the vote soon showed: only 1,368 votes for rejection were cast, whereas 1,473 were needed. The vote to reject failed, therefore, by 105 votes. But there were other angles to the matter: first of all, there was much confusion among the Fathers as to how you had to vote in order to reject the schema. I voted *Non Placet* (It doesn't please, reject it!). It was only later that I discovered that I *should* have voted *Placet*, (It *does* please me—to reject it!). Hundreds of the Fathers made similar mistakes, on both sides.

In view of this confusion in the voting, and also in view of the fact that, in any case, there was a substantial body of the bishops who had voted No Confidence in the schema, Pope John simply stepped into the picture and ordered the schema to be removed and a new one written by an especially appointed Commission, on which all sides would have adequate representation.

On this new Commission Cardinals Ottaviani and Bea would be joint-presidents. The new decree was to be rewritten more in harmony with the aims of the Council. It would be brief, pastoral and ecumenical in tone and it would be in touch with modern advances in Biblical science.

I took special pains in my "Rome Letters" to explain our special way of voting at the Council: *Placet* (Yea), *Non Placet* (Nay) and *Placet Juxta Modum* (Yea—but with this reservation which I herewith attach to my ballot). I felt it necessary to explain this procedure of voting with some care. After all, could you imagine the Louisiana legislature voting: *Yea, Nay* and *Sort of?*

While the debate on Revelation was going on, Archbishop Hallinan and I continued to seek information on the international scene and to exchange thought with other bishops, with observers and with *periti* over supper. These evenings proved most helpful. The Irish dinner was a great success, attended by Cardinal Browne, Archbishop Morris and Bishops Browne, Farren, Eugene O'Doherty, Fergus, Lucey, Rogers and Kyne.

Highlight of the evening was the arrival of His Eminence, Michael Cardinal Browne, a Curia cardinal who lives in Rome and who was personal theologian to Pope Pius XII. When His Eminence reached the front door of the Hassler Hotel where the party was held, he was met there, Roman-style, by two bell-boys carrying lighted torches. These boys conducted the Cardinal to the dining hall, but, as the Cardinal arrived, an electric shock ran through everyone in the hotel lobby. For the Cardinal, once inside the door, took off his great black cape and revealed his snowy white Dominican cassock, looking for all the world like the Holy Father! But the shock lasted only a minute; after all, Cardinal Browne is much taller than Pope John.

Council days were busy days occupied ordinarily with Council readings, Council participation, Council lectures and press conferences, correspondence from home, conferences with bishops, Observers, *periti*, visits to the houses of religious orders which work in one's home diocese, social events and receptions and, finally, sightseeing—if you could work it in!

Well, for example, I said Mass on a Sunday morning, once each session, at the General House of the Daughters of Jesus on Monte Mario. Afterwards I talked to the sisters about their associates who are doing such fine work in the diocese of Baton Rouge, most of whom come from Spain. After Mass I had breakfast at the convent, starting off (I suppose in Spanish style) with a bottle of cold beer! These good sisters rendered an excellent service to me; they would come to my hotel and see to it that my linen and lace robes and vestments were cared for and they would always bring them back to me beautifully laundered.

At each session, the U.S. bishops were tendered a reception by the American Ambassador to Italy, Mr. G. Frederick Reinhardt, and his wife at the Ambassador's residence in Parioli. The house is set in a lovely Roman garden and was once the scene of St. Philip Neri's activities when he was tutor to the children of a noble Roman family. The reception was a brilliant affair with some 200 bishops present in their flowing red capes, along with a large representation of people from the American colony in Rome. It was good to be there with these Americans enjoying a supper "on American soil." Newsmen were also on hand in numbers, cornering this or that bishop in the hope of finding a special story on the Council.

I had entered a petition for an audience with the Holy Father as soon as I reached Rome on October 9. By November 18, I had about given up hope of ever seeing Pope John personally. But even at that I was not so bad off as Archbishop Hallinan, who was carrying around in his pocket a sizable "Peter's Pence Collection" check for personal presentation to the Holy Father—which got him nowhere either! Then suddenly it was announced that the Holy Father would see all the U.S. bishops together that evening in the great Clementine Hall of the Apostolic Palace.

After we were all assembled, Pope John came in and spoke to us in a jovial and charming manner. He would stop every now and then and let Archbishop Cody translate his Italian into English, which the Archbishop did with the greatest of ease and even with a few of Pope John's lovely gestures. Finally, Cardinal Spellman arose and expressed our gratitude and loyalty to the Holy Father and, half-jokingly, extended to him an invitation to come to the United States for a visit. Pope John chuckled a great deal over this, thanked us and then smilingly said: "I have often thought of coming to America, but every time I do, there is a little angel who sits on my shoulder and says to me 'John, at your age, forget it!' "

The whole experience of meeting Pope John personally (for he came around and shook hands with each of us) was very moving. Pope John possessed an amazing combination of personal qualities: piety, wisdom, human feeling, sagacity, perceptiveness, great warmth and a sure touch in dealing with people. The entire city of Rome adored him. One bishop, when he saw the great devotion the Romans had for John and recalling how much they had also venerated his predecessor, asked: "What are they trying to do around here anyway? De-Stalinize Pius XII?" Every Sunday Pope John was out visiting in the midst of the people and he was the despair of the Communists.

Thus far the Council had spent fifteen daily meetings (October 22 to November 13) debating the Liturgy schema. Then it occupied the next ten daily congregations (November 14 to 23) with discussion of the schema on Revelation. On November 25, at the twenty-fifth daily meeting, the speeches began on the subject of the Social Means of Communications—Press, Radio and TV. It was also announced that the following subjects would be taken up next in order as follows:

> *Unity of the Church* (This was the document *Ut Omnes Unum Sint*, prepared by the Oriental Congregation, on the subject of union with the Orthodox.)
> *The Blessed Virgin Mary*
> *The Church*

It was later decided not to treat the Blessed Virgin in a separate schema, which might seemingly give her an unwarranted place in the program of salvation, but to incorporate the Council's views within the schema on the Church. By devoting a chapter to her within "the Church," the fathers showed her true role, while avoiding any appearance of giving Mary a role in the economy of salvation which was proper to Divinity. This decision, warmly debated, in addition to placing the Blessed Virgin in better perspective, had the additional effect of opening the way to ecumenical dialogue on the subject.

The debate on the Social Means of Communications schema lasted two days. Comparatively this discussion was listless, with most of the interventions sounding platitudinous: "The communications media can be instruments of great good but also of great harm. We must take every opportunity to use them to preach the Gospel. The schema must emphasize the rights of the Church in connection with the use of these media." And so forth.

However, a few striking thoughts were also presented: Here is a field in which to emphasize the role of the laymen since special training is necessary to be effective here and the priest should not be diverted to such work. We are living in a world "of the image" and less so in one of abstract thought, and we should adjust to this situation more rapidly and effectively than we are doing. The Church cannot protect people by insulating them against the influence of modern media; hence, the Church should drop her negative approach and boldly enter the field constructively. In the face of so much loss of human privacy, because of the activity of the communications media, the Council should consider the adoption of a "code of ethics" for the press, radio and TV.

The debate completed, the schema was adopted as a basis for fashioning a final text, with certain instructions to the Commission to shorten and rework the document, separating principles from practical suggestion, by a vote of 2,138 to 15.

The document on "The Social Means of Communication" was not generally regarded by the bishops themselves as one of the more impressive documents of the Council. Most of them, it seemed, had but little interest in it, feeling, perhaps, that the subject did not rate treatment at the Council. Indeed, more than one bishop suggested that a Vatican statement be substituted for it. Nevertheless, when the text came up for final voting, three members of the journalism fraternity, John Cogley, Robert Kaiser and Michael Novak, felt that the document was too restrictive, and they called for its rejection and revision in a mimeographed handout to the Fathers distributed in front of St. Peter's.

The three newsmen won themselves the nickname among the bishops of "the three children in the fiery furnace" because their mimeographed handout immediately got them into hot water with the Council Secretariat for using their position as newsmen to unduly influence the Fathers of the Council, who, the Secretariat suggested, would ask their opinion if they felt they needed it.

The Cogley-Kaiser-Novak statement was, however, certified as worthy of consideration by the signatures of three experts: Fr. John Courtney Murray, S.J., Fr. Jean Danielou, S.J., and Fr. Jorge Mejia.

The "three children in the fiery furnace" put forth these chief objections to the Communications schema: It was too "moralistic" and too vague; it oversimplified the problem of art and prudence and had little relevance to modern communications as they knew the field. Hence, it was a step backward. It emphasized the moral obligation of those who did the reporting but not the obligation of those who withheld information by means of authoritarian secrecy. It endowed the Catholic press with a near-infallibility and interposed an ecclesiastical authority between the reporter and his employer. Finally, it gave the state too much rope in controlling the press.

Most bishops to whom I spoke, however, felt that the newsmen had greatly overdrawn the picture and, by doing so, had enlisted sympathy for the schema, whatever its shortcomings.

On November 28, the Fathers had the rare opportunity of witnessing the Council daily Mass celebrated in the Ethiopian rite. The Mass caused a sensation both in St. Peter's and in the pages of the New York newspapers, one of which cried: "Bongo drums beat at the Vatican!"

The Mass was celebrated, in the classical Ethiopian language called Gheez, by Archbishop Yemeru of Addis Ababa, assisted by students from the Ethiopian College which is located on the grounds of the Vatican. It was carried out impressively, with great solemnity, and was marked, musically, by a chant, full of striking dissonances, which one bishop referred to as "progressive Gregorian."

I left my place down near the front doors of the vast basilica and went up near the altar to obtain a better view of the extraordinary proceedings. There I found myself beside an elderly Italian bishop.

The Ethiopian liturgy goes back at least to the fourth century and is one of the most ancient preserved in the Church today. It is a vibrant, living liturgy characterized by a continuous exchange between priest and people and by the liberal use of strictly local African melodies, vesture and usages. It offers an example of an appropriate welding of local custom to traditional forms of the Liturgy, a matter under discussion on the floor of the Council during the Liturgy debate.

But the solemn bringing on of the Gospel Book after Mass was the real climax. A steady beat of bongo drums began, accompanied by a clapping of hands and punctuated by what seemed to be a calypso-type native chant, as the great book of the Evangelium was carried in the utmost solemnity to its place of honor. As the drums beat and the tambourines were shaken, I looked about upon the vast throng in St. Peter's, everyone watching, wide-eyed and unbelieving. I have never seen an audience more entranced.

The Italian bishop beside me gulped, wiped his glasses, and just stared, apparently unable to believe his own eyes and ears. At last he uttered a moan, clenched his two hands, cast his eyes heavenward and groaned: "Mamma mia!"

The gathering could not help being deeply impressed by the strange but utterly living liturgy before us. Moreover, it came as a surprise to nearly everyone that the Church had fostered and encouraged the retention of this local rite over all these centuries. It served to demonstrate the sincerity of the Council's currently expressed desire that all the ancient rites of Holy Mother Church be preserved, that to lose them would be to forfeit a precious heritage. Little did I think that, less than four years later, I my-self would be celebrating Mass for 1,200 CYO boys and girls of my diocese to the tune of guitars and American spirituals!

On November 26, the Council went on to debate, at four daily meetings, the schema called *Ut Omnes Unum Sint*, a schema drawn up by the Oriental Congregation of the Vatican on the subject of reunion with the Orthodox churches of the East, which had once been united with the Church of the West but which has been separated from her for many centuries.

The separation of the two Churches was due in part to secular historical and political causes, namely, the shifting of political and military importance from Rome to Constantinople. But it was also due to the great differences in culture and language and to differences in the religious history and religious character of East and West. The East had not been evangelized by the West. It had had its own independent reception of the Gospel from the Apos-tles, and it had its own antiquity. Of all this the Eastern churches are immensely sensitive and proud. Then there came the decline of the East and the rise again of the West with the establishment of the new Holy Roman Empire beginning with the baptism of Clovis, king of the Franks, and reaching fulfillment with the crowning of Charlemagne.

Meanwhile, in the fifth century, certain Eastern churches had separated themselves from both Rome and Constantinople; while in the eleventh century a vast break took place between Rome and all the churches of the entire East. Only small pockets of Oriental Catholics of various rites remained in communion with Rome and these were regarded locally as disloyal to their nation as well as to their church. Today the Orthodox are approxi-mately one-fourth as large as the Catholic body—130 million to 540 million communicants.

And yet, the Orthodox have kept intact the main tenets of Christian doctrine. Only the matter of authority actually stands today as a really major block between East and West, in the sense that if this obstacle were removed, the other obstacles would be-come far less formidable.

However, many Council Fathers found the schema drawn up by the Oriental Congregation seriously defective in tone and approach and calculated even to antagonize rather than open avenues for dialogue and understanding with the Orthodox. It was urged that the tone was too authoritative and that such expressions as "return to the true fold" only served to irritate and harden the separation. It was advocated that a better approach would be to admit, first of all, that there had been fault on both sides in the original division of the eleventh century and later, without assessing who had been responsible. Then, great stress should be placed on the fact that Orthodox Christians possess the true baptismal character, the same faith and the same sacraments as the Christians in the West. Especially do they have a valid priesthood and episcopacy. Here, the Fathers said, exists a most promising field for fostering good will between East and West by considering the possibility of wider recognition of these truths in practice. Finally, when one came to the differences between the Latin and the Orthodox, these would clearly appear to be accidental rather than essential and could then be taken up in an entirely different atmosphere than that produced by the "return to the fold" approach.

As a consequence of these considerations, the schema was, in effect, rejected—that is, the question of reunion with the Orthodox, it was voted, should be treated elsewhere in other Council documents and not in a separate schema of its own. Thus, the question was eventually treated later in the Council in the decree on Ecumenism and also in the decree on the Oriental Churches.

Meanwhile, relations with the Orthodox were to receive a great boost from the personal work of Pope Paul. His visit to the Holy Land and his meeting there with the patriarch of Constantinople (Istanbul), Athenagoras, and their embracing of each other; and then later the mutual dissolution of any existing censures left over from the past by Pope Paul in Rome and Athenagoras in Istanbul on December 7, 1965, just before the end of the Council, have had tremendous impact in establishing improved relations and understanding, and in bringing the Orthodox into the Council at last.

Although I had nothing to suggest when Cardinal Tardini caught me by surprise back in 1959 with a request for suggestions on the Council, three years later, when summoned to a private conference with Cardinal Cicognani, in the office of the Secretary of State, I had recovered my tongue and was ready to make a number of recommendations about the Council when invited by His Eminence to do so. One of these recommendations was that any father of the Council who could gather a sufficient number of signatures should be permitted to appear before a Council commission where important decisions were often made, in order to further debate certain important questions. (This was eventually done.) And a second recommendation was that an official transcript of each day's proceedings similar to the U.S. *Congressional Record* be made accessible to the Fathers at some central place. (This was not done, although Council press dispatches were improved, which helped a great deal.)

As it was, you had to catch everything by ear and make notes of it. There were two difficulties with this system, as far as I was concerned: first, I just did not know that much Latin. I could understand the general trend of an address but often I missed the specifics and precisions involved; second, I was confronted with several varieties of Latin: *French* Latin—that is, Latin spoken with a French accent (like Cardinal Tisserant's); *German* Latin (like Cardinal Koenig's); *American* Latin (like Cardinal Cushing's) or *Italian* Latin (like Cardinal Ruffini's). Of them all, the Italian Latin was the easiest to hear and understand. Speakers like Cardinal Ottaviani and Archbishop Felici were clear, slow and utterly distinct when they spoke Latin, and it required little effort to understand every word they said—even the humorous side remarks for which the Secretary General eventually became renowned. Still, I had to listen very closely to get everything, and at times those of us who did not use Latin as an everyday conversational exercise (as do seminary professors and members of the Curia) had to turn and ask a neighbor what had provoked the laughter.

I had a bishop beside me, at one session, who enjoyed everything of a humorous nature, only he never laughed. When amused, he merely said repeatedly: "Whoo, whoo, whoo," sort of chuckling to himself.

Near the close of the Council, Archbishop Felici made the following announcement: *"Crastina die, in festo Sancti Nicolai (uti aiunt 'Santa Claus') Sanctissimus Pater donabit singulis Patribus ANULUM AUREUM in memoriam hujus Sacrosancti synodi— sed velint Venerabiles Patres in sedibus eorum manere, quia, manifeste, non est possibile accedere ad eos qui partibus hujus magnae Basilicae dispersi sunt."* But during the announcement, this whoo-whooing bishop had been distracted and was not listening closely. He became aware that something interesting had been said only when he heard the general laughter. So he leaned over and asked me what Felici had announced.

"Felici said," I replied, "that tomorrow is the feast of Saint Nicholas (commonly known as 'Santa Claus'); hence, the Holy Father will give to each bishop a gold ring as a memento of the Council."

"Whoo, whoo!"

"However," I went on, "Felici says that you must remain at your place to receive your ring. He says that he'll be damned if he is going to go chasing you all over this big basilica to make delivery."

"Whoo, whoo, whoo! . . . ."

Language-phones similar to those used at the U.N. and those we used at the International Congress of the Apostleship of the Sea in Liverpool in 1965, were repeatedly proposed. And it was frequently rumored that Cardinal Cushing, sponsor of all good causes, would raise the money to pay for them. This rumor had its foundation in the remark that Cushing had made, publicly, about his inability to follow the Council very well in Latin. Eventually, the Protestant observers did get language-phones. You could go down in their tribune, if you wished, and listen for a while over one of the phones not in use at the moment. But the Fathers did not get them. Speculation on the reason for this centered about the retention of Latin as the international language of Catholicism and the position that bishops simply *ought* to know Latin!

Cardinal Cicognani was Apostolic Delegate to the United States for a quarter of a century during which time he visited LSU while I was chaplain there. His Eminence called me in for a conference during the first session. He was most interested in our new Diocese of Baton Rouge and expressed great hopes for its future. Naturally, we also talked about the Council. I thanked the Cardinal for his kindness. He was, after Pope John, the man with the greatest responsibility for the welfare of the Church and the success of the Council. Yet, he found time to invite me in for an interview. But I had had previous evidence of the Cardinal's thoughtfulness. At my request, some time ago, he had constituted Monsignor Gillespie (our Vicar General) as a *Peritus Conciliaris*. Monsignor Pat went to the Council as my own *peritus* or expert. But now he became an Expert of the Council itself, so constituted by the Holy Father's Secretary of State and the Central Office of the Council. This entitled him to a passport and free access to the Council, to a copy of the confidential schemata, and to a listing in the Official Directory of the Council. This was a great help to me, for Monsignor Gillespie was a student of the matters under discussion and was equipped to give sound information and advice on short notice. It was a great honor to our diocese and to him that he was so named.

The weather in Rome all through November at the first session was *molto brutto* which, as you may guess, means very brutal—indeed, with a thin, icy rain all day, every day. But December, 1962, was cold and clear.

The twilight hours in Rome, beginning at 4 P.M. when all the little stores open after siesta, are a most attractive time of day. One afternoon in December, I took my walk in the Piazza Navona where a traditional "mercato di Natale" (Street Fair of Toys) was being held in preparation for Christmas.

The Toy Fair had a colorful, warm, and happy atmosphere with a backdrop of buildings that looked like something from an opera. The fair was simply jammed with "ragazzini" (little Italian boys and girls) all in a state of the highest excitement over the marvellous display of "giocattoli per bambini" (toys) and the twinkling, multicolored Christmas lights.

There was not a single Christmas tree or a single Santa Claus in sight. But there were just thousands of cribs, Josephs, Marys, shepherds, angels, etc. I find a deep strain of religion in Italian people; and their little street fair for children, while lacking the slick, mechanical toys we are familiar with in our big U.S. department stores, still had something far better—a genuine air of expectancy, which is really the spirit of Advent.

The absence of Santa Claus, though, alarmed me. I was worried that some American child might try to get his Christmas list to one of our bearded Eastern bishops coming out of the Council!

While the debate was in progress on Unity with the Orthodox, votes on the amended chapters of the documents on the Liturgy and Communications came up as sections of the text were revised and printed for resubmission. The rules required that there be no more discussion on these matters but only voting. However, if a Commission felt compelled, with the consent of the Central Commission, to introduce new material into a given text, then discussion had to be reopened. It was this rule which caused so much misunderstanding later on in the Council at the end of the third session when the text on Religious Liberty was not voted on but held over for further discussion and final voting at the fourth session. But this was not the case in the revision of the documents on the Liturgy and Communications, and so votes were taken on the revised texts as they appeared.

Meanwhile, we were already into the month of December with only a week remaining before the end of the first session which had been announced for December 8.

Chapter 6

The Early Debate on "The Church"
The End of the First Session

The first debate on the schema *De Ecclesia* (On the Church) was carried on during five daily Congregations, from December 1 to December 6, 1962.

By this time many of the Fathers were somewhat wary of anything prepared by a Preparatory Commission, but especially of a schema produced by the Theological Commission, the successor to the Preparatory Commission on Faith and Morals. After their experience with "Revelation," they had grounds for expecting that the schema on "The Church" would be written in the same old language and with the same old Council of Trent approach —in other words, that it would be another carbon copy of a theology textbook, calculated to freeze and harden forever the positions at Trent and Vatican I.

Sensing the atmosphere, Cardinal Ottaviani, chairman of the commission, first begged the Fathers not to prejudge the schema but to hear out the "relator" who was about to introduce it, Bishop Franic of Yugoslavia. "I know that some of the Fathers have their own schemas on the Church tucked into their hip pockets, but please listen to this one first!" the Cardinal said in effect.

The Cardinal's remarks were made in apparent good humor and brought laughter from the Fathers, but they failed to stem the tide of opposition to the schema. The objections were quick in coming.

The schema failed to treat the Church adequately even in its definition. It seemed to consider the Church merely as an organization on earth and not at all as a mystery. It was heavily larded with references to the Church's rights but had little to say about her apostolic mission and duties. There was little said in the schema about the role of the laity in the Church, about the holiness of the Church or about the relationship of the Church to our separated brethren and to the state.

It was Bishop De Smedt of Belgium who cited three essential faults in our past way of looking at the Church which he found perpetuated in the schema: (1) *triumphalism*, the tendency to lord it over others—over those who, for example, through no fault of their own, were not formal members of the Catholic Church—as though our own membership were somehow due to our own goodness; (2) *clericalism*, the attitude that only clergy count; that the laity must be regarded with suspicion and allowed to do only what the clergy tell them to do; and (3) *legalism*, the position that the approach to religion and the Church must be boiled down to well-defined laws and statutes which one kept as the essential attitude of a good Christian.

One bishop, who had been struggling to refine a schema and who had found implacable opposition in his Commission from the author of it, said that there was one more faulty attitude which he would like to add to the list, namely, what he termed "umbilicalism," the position that "This text is my baby and you had better not try to change one single word in it!"

The Fathers who were disposed to defend the schema were not wanting or silent. Rising one after another to speak on its behalf they stressed the dangers of straying from the traditional path and from the old scholastic approach which laid everything out so precisely and clearly. To abandon this time-tested formula would be to induce confusion and perhaps even heresy among the faithful. Moreover, everything said at Vatican II had to be framed in such a way as to take into account the central doctrine of Vatican I, namely, the infallibility of the Pope. Finally, regard for our separated brethren must not be carried to the extreme of placing taboos on such fundamental and tested Catholic teachings as those on the Church Militant, the Blessed Virgin Mary, and the Souls in Purgatory.

However, with the sentiment of the Fathers as a whole already clearly expressed by the overwhelming votes for the updating of the proposed texts on Liturgy and Revelation, the champions of renewal became more and more vocal. They now began to rise one after another to attack the schema on the Church:

The schema had to be radically changed if it were going to fulfill the express aim of the Council. It simply had to bring out the fundamental concept of the Church not primarily as an earthly organization but as *The People of God*, with the Pope, bishops, religious and laity all members of it, first and foremost, by baptism, before they were officials in this or that position. Moreover, to emphasize the episcopacy and to clarify its true nature and powers were in no sense to infringe on the primacy of the Pope.

The burden of the comment was mainly this: that the schema on the Church was simply out of touch with the purpose expressly stated by the Pope and the Council. It gave no evidence of intending to renew or update the teaching about the Church; it gave no sign of being aware of the place of the Church in the world of today. In short, it had to be radically rewritten on an entirely new basis.

The present Holy Father, as Cardinal Montini, Archbishop of Milan at the time, was one of those who asked for a rewriting of the schema by the Theological Commission and the Secretariat for Christian Unity jointly. His position was thought to express Pope John's own mind on the matter since Montini was regarded as one of the Pope's closest advisers.

Indeed, in the thirty-fifth daily congregation on December 6, the Secretary General announced that Pope John had decided to send all the schemata, especially those already discussed in the Council, back to be reworked by mixed commissions. When this had been done, the revised texts would be mailed to the bishops at home so that they could read them and then forward their suggestions and comments.

This procedure, it was thought at the time, would vastly speed up the rate of action. Seemingly under the new procedure the commissions would easily discover the mind of the Fathers, and could cut them down and revise them accordingly. Thus only one more session would be necessary to bring the Council's work to an end. Such was the widespread feeling among the Fathers at the time, especially since Pope John himself had publicly expressed this hope.

With this general feeling I could not agree. I felt that, with no schema yet promulgated, it was overly optimistic to expect all of them to be processed and promulgated in one more session. True, some Fathers spoke of one long session, lasting for perhaps four months, with all hands remaining on deck until the job was done. This idea seemed to me to be completely unrealistic, since the bishops could not remain away from their dioceses for so long a time, nor could they afford to be traveling back and forth to Rome from the ends of the earth. This would be especially true of the missionary bishops.

With this sharp exchange about the Church, the first session terminated its business. A general congregation was held on December 7 to which Pope John came and addressed the Fathers, followed a day later by a solemn closing ceremony. Here the Holy Father took occasion to sum up the work of the Council. As usual he was optimistic. He granted that the first session had had its difficult moments, but these he wrote off as due to the natural problems which could be expected at so large a congress of bishops from so many different nations and with so many different points of view.

When he turned to the conflicts which had developed, Pope John produced a phrase often used in Council affairs thereafter. He said that the Fathers simply had to have a "holy liberty" at the Council in which to express their minds, and that it was not surprising that this liberty should produce conflict at times. Pope John made it clear that he regarded this as very healthy. In other words, he did not want a dead Council on his hands. "After all," he said, "the Fathers cannot be expected to sing together like monks in a choir!"

In spite of the seemingly small amount of work accomplished, and in spite of the fact that the Pope had felt it necessary to send every single schema back for rewriting, many Fathers privately guessed that the Pope was actually delighted at the net results, now that the spirit of renewal was so clearly at work in the Council, under the guidance of the Holy Spirit. At the same time, he warned the Fathers that work at the next session simply had to be stepped up; the renewal called for was pressing and there was no time to lose.

It had been previously announced that the next session would open on September 8, 1963. Pope John expressed hope that the Council could be concluded by the following Christmas in view of the great expectations which people around the world held in connection with its work. Then, with a greeting to our flocks, Pope John blessed us all and quietly turned and left St. Peter's by a side door. I never saw him again, for by the time we returned to Rome for the second session, he had gone to his eternal rest.

Even before we departed from Rome the first evidence of the streamlining of the Council's work appeared. A booklet distributed to the Fathers on December 6 indicated that the number of schemas—originally 116, later reduced to 70—were now to be reduced to only 20!

I went home after the first session with a completely different outlook on the Council from the one I brought with me. Mainly, I was encouraged by two discoveries: first, that I could play an active part in the Council; although no expert, I was no mere observer either. Indeed, each bishop was made to feel that his every intervention and his vote were being taken as seriously and treated as respectfully as those of the most illustrious of cardinals. Second, it was clear that the Council had now embarked on a manifest course of genuine renewal of the Church in all her aspects and interests. And the very fact that no document had been produced for promulgation, far from being discouraging, was on the contrary Exhibit A of the complete openness with which Council affairs were being conducted and a demonstration that there was no railroading of business. Related to the second of these discoveries of mine was my conviction that the minds of the bishops were becoming better informed, more open, and more adjusted to the new experience of participating in an Ecumenical Council. At the end of the first session, there was far more willingness on their part to consult the *periti* and to listen to the observers than there had been in the beginning. There was also an infinite number of contacts and friendships made among the bishops in those short two months which could not help but work for the good of the Church.

Hence, as our autobus pulled away from our base at the Rome office of the NCWC and headed for the airport, a chorus of *A rivederci Roma* arose from a group of very happy American bishops and *periti* who had just closed a most important chapter in their lives and who were returning home highly aware of their instrumentality in the hands of God for the updating of the Christian life of their times.

As our chartered jet, carrying some 150 of us, landed at International Airport, a gentle snowfall began. Christmas was near and the snowfall was a lovely sight and an appropriate welcome home.

When Monsignor Pat and I reached Baton Rouge, we walked off the plane into a grand reception at the airport, with huge welcome signs, musical bands, and delegations headed by the mayor, the lieutenant governor of Louisiana, and our own diocesan officials. At the ensuing luncheon Monsignor Pat and I tried to summarize the experience we had been through, and then our first journey to the Council was officially over.

The next day we were back at our desks in the chancery. Outwardly, I suppose, we looked much the same as ever, but inwardly we were irrevocably changed in thought and outlook from the day when, only two months before, we had locked up our desks and headed out for Pope John's Great Council.

Chapter 7

A New Pope and a New Session

Early on the morning of June 3, 1963, I was awakened by a phone call from Fr. Robert J. Fangue, chancellor of our diocese, with the news that Pope John had died. Sad as the news was, it was no surprise. The world had agonized with the beloved Pope for days as he lay waiting for death, his bags, as he said, all packed and ready to go. In his death at 81 years of age he was as moving an example of Christlike qualities as he had been in life. To a cardinal who had come to comfort him, he said: *"Laetatus sum in his quae dicta sunt mihi: in domum Domini ibimus* (I have rejoiced in the things that were said to me: I shall go into the house of the Lord)," a familiar verse from Psalm 121.

The pontificate of John XXIII had been one of the shortest in modern times, lasting only four and a half years. Elected at the age of 76, the Pope had anticipated the brevity of his reign and had even remarked that other popes named "John" had served only briefly. Yet, by contrast, no pontificate in modern times had produced so profound a movement of renewal in the Church.

The Pope's waning condition had been communicated to the world, hour by hour, and millions were able to attend his funeral over television. For a moment, the Council was forgotten as humanity mourned the passing of a Father from their midst, a mourning brightened by the reflection that the Church, and, in a sense the world, probably had gained a new saint.

But when the funeral of good Pope John was over, interest returned again to the Council. Would the new pope continue what Pope John had started? Unless the new pontiff chose to recon-vene Vatican II, it would simply cease to exist, under Church law. And so speculation as to Pope John's successor took on added excitement.

The conclave to elect a new pope began on June 19, 1963. Quite unexpectedly, it reached a decision on June 21, 1963, just before noon. John Baptist Montini, the Cardinal Archbishop of Milan, was elected and took the name of Paul VI.

Immediately the new pontiff set out to reassure the waiting world of his intention to continue the work Pope John had begun. On the day following his election he named September 29, 1963, as the date for the opening of the Council's second session. By July 3 the Coordinating Commission was ordered back to work again.

Cardinal Montini carried with him to the papacy an interesting image and reputation. He was a trained Vatican official, capable and intelligent, a close associate of Pope Pius XII, and also one of the most trusted advisers of Pope John. In his see of Milan, Mon-tini effectively and directly reached the people of that highly in-dustrial and Communist city. When Pius XII wanted to make him a cardinal, Montini had urged him to look elsewhere around the world in the interest of the world-wide Church. It was Pope John who insisted that he accept the red hat.

Montini was also credited with having a powerful hand in the shaping of Pope John's *aggiornamento*. As a cardinal he had spoken twice at the first session and his weekly letters to his peo-ple of the Archdiocese of Milan had been frequently quoted. On his election to the papacy, then, it was anticipated that he would continue the work of renewal in the Church, however much he would add of his own flavor.

The job confronting Paul VI, however, was different from the one that occupied Pope John. It is one thing to get a Council started; it is quite another to bring it to a successful conclusion. Hence, there is a validity to the oft-repeated observation that it took a pope like John to start the Council but a pope like Paul to conclude it successfully. In fact some are now wondering whether Pope John would have been equal to the task of the delicate balancing, compromise and tightrope walking that Pope Paul has had to engage in to keep the fathers working together successfully and to step up the pace of business. Soon to be observed was the controlling hand not only of a competent, dedicated leader, but that of a highly skilled diplomat; the hand of a man who was serene and poised in even the most complex human situations, sure of his purpose and of himself, and unruffled by the unperceptive who had described him in the press as a Hamlet.

Long ago in Louisiana I had learned of Montini's interest in the ideas of Newman and Sturzo and of his activities with college students and in the area of social problems. Also in his background was his matchless record of apostolic action at Milan: a vast building program of new churches in the poorer sections of the city; the establishment of chapels in Milan's huge apartment houses; his bold action in going out into factories and market places to celebrate Mass "where the people were."

I was therefore confident that in Pope Paul we had a leader who, given sufficient time and latitude, would guide the Council to a happy ending. There was no disputing the fact that, on the surface, he did not always head straight down the field and do the totally expected thing. To carry the football figure further, he often did seem to take off in one direction and then unexpectedly reverse his field. But like a halfback who doesn't get a key block when he needs it, and who must then rely on his own reflexes, Pope Paul has advanced wherever he got the blocks and has adapted to the situation wherever he was unsupported. Above all, he managed to keep a remarkable balance, with no trace at any time of panic.

An excellent example of his tactics was his address to the members of the Curia, shortly before the opening of the second session. There the Pope employed praise and even reward (a raise in pay) to sugarcoat the bitter pill of reform, a tactic which was at the same time wise, fair, and successful. Others who wished to advocate reform might insensitively have run roughshod over the feelings of men who led the customary lives of dedicated, low-paid servants of the Church. Unlike Hamlet, Pope Paul mastered the delicate situation, before the whole world, with firmness, tact and great charity, and in doing so he won needed support and harmony, on all sides, as the Council headed into its second session.

Meanwhile, back at Baton Rouge, there was considerable interest in the Council on the part of both Catholics and non-Catholics. Like many another U.S. bishop, during the early months of 1963 I made many talks about the Council. To save time, I went "on the road" and addressed large gatherings in each of our seven deaneries. After this tour I accepted no invitations to speak to individual Catholic groups on the Council. I had work to do in a new diocese, and my Rome Letters, reinforced by my deanery appearances, I thought represented an adequate effort to keep my people informed. But I did accept every invitation tendered me to address non-Catholic religious groups and civic organizations, and I thoroughly enjoyed the experience. Perhaps the most stimulating of these was my "dialogue" with Professor James T. Nichols of Princeton Theological Seminary before some five or six hundred students at the State University of Iowa, January 8-9, 1963.

Professor Nichols spoke of his experience as a Protestant observer, and I of mine as a Father of the Council. After we were done the students made the most of it, throwing us every curve ball they could think of. At one point I was asked to compare Cardinal Ottaviani and Cardinal Bea. I complied, with emphasis on the fact that the assignments of the two cardinals were quite different: Ottaviani's job was to safeguard matters of doctrine, while Bea's was that of making congenial contact with our separated brethren. One was a policeman, the other a good-will ambassador. In such a context, wouldn't it be difficult for any policeman to win a popularity contest, if he did his duty?

Meanwhile, some of the revised schemas began arriving by mail: those on "The Church," "The Blessed Virgin," "Bishops," "The Apostolate of the Laity," and "Ecumenism." In Latin, they were for me slow reading. Some I read in my library and some I took for study to the greater isolation of the Gulf Coast near

Biloxi, Mississippi. Under what contrasting conditions and in what different scenes and circumstances were my fellow bishops around the world examining the same texts? I tried to picture the bishops in my own row at the Council: Bishop Piche still frozen in among the wilds of northwest Canada and Bishop Karroum amid the hot sands of Syria; or Bishop Denning in the bursting neighborhoods of Flatbush, and Bishop Pepen y Soliman in the relaxed tropical atmosphere of Santo Domingo—all of them going over the same schemas as I and anticipating with me our reunion in September.

After ocean-hopping twice the first year in the tight, straitjacket seats of trans-Atlantic jets, Archbishop Hallinan and I agreed to journey to the second session the way the Fathers went to Rome for Vatican I in 1869—by ship. We favored more elbow room and more leisure to meet with other traveling bishops and *periti,* to continue our reading and to discuss issues expected to arise at the forthcoming session. Besides, a restful five-day ocean voyage would perhaps offset the hectic experience of getting ready for departure amid an avalanche of memoranda and last-minute diocesan business.

All our expectations were dashed by cold winds and a sea so rough for five straight days that nearly all passengers were kept out of deck chairs and more than a few out of the dining room as well. It is difficult to celebrate Mass, I learned, on a rolling ship. When the candlesticks began to slide on the altar I started to worry. I am a believer in participation in the Mass, but I draw the line at altar fixtures!

There was, however, plenty of time to read in the library of the ship and *The Council in Action* by Hans Kung, *Pope; Council and World* by Robert Kaiser, *Time* correspondent in Rome; *Twelve Council Fathers* by Walter J. Abbott, S.J.; *The Johannine Council* by Bernard Haring, S.J.; and *The Renewal of the Liturgy* by Rev. Frederick R. McManus all came in for serious attention.

One of the gray days at sea was brightened by a good, long session with Professor Paul Tillich, the prominent Protestant theologian who died soon after the end of the Council—a man ranked in Protestant circles with Professor Karl Barth and Professor Reinhold Neibuhr. On this voyage he was on his way to lecture in Germany. Professor Tillich was optimistic about current ecumenical trends within Catholicism; he was quite emphatic, however, about the need for definitions at every step of the way. He left us at the dock with the parting words, "God bless Pope Paul." There were wide differences, of course, between this German-born philosopher-theologian and ourselves. But there was also between us an immense reservoir of good will and desire to understand, love and cooperate. It was a part of my education to have had an encounter with the mind of such a man as Paul Tillich, whose presence exuded charity, honesty, and genuine good will.

Accompanying Archbishop Hallinan and me on our voyage were two priests from Baton Rouge: Monsignor Paul J. Gauci, a native of Malta, and Father Paul Landsmann, a native of Germany. Both were prominent pastors of our diocese and excellent traveling companions. In Germany, we depended completely on Father Landsmann as interpreter.

Only once did Father Landsmann break down in his role as interpreter. Having landed at Le Havre, we had gone on to Paris, where we rented a small car for the drive through France and Luxemburg into Germany. As darkness fell the first evening after entering Germany, oncoming motorists began to protest the brightness of our headlights, blinking their lights at us over and over again. We were puzzled, for our lights were on "low." At length we pulled into a service station and Father Landsmann directed the attendant, in impeccable German, to adjust the *lampen*. But the attendant could find nothing to adjust. He puzzled over the matter a while, went all around the car, and scratched his head.

Then finally he peered inside the car. There, Archbishop Hallinan and I were installed (all 400 pounds of us at the time) on the back seat. The attendant withdrew his head with a cry of discovery. He had located the trouble—and it was *not* in the headlights! The headlights were shooting their rays into the eyes of oncoming motorists for a simple reason: *"Die schwei dicken herren de hinden!"* ("Why, you've got both of the stout ones on the back seat!")

The visit to Germany further fed our interest in the Liturgy—a subject still being treated at the Council. The debates were over, but the voting was unfinished and the Liturgy Commission was still operating. First of all, we visited the Liturgy Institute at Trier, formed by the German bishops. Monsignor Wagner, the director, was a member of the Liturgy Commission on which Archbishop Hallinan sat. We also paid a visit to the famous Abbey of Maria Laach where the modern liturgical movement had its birth. And, finally, we each had the memorable experience of celebrating the *hochamt* or special German-style high Mass. Archbishop Hallinan was celebrant at Idar, across the river Hahe, and I was celebrant at Oberstein, the home of Father Landsmann.

At these Masses everyone participated in prayer and song with great vigor. The *hochamt* is a Mass with singing and prayer in the vernacular. It was designed to counteract the influence of the Protestant reformers of four centuries ago who had so successfully introduced the vernacular, singing, scripture reading and preaching into divine worship. I shall never forget, after I had intoned the "Gloria" in Latin, the way the people took it up, with a rendition of "Holy God, We Praise Thy Name"—in German!

"Why is the Rhine so beautiful?" asks a well-known German song. And well may the song praise it. The great river is a marvel of scenic beauty, even on a cloudy day, as it curves between mountains studded with castles and dominated by the famed Lorelei rock-peak. Following our Rhine trip, we stopped at lovely Lake Lucerne in Switzerland, and then we took a train through the gorgeous Alpine country into Milan. The last leg was a one-hour plane hop to Rome.

It was good to be back at the Council again. By this time, we had had enough travel and reading and were anxious for action. Along the way we had been devouring every newspaper account and every magazine article on the Council we could find. We had been reading about the new Council rules, the new Protestant observers and the Pope's address to the Curia. Now we were eager to make contact with our friends at Rome and get their reactions to all the between-the-sessions news. On Thursday, September 26, three days before the opening of the second session, we reached our old home, the Residence Palace Hotel.

The bishops and other Council personnel were now beginning to arrive in Rome in large numbers. The atmosphere this time was quite different from that of the previous October. This time there was more confidence. The scene, the language, the Council procedure, and the various officials were now familiar. Most of all, outworn views of Council figures and national differences and issues had been changed or discarded. A year ago the atmosphere had been one of uncertainty with an eye to spectacle; this time everyone seemed to be confidently preparing for business.

Perhaps the greatest difference was to be found in the turning of the pages of history. A year before, "a man sent from God whose name was John" had unleashed a force that caught us all up, as it were, and plumped us down in a new era, in a wonderful new world of renewal. Then Pope John died, and we were left to ponder on the strange ways of Divine Providence which had given us such an aged pontiff who could act with so youthful and vigorous a spirit, and whose great legacy to the Church was to be his great Council representing an irrevocable turn in history. Now Pope Paul was at the helm, and the eyes of the entire world were upon him. He was not another Pope John—not many such are vouchsafed—but he had superior qualifications that made him outstanding when the conclave convened, and the College of Cardinals lost no time in choosing him for the Supreme Pontificate. Hence, his address to be made at the opening of the second session was the subject of great speculation as the Fathers and their attendants poured into Rome by the thousands.

The bishops were instructed to assemble again at the Vatican Museum for the opening ceremony, as they had done the year before. As we entered the first hall of statues, the old Romans looked down on us just as disdainfully as they had a year ago. (I began to vest at the foot of a statue of Julius Caesar who looked a little bleary-eyed.) Simplicity marked the proceedings. There was no procession through the Piazza of St. Peter's as there had been in 1962. The bishops walked directly into the aula, the great nave of St. Peter's, where their Council stands had been waiting for them all year.

The Holy Father entered the basilica on the *sedia gestatoria* with his usual entourage. I noted that his tiara was the same bullet-like, simplified one with which he had been crowned. Hardly had he entered the basilica than he dismounted and walked to the great Bernini altar with rapid steps, yet with a calm and solemn bearing, acknowledging the plaudits of the assembly with cordial but restrained gestures. There was no mistaking the deliberate effort to reduce unnecessary formality and to promote a simple and unpretentious climate.

After the Mass, the new Fathers were introduced, including 75 Apostolic Administrators who were attending the Council for the first time. The Profession of Faith followed, after which the Holy Father delivered his long-awaited address lasting more than an hour. The bishops walked out of St. Peter's with the assurance that Pope Paul meant business and that he was going to see to it that the Council moved along with dispatch. That was my impression then, and that impression was to remain unchanged to the end.

The Holy Father early in his address looked up and spoke directly to Pope John, acknowledging his enlightened and loving leadership. Then in language easy to follow, he set forth four objectives for session two, as he saw them: (1) Awareness of the Church; (2) Self-reform; (3) Unity with other Christians; and (4) Dialogue with the World.

Awareness of the Church had reference to the first topic to be debated—the nature of the Church—including the relationship which exists between the Pope and the bishops, and the roles of priests, religious, and laity in the Church. It also refers to the link which binds us to our separated brethren, first those who are Christian, and then those who are not.

On Self-reform, the Pope used terms heretofore almost suspect among Catholics. For he asked forgiveness of those who might feel that they have been injured in some way in the past.

While insisting on the Church's substantial fidelity to her mission, he proposed to correct human failings and improve methods which were out of date.

Only then, the Pope said, can we move forward toward the blessed goal of Christian Unity.

Then he went on to speak of the Church's Dialogue with the Modern World—with the intellectuals, with youth, with leaders of government, with the workers, with the poor and suffering, and with those innumerable men and women who feel isolated in a troubled society. The Church has a loving interest in all these persons and in many others besides.

Back at the hotel I wrote a Rome Letter full of enthusiasm for Pope Paul. I felt that the Council was really on its way, but I also realized the enormous amount of work to be done, if Pope Paul's four objectives were to be realized. I cannot resist indicating here what a good prophet (on September 29, 1963) I turned out to be:

> It is still my guess that we will be coming back to the Council every fall for some years. But it looks as if we will conclude the Liturgy schema this time.

We did indeed return to the Council for two more sessions, and the Constitution on the Liturgy was indeed promulgated at the end of the second session.

One of the facets of our happy experience in returning to Rome was simply that it seemed so good, so natural, to be back again. It was like having two homes, one on the Mississippi and one on the Tiber; each was a joy to return to. The old familiar haunts of the previous year, the well-remembered streets on the route of our morning bus to the Council, all the friendly people in Rome we came to know so well, the daily climb up to the main door of St. Peter's, and the old-school scene inside—all of these gradually made some kind of *Romano* of me. Even as a tourist attraction, the Eternal City cannot be excelled. But when one has lived there any length of time and has had an opportunity to savor its inexhaustible religious, historic and artistic riches as well as the tempo of daily life and the affability which greets you on all sides, one soon discovers that he has fallen in love with the place.

I came to like the pace of Roman life. I found it very agreeable. Everything is closed from noon to 4 P.M. After a few false starts, one remembers this and quits trying to visit offices, shops or places of interest between those hours. The lesson is this: go and take a "siesta" like everybody else. But, come 4 P.M. and there is nearly always something to be done "in town." The whole city springs to life at that hour and remains alive all the evening. For us, most evenings meant gathering with a different group for dinner (never before 8:30 P.M.) according to subject of interest at the moment. The drive to and from the agreed-upon restaurant was always enjoyable—through ancient, narrow streets or along beautifully monumented boulevards, crowded with the most happily talkative people on earth. Signs of religion and history are everywhere in Rome: some 400 churches, little street-shrines with tiny electric candles, together with the awesome ruins of the ancient Romans and the great baroque buildings of the Renaissance.

At the second session, I advanced 138 places in St. Peter's (from S.918 the first year to D.849 the second). This seems as though I advanced only 69 notches, but seeming net difference has to be doubled, for the numbering progresses by one on each side. At the end of the Council my number was D.802 indicating that I had advanced 232 places.

Pope Paul announced at the start of the second session that, as a symbol of our union with him in the reform and renewal of the Church, we may wear our *mozettas* over our *mantelettas* at the daily meetings. Only a bishop who is head of a diocese, ordinarily, may wear the short, elbow-length purple *mozetta* cape— and then only in his own diocese. Outside his diocese, he wears the *manteletta* cape, like a monsignor. Getting to wear a *mozetta* in the presence of the Holy Father himself gives one a feeling similar to that of wearing your father's watch for the first time, or one's first pair of long pants. The Pope's gesture was more than simply a Roman fashion note; it had significance in view of the great question under debate at this session, namely, the collegiality of the bishops with the Pope in the government of the Universal Church. The gesture was, then, a graceful nod toward collegiality. Many residential bishops did not realize they might be able to use the *mozetta* in Rome and so had left it at home, but the auxiliary bishops (who can never wear the *mozetta* otherwise) seemed, to a man, to have had the *mozetta* handy, smelling of hope-chest mothballs.

Between the first and second sessions of the Council, in August 1963, the bishops of the United States met at Chicago to gain perspective on their work at the Council. Previous to this meeting, however, the Administrative Board of Bishops had made the decision to issue a "Council Digest" in English beginning with the second session. I have already said that the lack of a daily record, similar to the *Congressional Record*, had seemed to me a major defect of the organization at the first session, and that I had complained about it to the Secretary of State, Cardinal Cicognani. I had also urged it to Archbishop Hallinan, who shared my feelings. At the meeting of the Administrative Board Hallinan requested the bishops to authorize a daily digest in English of Council speeches and action, that could be delivered the same day to the Rome residences of the U.S. bishops. This request was approved and Archbishop Hallinan and Archbishop Krol of Philadelphia were appointed to carry out the project. At Archbishop Hallinan's request, I agreed to work with him on it and brought to Rome two of our priests, Father Robert Fangue and Father Stanley Ott, to assist the Rome NCWC Office, under Monsignor Paul Marcinkus, with the job.

A group of young American priests, students of the North American graduate house of study in Rome, who were already official "transcriptors" (recorders of Council speeches), each day set forth the core of each speaker's argumentation and recorded all Council actions that day. Father William Leahy of Philadelphia was the spark plug of the unit, whose work was so well done that I never once heard a complaint, though boiling down a bishop's remarks can be tricky business!

Monsignor Marcinkus' office then had the material typed, mimeographed and delivered, without fail, each evening to every U.S. bishop throughout the last three sessions of the Council. Bishops from other countries soon began coming to the office; at the end of the Council, more than 800 copies were being printed every day. It is a pity that the coverage was not complete, omitting as it does the first session; the three bound volumes I possess are invaluable.

During the Council I coded each talk, according to my view of its merits, using a system of underscorings, x's and, at times, even exclamation points. Then I enlisted the interest of my younger cousins at home, Regina Schmidt and Jacqueline Hatrel, in making a complete card index of every intervention of importance given at the last three sessions, together with the rating I had given it.

To be fair about it, some credit for the Digest idea should go to Monsignor MacReady of the Venerable English College in Rome. During the first session, MacReady used to issue mimeographed summaries of the Council speeches, not regularly, but from time to time, for the benefit of the British bishops. I saw a copy of his work and picked up two complete sets, giving one set to Archbishop Hallinan who said, "Why can't the American bishops do something like this?" And with that the Council Digest idea was born. Once the U.S. Digest began appearing daily, the English bishops simply subscribed to it and ceased their own efforts. Some bishops have said that the Digest was one of the major accomplishments of the U.S. bishops at the Council; at any rate, I know of no other national group of bishops who issued anything comparable to it.

This is a good place to recognize the splendid work that Monsignor Paul Marcinkus and his staff did for the U.S. bishops throughout the Council. There was simply no limit to the assistance they provided: they offered secretarial service, they made purchases, they arranged travel, they did mimeographing, they changed money—but, above all, they made the Rome NCWC a pleasant place for the U.S. bishops to visit. Monsignor Joseph E. Emmenegger and Father Robert F. Trisco gave Monsignor Marcinkus excellent support which he needed, for he was also much in demand at the Vatican as Pope Paul's top interpreter in the English language.

What transpired at the Monday meetings of the U.S. bishops would, I am sure, make an interesting report. But we met with the understanding that our discussions and decisions were to be completely confidential. Only under such an understanding could the bishops venture to make reports or to express opinions. Hence it was and is strictly up to the officers of our Administrative Board of Bishops to release information to the public concerning the exchanges and decisions of our Monday meetings.

Good press coverage of the Council itself for the people back home was a major concern of several U.S. bishops from the very start. But at first there was little or no organization of press relations. Once the scene had been explored and had become familiar to American officials, however, U.S. press relations became the best of all. As it worked out there was first a mimeographed press release issued by Father Edward L. Heston, C.S.C., head of the English Bureau of the Council Press Office. This was not a translation from someone else's Italian. It was an original report based on Father Heston's own notes and those of his associates. The release was handed out to reporters each day at 3 P.M. This took some doing. After all, the daily session in St. Peter's only broke up at 12:30 P.M. and, as already mentioned, condensing the speeches of bishops on highly explosive topics is like operating a mine sweeper, especially with so little time in which to do the job. But the English press bulletins were extremely well done, and I heard nothing but praise for them from the Council reporters.

Following the press release handout, at 3:30 P.M. the press people were welcome at the USO at the opposite end of Via della Conciliazione, where they could shoot questions to an American panel of experts. Among those who served as panel experts were the following: Father Francis J. Connell, C.Ss.R., Moral Theology; the late Father Gustave Weigel, S.J., Ecumenism; Msgr.

George G. Higgins, Sociology; Father Bernard Haring, C.Ss.R., Moral Theology; Father Robert S. Trisco, History; Father F. Mc-Cool, S.J., Scripture; Father George W. Shea, Dogmatic Theology; Father John King, O.M.I., Theology; Msgr. Mark J. Hurley, Education; and Father Frederick R. McManus, Canon Law and the Liturgy.

Thus the press was given every possible opportunity to get the news and to get it straight; and top reporters from the big U.S. papers did exceptionally good stories, day after day. The late Milton Bracker of the *New York Times* and Sanche de Gramont of the *New York Herald Tribune* were especially capable journalists whose releases were always accurate and very clear. Their performance never ceased to amaze me, for neither reporter was at home in Latin, and many issues could be understood only with difficulty without Latin. To their credit, their lack of this ancient tongue never showed through in their stories.

At the start of the second session a new rule on secrecy was promulgated. As I understood it, the contents of the schemata as printed in advance and the remarks made at Commission meetings remained under the rule of secrecy; however, the speeches in the aula could be reported—but in doing so "prudence" should be used. At the first session, there had been a sensation when *The New Yorker* came out with its first "Letter from Rome." In Rome, the issue was bought up in a single day and you had to have connections even to see a copy. The cause of the sensation was that *The New Yorker* and those who contributed the material were the first English-speaking group to run around the end of the rule of secrecy, although, to tell the truth, there was no more violation in the "Letter" than one could find every day in the French newspapers. But along with the violation of secrecy, *The New Yorker* also managed to inject a flavor of high-level intrigue—a journalistic combination that is simply irresistible. Even the first volume of Xavier Rynne's series of books, built upon *The New Yorker* articles, still had the cloak-and-dagger mystique going for it. Later, other imitative books followed, but the spell was broken. Thumbing through Xavier Rynne's first volume today, one wonders how it could ever have been re-

garded as such an exciting exposé. So much relaxation of the rule
of secrecy took place in the light of experience that Rynne now
seems very tame reading indeed. Still, at the time—a short four
years ago—his first "Letter" was sensational.

Later during the second session I talked to that "mild professor
of church history" in Rome, a Redemptorist priest who is widely
accused of writing the "Letters" and the Xavier Rynne books.
(Nearly every writer of books on the Council taxed him in a
similar fashion, and got a slightly different version.) "I am not
Xavier Rynne," he protested. "Indeed, my Redemptorist con-
frères think it preposterous that I be judged having the talent to
write such a book!" He added that he had stated to the authorities that he had not written the book. I dryly countered that no
one had accused him of actually writing the book; everyone
knew that the material had gone through the usual *New Yorker*
editorial process of rewriting basic material and shaping it for
popular consumption. The real question was this: Who fed them
the material? But really my line of questioning was immaterial:
anyone could easily have done so. The French newspaper *La
Croix* every day carried everything Xavier Rynne had to say, and
perhaps more. Anyone who subscribed to the *French* concept of
Council secrecy could have supplied *The New Yorker* with abundant grist for its mill.

At the second session the Council officials lost no time in getting the Fathers down to business. On the day following the
opening of the second session, September 30, the great debate on
the Church, which had been postponed for almost 100 years—
ever since the approach of Garibaldi's troops broke up Vatican I
in 1870—began. Immediately the big artillery from many countries (Frings of Germany, Siri of Italy, Silva of Chile, Rugambwa
of Tanganyika, Ruffini of Italy, Maximos of Antioch, *et al.*) was
wheeled into firing position and started to blast away in an exchange due to last a whole month—half the length of the second
session.

Chapter 8

"De Ecclesia"

The schema on the Church, which had been mailed to us for our examination during the summer of 1963, was a brand-new text. The old text had been completely revised according to the decision of Pope John, who, after hearing the speeches of the first session, had ordered all the Council texts redone, with an approach and in a tone more in harmony with the evident spirit of the Fathers as a whole. And the new text clearly reflected the difference between work of the Preparatory Commission, which had written the old text, and that of the Council Commission, which had written the new. As a matter of fact, the promulgated Constitution on the Church eventually followed the general lines of the revised text. While the revised text before us had only four chapters and the constitution ultimately had eight, the order, approach and language were identical.

To return to September 30, 1963: the revised text was only a proposal for debate. Cardinal Browne introduced the schema with a *relatio* or explanation of what the schema contained and of the thinking behind it. In this connection, he made reference to the fact that some 372 amendments had been submitted to the Theological Commission on the introduction and first two chapters alone!

The four chapters of the new schema treated:

Chapter I   The Mystery of the Church
Chapter II   The Hierarchy, especially the Bishops

Chapter III   The People of God, especially the Laity
Chapter IV   The Call to Sanctity

A preliminary discussion, prior to taking the vote on whether to keep the revised schema as a basis for discussion, was short (less than two days) and touched upon a wide assortment of ideas: from the complaint that there was too much stress on infallibility in the document, to a plea that non-christian observers be admitted to the Council. Pros and cons as to whether the treatise on the Blessed Virgin Mary should be a separate schema or incorporated into the Church schema were also heard. Still, there seemed to exist a clear consensus in favor of the schema as an acceptable basis for the main discussion. The Moderators quickly sensed this and called a vote, before the second day of debate had ended, on this question: "Does this schema please you, in general, as a basis for pursuing the discussion chapter by chapter?" It did: only 43 Fathers were opposed, while 2,301 voted for acceptance.

At the same time the Fathers were informed that when the Council had finished discussing the Church and the Blessed Virgin Mary it would then take up the following subjects: Bishops, Apostolate of the Laity, and Ecumenism.

And so the month-long debate at session two began. The debate on the Church was to be carried over into three and a half days of the third session. Voting on *De Ecclesia* also was carried out at the third session to a final vote of approval on the text as a whole, as revised: for—2,134; against—10. Students today have many complete sources to which they may repair for thorough study of the great debate. Here I shall merely summarize the principal issues that occupied the attention of the Fathers who rose to speak on the Church.

(1) *The Definition of the Church:* With due attention to the charge of the Holy Father that the Council give special attention to the pastoral and ecumenical character of its work, many Fathers rose to insist that the definition of the Church be expressed more in Biblical than in professional scholastic language. Such language was described as the "sterile terminology of past centuries," unintelligible to the average Catholic and foreign to the non-Catholic. On the other hand, the abandoning of the terminology,

so familiar to the Fathers from their seminary days, caused certain concern: they complained about a loss of precision, about loose statements and vague expressions in theological matters which, they felt, could be disastrous. One bishop was so disturbed by the substitution on Biblical terms for the old scholastic definitions that he asked sarcastically: "And what is the theme song of the Council going to be: 'Should auld Aquinas be forgot'?"

Nevertheless, there was strong feeling in favor of the more pastoral and more ecumenical terminology as well as for expression which would make clear to the non-Catholic that we do recognize the many links they have with the Church and that these links are respected by us. This could be done, it was urged, by coming right out and calling denominations of separated brethren "churches" as they wished to be called.

The other issues also had their pros and cons:

(2) *The Collegiality of the Bishops* is a concept whereby the bishops share, by their very office, in the government not only of their local diocese but in that of the Universal Church under the leadership of the Pope. Those opposed to the notion held that bishops may do this, but not by their very office, only by reason of an invitation from the Pope, since Christ founded the Church Universal on Peter alone and not necessarily in his role as one of the Twelve. Those who favored collegiality argued that the Church was founded on the Twelve, with Peter at the head, and deduced that helping Peter's successor to govern the Church Universal today, either at an Ecumenical Council or outside of one—say, through a standing postconciliar representative body of bishops, like the U.N. in organization—was only continuing what happened at the Council of Jerusalem in the first century and what has happened at twenty ecumenical councils since.

After Pope Paul's opening address and the matter of the wearing of *mozettas*, I felt the voting would be heavy for collegiality.

The main objection brought against the doctrine of collegiality was the danger involved: there was fear that the authority of the Pope would be weakened by emphasizing the concept of the authority of the bishops in the care of the Universal Church. It was further thought that unity might suffer, and even that the bishops might find themselves confronted with disobedience as a result of seeming to minimize authority at the highest level. Moreover, civil authorities might move into the vacuum created by the failure to center complete authority in the Roman Pontiff. However, the sentiment in favor of collegiality ran strong among the Fathers, spearheaded by such leaders as Liénart and Frings, both of whom made important interventions on its behalf. Some of the sentiments expressed were striking:

> Peter cannot be regarded as outside the College of Bishops or against the College.
>
> Collegiality is just as clear in ancient tradition as are the doctrines of Papal primacy and infallibility or the Assumption of Mary.
>
> A bishop's jurisdiction exists in the whole Church by divine right, whereas his jurisdiction in his diocese exists merely by Church law.
>
> If Peter is to confirm his brethren, then the brethren will have to be closer to him, as the Italians are, and the only way to do this is to internationalize the Vatican Curia.

(3) *The Permanent Diaconate:* At present a deacon is a cleric whose next step is ordination to the priesthood and who can preach, baptize, give Holy Communion, and sing the Gospel at Mass. But in the early Church, the deacon had a permanent role in the Church and did not necessarily go on to the priesthood. Later, St. Francis of Assisi remained a deacon all his life. The proposal was to permit—for the benefit of bishops who need it, say in mission lands where priests can reach their flocks with Mass only a few times a year—a permanent order of deacon, who might even be a married man with a family. Such a man, ordained to the diaconate, could, by his power of orders, serve the people in the ways listed above, especially during those long periods when the parish priest is far away. Opponents feared that such a revival of the permanent, married diaconate would operate against vocations to the celibate priesthood. However, I felt at the time (as I wrote home) that enabling legislation should be passed for the benefit of those bishops who can use such deacons without proportionate difficulty over vocations to the priesthood.

(4) *The Priesthood:* There was widespread feeling that the Council must make a strong presentation on the modern priest-

hood. It would not be appropriate to issue a schema with a proposed 9 pages on the role of the bishop and 7 pages on the role of the laity, but only 1½ pages on the role of the priest. And, eventually, there was a separate decree on priests.

(5) *The Laity:* The main concepts of the laity presented in the "new" theology and set forth in the schema *"De Ecclesia"* were as follows: Whereas the ordained priest is clearly conscious of his sacred mission and of his "consecrated" state through the reception of Holy Orders, the laity, on the contrary, seem little conscious of their mission to continue the work of Christ, or of the fact that they, too, in a definite sense, lead "consecrated" lives through the reception of Baptism and Confirmation, which constitute them in a supernatural state in which they are possessed of certain powers to project the presence of Christ into their life-situations, the greatest of which is their power to offer the Holy Sacrifice with their priest.

In the debate on the laity, there was heavy attack on these concepts. The mission of the laity, it was argued, does not come directly from Christ, but rather from the hierarchy of the Church. Charisms, or special gifts with which to carry out the Christian mission, are not common; they are, on the contrary, very rare. The layman does not participate sacramentally in the priesthood of Christ; he participates only in a metaphorical, not in a literal sense; he offers a sacrifice only of "service" whereby he cooperates externally with the clergy.

The defenders of the schema leaped to reply: The laity had been waiting four hundred years for a positive statement from a Council regarding their place, dignity and vocation. The laity realize full well that the ordained priesthood differs from theirs, and they know how it does so. Nevertheless they need a declaration of the theological nature of their state and their role as baptized and confirmed Christians. It is simply not enough to say negatively that they are neither priests nor religious.

Moreover, the laity need something beyond a mere juridical and abstract notion of their position in the universal communion of God's sons. They need a definition of "the laity" which will come to have a vital and a personal effect upon their lives.

The laity—the case continued—need to shed the "rampant individualism" which has led so many of the faithful in the past to concentrate too much on their own individual consolation and security in their piety. They need to be introduced to a more concrete and vivid community experience, a more profound understanding of the place of the baptized and confirmed Christian in the Christian body.

Then the laity need to get a dynamic view of their role in the Church: that from their baptism and their confirmation they receive from God a mission, all their own, which is under the guidance of the hierarchy but does not flow from it, the mission to continue the work of Jesus in their lives, according to their state and according to the teachings of the Church, whether they are mandated by the hierarchy to do this or not. When mandated by the authority of their bishops to do a certain work, this becomes Catholic Action, the participation of the laity in the work of the hierarchy; and this must, of course, continue and be strengthened. But, side by side with Catholic Action, there must also exist the awareness by the Christian of who he is because of his baptism and confirmation, a child of God empowered to offer the Holy Sacrifice and to project the presence of Christ into his own life and then into his life-situation.

Finally, the mission of the laity to continue the mission of Christ in their lives can be understood by reflecting that Our Lord carried out a three-fold mission: as priest, as prophet and as king. Thus the laity, too, engage in *priestly* work when they offer Mass with their ordained priests, administer the sacrament of matrimony, confer baptism in emergency, and bless their children; they engage in *prophetic* work whenever they give witness, by their words and example, to the ideals and the spirit of Christ; and they share a *kingly* role ("you are a *royal* priesthood") when they labor to bring the elements of the world into harmony with God's law. To tackle this responsibility the laity need to have emphasis placed on their initiative and on their freedom; especially do Catholic intellectuals need to have their right to freedom of investigation vindicated. Nor are charisms rare among the laity; they abound and are everywhere in evidence.

The debate of *De Ecclesia* centered chiefly on the above five main topics, but it also touched on many other less important issues. To me it was not only extremely interesting but served as a real refresher course on the subject of the Church.

During the course of the debate a few Fathers denied Collegiality as a fact; those who opposed the notion, however, did so only when it was presented as a matter of divine law. These felt that Collegiality had always been and must always remain a mere Church arrangement which the Pope could, if he wished, completely dispense with. Indeed, many of these speakers seemed inclined to feel that, with the definition of Papal infallibility, in 1870, collegiality of the bishops and even ecumenical councils was no longer necessary. They seemed to have strong views that the strength of the Church was centered in primacy of the Pope alone in teaching, and in the centralization of the government of the Church in Vatican discasteries, in practice. The declaration of collegiality as a matter of divine institution, was, therefore, of prime importance for the future of the Church, both in its doctrine and in its practical life.

On the other hand, many bishops urged that the doctrine of collegiality did no violence to the primacy of the Pope. These Fathers felt, moreover, that the doctrines of the primacy and infallibility needed better, clearer and more up-to-date treatment. First of all, at Vatican I these doctrines had been treated without reference to the relationship of the Pope to the bishops. Second, the doctrines had been interpreted by many in ways that led to a misunderstanding of the office of bishop and to an over-centralization of Church government in Vatican bureaus. Hence, the doctrine of collegiality, far from hurting the primacy and infallibility of the Pope, would, on the contrary, help greatly in clarifying and in strengthening the Pope's position. After all, it was because Pope John felt the need of conferring with all his fellow-bishops throughout the world that he had called an Ecumenical Council. What he wanted done in the Church could not be accomplished by simply consulting his Vatican departments. And, as a matter of fact, the acceptance of Collegiality has indeed gone far to improve the position of the Papacy in the modern world. For it has helped greatly to bring the bishops into strong and loyal contact with their leader and head; it has produced a strong image of the Pope as the Father of Christendom and, indeed, of all the world; and it has given the bishops who, after all, are those in closest touch with their own dioceses, a reasonable voice in the making of policy which will affect those dioceses. All of this will contribute powerfully to the honor and strength and respect which the Papacy possesses. At the same time, it has already helped the Pope to seem less strange, less foreign, more human and more accessible to all men, while yielding nothing of his supreme authority to teach and govern which is the prerogative of his office.

An issue of the first magnitude at the second session was that of clearly stating that the office of bishop was distinguished from the priesthood not merely by reason of *jurisdiction* but also by reason of *sacramental completion*. This concept bolstered the notion of Collegiality from the other direction by aligning it more clearly with the position of the Pope in so far as he, too, is a bishop.

It must be confessed that despite the intellectual excitement inherent in the basic issues, the debate on the second chapter of the schema *De Ecclesia* was the longest and at times the dullest of the Council. Still, side by side with this was the fact that, more and more, a single bishop would rise to speak for many others, frequently for the entire hierarchy of a nation. This helped save valuable time in advancing the debate and in avoiding a measure of repetition and, in addition, it gave the speaker's remarks much greater weight. Still, the second session, as will be indicated later on, was at times the most tedious of all.

During the debate on *De Ecclesia* and the later debate on Ecumenism, the Liturgy Commission had been meeting regularly and had begun to send up material to be voted on, between speeches. This was carried forward so consistently and with such determination that, at the close of the second session, the work on the Liturgy had been completed and the constitution on it made ready for promulgation. The same interjection of voting motions was used later for the decree on communications. Every now and then the Secretary General would halt the discussion and ask the Fathers to vote on provisions for the Liturgy and the communications document, so that it was hardly possible for one to leave one's place for any length of time. During the first 41 daily meetings of the second session, my notes record that I did not miss a single daily congregation nor miss a single vote. Nearly all votes at this time were overwhelmingly in favor of each chapter as revised. The new liturgical changes were passed with *bis mille* (2,000 or more) votes all the way.

There were only 77 African bishops at the Council, but they did make themselves heard from. They had a patriarch, a cardinal, 19 archbishops and 56 bishops in their very lively and active national group. Seventy-one were Negroes and only six were white. Many of the Negroes seemed so young as to look almost like altar boys; but actually they were highly educated men, many of whom surprised people like me from the Deep South with their clipped British accent. The Congo led all African nations with eleven bishops. The Council concerned itself greatly with the needs of emerging nations and missionary lands and the Africans had much to teach us in these departments. Hence, many lectures were given during the Council by bishops and experts from African countries.

At the first session only one Catholic layman attended the Council—M. Jean Guitton, of France. The cry was raised at once that, since so many non-Catholics were invited in the persons of the observers, more laymen and, indeed, laywomen also be given the same honor and opportunity. At the mention of laywomen, voices were raised immediately all over the world on behalf of religious sisters (although I do not recall that the spokesmen for religious brothers made much noise on their behalf!). At any rate, the voices were heard, and at the second session we had fifteen laymen as auditors including Jim Norris, the well-known executive in the U.S. bishops' overseas relief program. Norris had distinguished himself during and after the war in this field, and in the course of duty had become well acquainted with Monsignor Montini, now Pope Paul VI.

The question of bringing women auditors into the Council inspired our good friend, the bishop who did the limericks at the second session, to recognize the efforts of Cardinal Suenens of Belgium in favor of having lady auditors:

> Said Suenens at one "congregatio":
> I am tired of this "segregatio."
> These Fathers are churls.
> I say: bring in the girls,
> Even though it does cause "admiratio"!

Women auditors did eventually make it to the Council, which I shall go into later.

Life in Rome during this second session was full of a variety of extracurricular experiences for me. First of all, I found that Loyola University of Chicago had a branch in Rome at which some of my students from Baton Rouge were enrolled for a one-year course for overseas students. I found that the old Newman spirit runs strong in a man even after he is too old to stay in the active arena of the University campus. And so it was a pleasure to have a gang from Loyola come over on Sundays for Mass, breakfast, a swim at the Hilton, and lunch. After lunch I would say: "Well, I suppose you students had better get back to Loyola and do some studying," a remark greeted without enthusiasm on their part. Their visits were always an agreeable throwback to my days at LSU, and I invited them over on as many Sundays as I could.

All sorts of other things happened: My friend, Bishop Leonard Cowley of St. Paul, Minnesota (a former Newman chaplain at the University of Minnesota), went to Salvator Mundi Hospital in Rome for a simple checkup. And who was his first visitor? Pope Paul! (The Holy Father happened to drop in; he consoled the good bishop without the knowledge that he was just in there goldbricking from the Council!) Then, Bishop Leo P. Smith of Buffalo suddenly died of a heart attack and I attended his funeral Mass in Rome, little thinking that I would be appointed to succeed him as national director of the Apostleship of the Sea Conference of the United States.

This appointment was due to change my way of life markedly.

It was to send me all over the United States, visiting sea chaplains, sea clubs and sea conventions, and it was to take me to the Catholic International Congress of the Sea held in Liverpool, England, the following summer. It was also destined to involve me in the question of the reorganization of the whole international approach to the spiritual care of seamen, which came up for discussion at many meetings in Rome at the Consistorial Congregation during the fourth session of the Council.

The job is a challenging one in which there is little general encouragement and meager visible results. Yet the U.S. bishops have given the Conference every possible support and the rest, now, is up to us who are in the field.

Some of the startling local results of my appointment as national director of the Apostleship of the Sea were these: First, I started using the ferry to cross the Mississippi River at Baton Rouge, instead of the Huey P. Long Bridge. Next, I discovered that 40,000 seamen were coming into the port of greater Baton Rouge every year, and that the churches of Baton Rouge were doing little or nothing to make them welcome or to discover their spiritual needs and assist them, apart from the interest which the local parish priests might exhibit. Naturally, none of this registered with me as I knelt near the bier of Bishop Smith and prayed for the repose of his soul. I might well have prayed also for the divine guidance of his successor!

There are 76 priests assigned to the care of seamen in the U.S.A., only four of them full-time chaplains; and there are 7 Catholic Maritime Clubs of various sizes, offering a variety of services. Today, however, the trend is to establish "community" centers for seamen, rather than strictly denominational clubs. The reasoning is that it is far better to have one really good community center in which religious leaders of all denominations function, with support of the community, than to have several mediocre denominational clubs all of whom make their own separate appeals to the business and community for support.

The Paulist House in Rome was a Mecca for everyone interested in the ecumenical movement. This was partly due to the fact that the Paulists have a natural interest, because of their basic mission, in matters ecumenical, and also because Father Thomas F. Stransky, the Paulist, is Cardinal Bea's secretary and a prime aide to the Protestant observers. Sunday evenings at the Paulist House brought Paulists, Protestant observers and Catholic bishops and *periti* together regularly for a social hour and dinner.

The Paulists did a great service here, which has advanced the cause of ecumenism in the Church of America incalculably, in my opinion. Dr. Outler, Dr. Brown, Dr. Lindbeck, Canon Pawley, Dr. Quanbeck, Dr. Horton, Bishop Corson and many, many others were regular guests on these Sunday evenings, along with a wide assortment of Catholic bishops from the U.S. and their attendants, all of whom got to know the observers personally. These observers were fine men, highly educated—even in Latin and Catholic theology!—but above all they were relaxed and congenial and animated with a true religious spirit. One couldn't help feeling edified and elevated in their company. They were restrained, urbane, yet so clearly convinced of their own positions, that one could meet them only in terms of respect and admiration.

In the end there developed a solid and intimate friendship between many a bishop and these Christian gentlemen, scholars and ministers. There has been no change in our Catholic position that they, unwittingly, possess only a limited possession of the divine deposit of the Christian faith. Yet who can deny that they have, in many ways, responded to God's grace most impressively?

What has impressed me the most was their attitude, their readiness, in spite of former slights and offenses on our part, to forget past mistakes, theirs as well as ours, and to start out afresh in a new climate of Christlike charity and cooperation.

We will come to the subject of ecumenism later on, and go further into this question. But at this point during the second session there was inaugurated, mainly by the Paulist Fathers of Rome, a very important program of contact with the Protestant observers which, I feel, will bear great fruit for years to come in the life of the Church in America.

One of the bishops with us at the Residence Palace had said a public farewell to his people at his cathedral before leaving for

Rome and the Council. As he came up the steps to enter the cathedral a little girl of fourteen ran up to him and gave him an envelope. The bishop looked at it; it was addressed "His Holiness, Pope Paul VI, Vatican City." "Please give it personally to the Holy Father for me when you get to Rome, will you, Bishop?" the little girl pleaded. Taken by surprise, the bishop replied, "Why, yes, yes, of course," and went on into the cathedral. When he got to Rome, he began to realize what he had promised. Faithful to his word, he went to see Cardinal Cicognani, the Papal Secretary of State, and presented the little girl's letter. His Eminence explained that it was his duty to open all such messages, and slit open the envelope in the bishop's presence to read a touching message from a little Midwestern school girl to the Vicar of Christ:

"When Pope John died," she began, "I was very sorry and I even cried for him. He was so good. But after the voting for a new pope started and after a week you were elected, I was happy again because I know you will make a good pope too!"

"Hmm," said Cardinal Cicognani, "a week? It took only a day and a half!"

"You are doing good work," the letter went on, "especially by letting us have the Mass in English. I think the children will get a lot more out of it."

His Eminence made no promises, but the American bishop felt that one day the Holy Father might perhaps, in the midst of his many official papers, find a letter of encouragement from the little girl back in the U.S.A.

At one press panel meeting, Archbishop Hallinan was asked this question: "In view of the big votes now being cast for almost every reform of the Liturgy, is it not possible that the Liturgical Commission has not gone far enough in its reform provisions?"

The Archbishop fielded the question neatly. I admired the readiness with which he answered the question as follows:

(1) The Council passed mainly *enabling* legislation and the doors are open to even further reform; (2) the commission had to look two ways: toward reform but also to *passage* of the schema on the

floor of St. Peter's. It could not afford to push its luck. (3) The Council does not operate like an ordinary parliament in which politicians are trying to get a favorite measure passed: many a bishop revised the attitudes of a lifetime on certain reforms, once he saw the mind and spirit of the Council. Hence the big votes which were all but unanimous on most points.

As we Americans moved about on weekends and holidays at the second session, visiting many parts of Italy, France, Germany and Spain, I began to pick up a lot of interesting cultural items. One had to do with dubbed-in titles of American movies shown in European countries. In one Western, a bad-guy gunman swaggers up to a frontier bar in the early Oklahoma territory and loudly demands: "Gimme a shot o' red-eye." Being interpreted in French, in a dubbed-in movie title, this comes out: "Un Dubonnet, s'il vous plait"! And then there was the half-naked American Indian approaching the Confederate officer, in a Civil War film, with upraised hand saying (in the dubbed-in German title): "Wie gehts!"

The Constitution on the Church was easily the most important and far-reaching in its consequence of any document enacted at the Vatican II. Its text merits reading and re-reading by any person interested enough to read this far in this book. Originally I had planned to set forth the highlights of *De Ecclesia* as a conclusion to this chapter: now I feel that this would be a mistake. The reader would do much better to go directly to the text of the constitution itself or else to consult the excellent summary of the constitution by Virginia Mary Heffernan, staff researcher of *The Long Island Catholic*, Rockville Centre, published by the America Press, New York, for fifty cents.

Instead of highlighting parts of *De Ecclesia*, let me set down here certain interesting and important effects the constitution will have on the Catholic life of our times, as I see them.

The problem of educating our people in the content of the *De Ecclesia* is a formidable one: where does one start? I started by scanning all the diocesan newspapers I receive for hints from the more imaginative and energetic bishops in various parts of the

country as to how to proceed. At Atlanta, as one might anticipate, there has been a lot of imaginative action. Now as this book
is being finished, congresses of the laity, religious and priests are
being held (May, 1966) as a prelude to a Diocesan Synod. "Observers" from the ranks of our own Baton Rouge laity, religious
and priests, are present to watch Archbishop Hallinan's program
in action.

The point is that such an unusual procedure is one of the direct
products of *De Ecclesia*. The thinking behind these congresses
follows this line: If the Pope was *disposed* to go along with a two-
thirds consensus of the bishops of the world (while of course re-
serving all final decisions to himself) why could not local bishops
do the same? Why should not I also be disposed, I ask myself, to
go along with a two-thirds vote of the laity, religious and clergy
of my diocese on matters they actually know much more about
than I do? However, since I am ultimately responsible, I cannot
completely relinquish or abandon the authority intrinsic to my
office as bishop. In other words, while I retain a veto, the understanding is that it will be used sparingly and that I am, in advance,
"disposed" to go along with anything two-thirds of my congresses endorse.

Another interesting effect of the Constitution on the Church is
its direct effect on the Church's use of the laity. In this respect
many important developments are in the offing. It would be tedious to attempt to list them all, but let us take just one—for example, the new discussion of the powers of parochial school boards.
This subject was the main topic of the sessions of the National
Catholic Education Association this year in 1966. The new
thought on this subject adds up to this: in the past school policy
was usually made by the pastor in consultation only with the principal of the parochial school. Yet, rarely does a pastor have adequate qualifications as a professional educator. In his parish, however, there exists, in most cases, highly trained educators who at
the same time are excellent Catholics. The use of their special
competence can improve local school policy immensely. One of
the effects of the Constitution *De Ecclesia* therefore is the encouragement of the involvement of such dedicated and compe-

tent lay Catholics in the formation of parish school policy. Again the man who is ultimately responsible, the pastor, must retain a veto. Still he too ought to be "disposed" to go along with two-thirds of his parish school board, and only rarely will he exercise his veto, as, for example, when he possesses confidential information, as pastor, which the board is not privy to.

In the realm of church government, *De Ecclesia* will lead to radical improvement. The proposed reorganization of the National Catholic Welfare Conference, which is actually the national body of bishops for the United States, is vast, goes to the roots, and is already begun. And, while the Church will still heavily depend on the dedicated service of the highly trained servants in the various Vatican departments of the Roman Curia, these officials will no longer have so much influence in policy-making at the top level. Rather will they be executors of policies made by the Pope in consultation with his brother bishops in the worldwide Synod of Bishops due to meet for the first time in 1967.

Vatican dicasteries will therefore be the agents, not only of the Pope individually, but also of the Pope as the head of a body of bishops from across the world with whom he sits down, as duly appointed successors of the Apostles, without relinquishing one whit of his supreme authority to teach and govern.

Here is to be found the principal difference in the future conduct of Church government, thanks to *De Ecclesia*. Whereas formerly the Holy Father forged top Church policy with the aid of prefects and pro-prefects (and sometimes even lower officials of Vatican offices), in the future he will arrive at such important policy decisions in conference with his brother bishops, and the Vatican offices will serve mainly to carry out the decisions arrived at. There was never any doubt about the supreme authority of the Pontiff when he made policy with the prefects and pro-prefects, and there will be none when he sits down to make top policy with the assistance of his brother bishops. They, because of their high office which is from Christ, understand more profoundly and appreciate more effectively than does the Roman Curia the nature of the Holy Father's primacy and infallibility in the Church of God. Moreover, they will be in a position to provide the Holy Father with advice which is broader and more up to date than the Curia could offer. Further they will not be inclined to promote the concentration of *all* decisions in Rome, as the Curia has shown itself in the past inclined to do.

Cardinal Bea spoke to the heart of this matter at the second session of the Council. The principle of "subsidiarity," he said—a principle which the Church itself has urged on the nations of the world—must now be applied to herself: Nothing should be done in Rome which can just as easily or even more effectively be done by the national body of bishops or by the local Ordinary.

Examples are easy to find where the opposite held true. How could a Curia official determine better than a local Ordinary whether or not there was need for a parish priest to say three Masses on a given Sunday, under given conditions? Yet it was only recently that local ordinaries were given the right to decide this matter, according to their own judgment, without recourse to Rome. And how can realistic regulations governing fast and abstinence ever be made in Rome to govern alike every country in the world?

The spirit of the Constitution on the Church will in time prevail, and its principle of "subsidiarity" govern the life of the Church. Because the Constitution offers this prospect, it can affect almost every aspect of Catholic life and the implementation of almost every other Council document.

For these reasons the constitution *De Ecclesia* has been hailed as the most important document to come out of the Council and has been cited by Pope Paul himself as the one schema which will probably be recognized as "the crowning achievement" of Vatican Council II.

Chapter 9

The Story of an Intervention

During the course of the Council I entered several *written* interventions, but only once did I make a *spoken* intervention. This does not count the time during the fourth session when I was called upon in St. Peter's to make a spoken intervention—and wasn't present! But we'll come to that later.

Friends have often chided me for "holding back" at the Council, for not speaking more often. The truth is that usually when I was prompted to intervene on behalf of a good cause, I found either that my point was of insufficient general interest to take up the time of the Fathers on the floor, or that other American bishops of greater stature than I were available to make the presentation. Under the circumstances, there was no point in my prolonging the discussion by useless repetition. Further, as long as my feelings and positions in a debate were being expressed, and as long as the U.S. bishops were being heard, it was sensible for me to restrict myself to written statements.

When, however, racial equality became the subject for discussion, the situation changed abruptly. Now a spoken intervention on my part was clearly in order. I was a Southern bishop and the subject was in my bailiwick. And here was an intervention which simply had to be spoken on the floor of the Council in order to achieve needed effect. No written intervention would do.

This spoken intervention of mine was made during the second session. Here is how it came about.

I was sitting at my place in the aula reading over the text of the schema *De Ecclesia,* while a number of repetitious speeches were in progress on the floor. It was October 15, 1963. While scanning the chapter on "The People of God" my eye caught a phrase that arrested my full attention: *Nulla est inequalitas in Christo et Ecclesia, spectata natione, sexu vel condicione sociali.* ("There is no inequality in Christ or in the Church arising from nationality, sex or social condition.") The passage went on to quote St. Paul to the Galatians, 3:28: "There is neither Jew nor Greek; there is neither slave nor freeman; there is neither male nor female. For you are all one in Christ Jesus."

I reread the Latin text. The more I pondered it, the more I felt it needed clarification. And the clarification I felt called for centered on one Latin word in the text—the word *natione.*

The Latin word *natio* (the nominative case; *natione* is the ablative form) is broad enough to cover the notion of "race," and in this particular context, *in Latin,* it clearly did so. But how would the word be understood in an English translation? There *natio* would probably be translated as "nationality" and the statement would come off: "There is no inequality in Christ and the Church because of *nationality,* sex or social condition." In translation, then, the notion of "race" would be completely lost; for the word "nationality," as commonly understood, refers to distinctions between such groups as the Germans, the Irish, the French. It does not refer, ordinarily, to distinctions between the white, brown, black and yellow races.

Coupled with this concern was an even graver one: if the translated text used the word "nationality," it might appear that the Council had deliberately sidestepped the question of race when speaking of the equality which exists among the people of God. The statements of the U.S. bishops on racial justice would then seem to be more advanced than the statement of the Council itself. This might be used to our disadvantage by certain segregationists seeking to cause confusion: they might try to make it appear that the Council had failed to support our own bishops' religious and moral stand on the question. I felt that it was most important that the Council be every bit as explicit as the U.S.

bishops had been, not only in the Latin text, but also in the English translation.

After I had sensed the need for an intervention there came to me a moment of doubt that my apprehensions were well founded. Let me go to the coffee bar, I said to myself—it was past 11 A.M., anyway—and consult some knowledgeable people. The first person I came upon was Cardinal Meyer of Chicago, who was kind enough to listen. After glancing over the Latin text, he at once agreed that it should be made more explicit. He suggested that I work up a spoken intervention, to be given in the name of the U.S. hierarchy. When the morning session was over, I returned to the hotel and drafted an intervention. Father William Leahy kindly cast it into acceptable Latin for me. (If I was going to make my debut in Latin before all the Catholic bishops of the world, I wanted an expert in Latin at my elbow!)

The U.S. bishops were to meet on Friday, but I had already planned to fly to Malta on that day. So I asked Bishop Warren L. Boudreaux of Lafayette, Louisiana, to present my proposal to the U.S. bishops and to learn whether the bishops would endorse my intervention. Bishop Boudreaux was good enough to do so. The reaction from the bishops was this: they wanted to hear a digest of my text before endorsing it. On my return from Malta on Sunday evening I received Bishop Boudreaux's report and composed a digest of my intervention, which I then submitted to the U.S. bishops at their regular meeting the next day.

Archbishop (now Cardinal) Shehan of Baltimore then moved that I be authorized to give my intervention in the name of the hierarchy of the U.S. and his motion was carried unanimously. This expression of approval and solidarity was exhilarating, but one thing more was required. So I explained to the bishops present that I also needed to obtain precedence at the microphone, that is, I had to have a chance to be heard before debate on the third chapter on *De Ecclesia* was ended by cloture. This would require a list of names endorsing my petition to speak. I passed two sheets of paper around the meeting hall and obtained 147 signatures, probably all the signatures of those attending.

Now I was set. The next morning, Tuesday, just before Mass, I went up to Cardinal Suenens, the Primate of Belgium, who was the Moderator for the day's meeting. I explained to him the nature of my talk and the fact that I would be speaking for the entire U.S. hierarchy. The Cardinal arranged for me to speak on Thursday—two days hence.

Between Tuesday and Thursday I worked further on my talk, adding ideas which I had previously overlooked. On Tuesday, I had handed in a summary of what I would say, as the rules required. Now I found that my final text would be much changed from the original. I had also heard in the meantime that the Fathers would probably feel that the race problem was so limited in scope (affecting mainly only the United States, South Africa, Rhodesia and, to some extent, Australia) that it would be regarded as a *local* rather than a universal problem.

The Fathers, I was informed, would probably find it difficult to understand how this issue could become a matter of conciliar concern. Since the Latin text says that there is no inequality among the people of God because of nation, sex, or social condition, they would probably feel that such a statement fully covered the field. "Nation" would probably satisfy them, although it would be much less explicit than an English-speaking bishop, with a racial problem in his own country, might wish.

A further problem arose in my search for the word in Latin to express the precise idea of "race." I found myself confronted with a curious difficulty: there was no such word! Conferences with more Latin scholars produced only two possibilities: *gens* and *stirps*, neither of which necessarily means "race" in our sense. In a certain context they could be made to signify "race" but that was not their basic meaning. *Gens* means "people." *Stirps* means "trunk" or "root" (in a broad sense, "ancestry"). The Romans had no word for race. They simply failed to make this distinction among men. They did make the distinction of "Roman" and "non-Roman"; and the distinction "Jew" and "Greek," but not the distinction "white" and "black."

Finally I decided to ask Archbishop Felici, the Secretary General, another expert Latinist, to advise me as to which was the more appropriate. Felici had no hesitation in doing so. *"Stirps, stirps!"* he pronounced. Still, I decided to insert in my text, after *stirps* (as a kind of parenthesis), the word for "race" as it is known in English, French, Italian and German.

On Thursday, October 24, 1963, at exactly 10:43 A.M. I rose in the aula and delivered my eight-minute intervention. Knowing how difficult the Fathers from other countries found Latin spoken with a U.S. accent, I tried to speak slowly and to enunciate clearly. As spoken interventions went, it was a short speech, going like this:

> Venerable Brothers: On page 5, lines 20 and following, of this III Chapter, we read: "Therefore, there is no inequality in Christ and in the Church, with respect to nationality, social condition or sex" (*spectata natione, condicione, sociali, sexu . . .*)
>
> And then, in order to strengthen this statement with testimony from the Bible, the words of St. Paul to the Galatians are quoted in which he states that among Christians "there is no such thing as Jew or Greek; slave or free man; male or female."
>
> I would propose, and this with the agreement of 147 bishops of the United States, that (in the first part of the series) on line 21, there be added some mention of *race* (*stirps*, Latin; *race*, French; *razza*, Italian; *rasse*, German), so that the phrase might read *"spectata stirpe vel natione"* or something on this order, as indeed already noted in the booklet of emendations on this III Chapter, page 7.
>
> My *reasons* for making this proposal are the following:
>
> *First*—If this addition, which refers directly to equality, regardless not merely of nationality but also of race, were introduced into the text of the Schema, then our Council would go squarely and explicitly on record for that equality which all the members of the Populus Dei enjoy, by right, in the economy of Christianity. Besides, all discrimination, based solely on race, would be explicitly branded as irreconcilable with that truth according to which we believe that God created all men with equal rights and equal dignity.
>
> *Second*—This emendation makes the Schema even more harmonious with the thought of St. Paul cited in the text in which the Doctor of the Gentiles wishes to lay down the proposition that all opposition between "Jew" and "Greek" has ceased to exist among true Christians. It would seem that, in the context, the terms "Jew"

and "Greek" are to be better understood as referring to a distinction of religion, culture, *and race*, rather than merely to what we might describe as "nationality."

Third—Because of actual conditions in the United States and similar conditions in other parts of the world, Fathers now here at the Council, at home frequently find themselves faced with serious problems stemming "*ex praejudicio razzistico*" (vulgo: "racial prejudice" or, as I have it, "*ratione stirpis*"). The bishops of the United States are striving to instruct their people in matters of social justice and charity, and they have issued several public statements setting forth the doctrine on these matters. Now should the Council, speaking of the Populus Dei, make an explicit and solemn declaration on the fundamental principle of the equality of all races, the aid and comfort given thereby to the Bishops in their efforts to teach the people would be tremendous.

Fourth—Such a declaration on the part of the Council would bring great consolation to all those persons in the world who are deprived of equal liberty and who are burdened and humiliated purely because of their race.

Fifth—Such a Conciliar pronouncement in this Schema would also provide a doctrinal foundation for future decrees in which the principle of the equality of all races of men, in the context of modern times, could be applied much more readily and with much more effect on a practical basis.

Therefore, because of the above reasons which deal with an urgent, pastoral need of our day, I ask the Fathers of the Council that a solemn, doctrinal declaration of the equality of all men, regardless of race, be given in this Chapter on The People of God.

Gratias. Dixi.

That afternoon at 3:30 I went down to the USO to meet the press. After telling the story behind the intervention, I entertained questions. The first came from Paul Blanshard, author of the well-known series of anti-Catholic books beginning with *American Freedom and Catholic Power*, intended, no doubt, to be a real curve: "How will your intervention affect interracial marriages in Louisiana?" I answered by pointing out that the intervention referred only to the *doctrinal* matter of equality and did not propose to discuss all the various practical effects that might flow from it; further, there was no canonical prohibition in the Church, even now, against interracial marriages; finally, since the choice of a marriage partner was a highly personal matter, I did not anticipate any great immediate change in the racial pattern of marriages in Louisiana.

Some of the U.S. bishops at the Monday meeting would have had me use the word "color" in face of the difficulty of finding a word for "race," and some of the reporters brought up the same point. Both times I maintained the position that to use the word "color" would only confuse the issue, since color is but an accidental manifestation of racial difference. For example, it is not unusual to find a Negro with a far lighter skin than some persons from India.

The questioning continued for forty-five minutes in a room crowded to the rafters with reporters; this was the first time in the two sessions of the Council that any intervention had been given expressly on the race issue as such. What most intrigued the reporters was the fact that I had stated in my intervention that I spoke for 147 U.S. bishops, the number of those whose names I had collected on my two sheets of signatures. I made a mistake in specifying "147." I should have stated that I spoke for the entire U.S. hierarchy, which I actually did. When I said "147 bishops" the press naturally wanted to know: "What about the others? Did any of them hold out?" I had to explain that the number referred to the 147 bishops who had attended the bishops' meeting on Monday, and that I had not attempted to contact the others. Besides, the repeated statements of the U.S. bishops on the race question surely spoke for themselves.

Early the next morning I left for London and Dublin on a weekend journey to see my Irish seminarians. During my trip I could not help but wonder how my intervention had been received in the press. On landing at Dublin I found out: the *Irish Press* ran a banner headline which cried: RACE NO BAR IN CHURCH.

The Dublin handling of my intervention was an indication of the interest which the world press would take in it. All the major newspapers of the world gave it front-page coverage (the *New York Times* also printed my picture); but my own hometown

papers (protecting me, as usual, from my own imprudence) assigned me rather limited and remote space (I believe on page 5).

Sanche de Gramont, writing in the *New York Herald Tribune*
on October 25, 1963, made this observation: "Bishop Tracy said"
(in his press interview): "While racial problems are, admittedly,
circumscribed to certain areas of the world, nevertheless, here in
Rome, I am bombarded with questions on the racial issue, from
taxi drivers to bishops, once they find out I am from Louisiana.
Still, the majority of Council Fathers, it seems, find it difficult to
understand why this should be a matter of conciliar concern."

The latter opinion of mine, which I confess I had bought second hand from some advisers, I later felt compelled to repudiate.
The Council Fathers, as a matter of fact, were anxious to have the
question of racial justice settled, once and for all, on the international level. In *experience* the racial problem was restricted to
certain geographical areas; in *interest* the problem knew no restrictions whatsoever. On the contrary, it was a matter of prime
international concern.

What first stirred me toward a realization of this fact was the
generous applause of the Council Fathers which greeted my remarks. I had been led to believe that my motion would meet with
general indifference; on the contrary, it met with warm and general approval. You may well imagine, then, the surprised and delighted feelings with which I returned to my seat.

Here to me was an unexpected open door; here was a broad
vision of charity: the bishops were ready to meet the problem of
racial injustice throughout the world, wherever it might exist,
and even though they might have no trace of such a problem in
their own back yards!

Regarding my own back yard, namely, the Diocese of Baton
Rouge, I am happy to state that, by diocesan statute, all our
Church institutions, organizations and activities are open to all
our Catholic people. However, I have long felt that the elimina-
tion of racial barriers, while strictly necessary in justice, would
nevertheless open up other equally difficult and fundamental
problems, most specifically those attendant upon the elevation of

many of our people from their present substandard level to a decent economic, social and educational condition. In tackling this deplorable condition our national anti-poverty programs are proving to be of immense effectiveness. They are providing thousands of children in our diocese with dental, medical, nutritional and educational care for the first time in their lives. They are opening the way for persons who are illiterate to learn basic reading; for persons whose education is substandard to obtain instruction; for persons lacking a basic skill to achieve vocational rehabilitation. At the moment, in Baton Rouge the vast majority of the children and adults so aided are the deprived members of the Negro race. Whoever the underprivileged beneficiaries may be, the important programs operating now in their favor are generally endorsed and well supported by the community at large.

My plea to my flock to be Christlike in this matter of human relations was made in a pastoral letter dated May 23, 1965, in the following words:

All we ask is that our Catholic people remain steadfast in their confidence in our leadership, guided as it is by the very highest religious considerations and fortified daily by prayer and earnest consultation with persons of the highest integrity.

In everyone's life there comes the "moment of truth"—the "moment of conscience." That hour has now arrived for us on this issue of racial charity. Let us, therefore, put our trust in God who can help us to achieve something of His own love and goodness to all men.

Prayer is our great recourse. For no one, in his moments of encounter with the Lord God in prayer, can yield to such degrading attitudes as dislike, discrimination, hatred or simply unfeeling neglect toward any human being on earth. Such prejudices and evil feelings cannot enter the sacred sanctuary of our minds once we are alone with God, our Maker and our Judge.

Let us, then, shed the old man of racial prejudice; let us cast off the old bonds of guilt. And, let us arise anew to a truly Christian world of generous giving of open love to all members of the human family.

Your Diocese, your Bishop and your pastor will show you the way. Put your trust in God and you shall not be confounded.

I thank God that this message has been generally accepted throughout the diocese.

To return to Rome: my intervention was accepted. The change it proposed is now to be found in the official text of the "Constitution on the Church," Chapter 4, No. 32, as follows:

> . . . There is, therefore, in Christ and in the Church no inequality on the basis of *race* or nationality, social condition or sex, because "there is neither Jew nor Greek; there is neither bond nor free; there is neither male nor female. For you are all "one" in Christ Jesus.

The passage is now to be found, however, not as formerly in the chapter on the "People of God," but in the chapter on "The Laity." The important point is that the very highest authority of the Church has now vindicated in a most solemn and explicit manner the principle enunciated by the U.S. bishops in their public statements "that all men are created with equal rights and equal dignity."

Chapter 10

"Bishops" and · "Ecumenism"

The period October 28 to December 4, 1963, was characterized by fascinating subjects and developments on the one hand and tedium and frustration on the other.

The all-engrossing subjects were "Bishops" and "Ecumenism"; the interesting developments were the continued voting on the Liturgy, the disposal of the treatise on the Blessed Virgin Mary, and the celebrated test vote on the "five propositions," a vote which has been called a "turning point" of the Council. The tedium was caused by lengthy debate and a return on the part of some bishops to the attack on collegiality, a matter on which a consensus of the Fathers had already been clearly established. The frustration grew out of an emotional atmosphere engendered by failure to get the subjects of "The Jews" and "Religious Liberty" on the floor for approval as a basis for discussion. These had once been Chapter IV and Chapter V respectively of the schema on Ecumenism; now, however, they had been separated from the first three chapters and in the process they disappeared from the agenda of the second session.

The sequence of events at the opening of this period ran as follows:

October 28: Mass by the Pope and sermon by Cardinal Suenens for the fifth anniversary of the election of Pope John.
October 29: Vote to dispose of the treatise on the Blessed

Virgin; distribution of copies of five "propositions" to be voted on.

October 30: Vote on the five propositions.

A number of journalists claimed to see a connection between the events listed above—namely, this: that by solemnly emphasizing Pope John and his brief reign at this juncture of the Council, and by having one of the four Moderators, Cardinal Suenens, preach the sermon at the Mass, the Pope was going out of his way to make a point. He was indicating to one and all, it was theorized, that the Council would continue to move in the direction initiated by Pope John and that the disputed decision of the four Moderators to call a test vote on collegiality (in the form of the five propositions) was going to be sustained as far as he was concerned.

This is the type of unsustained supposition, the kind of "inside" story which made its way into the press constantly all through the Council. These stories made interesting reading, but one could never tell how reliable they were; they frequently sounded plausible but there was always the nagging suspicion that they were based on conjecture and gossip.

At any rate, the Fathers voted to incorporate treatment of the Blessed Virgin Mary into the document on the Church. But it was a very close vote: 1,074 to 1,114. As mentioned earlier, there was a need to indicate clearly the role of Mary in the entire divine program or history of salvation, a role subordinate to that of Jesus, the God-man and Saviour. There existed in the Church, as a number of Fathers testified, an unfortunate tendency among certain peoples, and especially among the uneducated, to exaggerate the role of Mary at the expense of Christ. Such exaggeration induced confusion in the popular mind; besides, unnecessary obstacles were thus thrown in the way of Christian unity and understanding by what may have seemed to outsiders as Church approval of this exaggeration.

On the other hand, no one wanted to appear to be lukewarm in his love, devotion and loyalty to the Blessed Mother. And relegating her to a mere chapter in "De Ecclesia," instead of giving her the honor of having her own document, was widely interpreted as being just that. In addition to their arguments, those who advanced the cause of a separate schema for Mary did so often with an active canvassing campaign for votes. I received daily mimeographed messages in my hotel mailbox requesting me not to treat the Mother of God in so shabby a fashion as to deny her the tribute of a schema of her own. This, to me, reflected the same mentality as that urging the use of such exaggerated titles for Mary as Co-redemptrix. True, such a title is capable of a completely orthodox interpretation; still it serves to confuse people: it requires constant explanation, and it casts unnecessary blocks in the way of those who sincerely seek to understand Catholic teaching and devotion on Mary, the Mother of God. It is a doubtful honor to Our Lady to give her titles which may please us, but which cannot really please her, in themselves, since they serve to becloud rather than clarify the teaching of her Son.

The Fathers did vote, in the end, to incorporate the treatise on the Blessed Virgin Mary into the schema "De Ecclesia" so that Our Blessed Lady could be seen more in the total context of the history of salvation, and to insist that true devotion to Mary cannot exist apart from the living of a fervent Catholic life. However, this proposal managed to only squeak by; it won by only 40 votes.

On October 30, 1963, the Fathers were called upon to vote on the five famous "propositions." These propositions were statements of basic positions on the episcopacy, its sacramental and collegial character and its relationship to the Pope. Included was also a statement on the diaconate as a distinct and permanent grade of Holy Orders.

The reason for placing these propositions before the Fathers for voting was this: Within the Theology Commission, no agreement could be arrived at on the five questions clear-cut enough to produce a revised text for the Dogmatic Constitution on the Church. There was the accusation, made even on the floor of the Council by Cardinal Lercaro, that some commission members instead of seeking to produce a text in harmony with the sentiment of the Fathers generally as voiced in the debate on "De Ecclesia," were re-debating the whole matter in commission in an effort to have the schema adhere to what they considered traditional and therefore safe positions. (Indeed, it took considerable effort to even get the five propositions before the Fathers for voting; and, even after the propositions were voted through favorably by more than eighty per cent of the Fathers, the propositions were still disregarded and disparaged by some as wholly unofficial!) However, Cardinal Lercaro urged, we must not live in the past; we no longer need to fear an attack on the Pope's authority; there are no separatist movements afoot today; all the Fathers are solidly back of the primacy and infallibility of the Pope.

The substance of the five propositions and the vote on each were as follows:

> 1. That Episcopal Consecration constitutes the highest grade of Holy Orders.
> For—2,123; Against—34; Invalid—0.
> 2. That every Bishop legitimately consecrated and in communion with the other Bishops and with the Roman Pontiff is a member of the Body of Bishops.
> For—2,049; Against—104; Invalid—1.
> 3. That the Body or College of Bishops, in exercising its power of teaching, sanctifying and governing, succeeds the College of the Apostles and that, united with its head, the Roman Pontiff, and never separately from him, does enjoy a share in the full and supreme power of the Church.
> For—1,808; Against—336; Invalid—4.
> 4. That this power comes to the College of Bishops by divine right.
> For—1,717; Against—408; Invalid—13.
> 5. That a permanent order of Deacon be restored.
> For—1,588; Against—525; Invalid—7.

If you are curious about the "invalid" votes, this is the answer. Votes could become invalid in a number of ways: for example, by not being marked properly with the electronic pencil, or by one's voting *placet juxta modum* (yes-but) on a matter that admitted only a straight *placet* or *non-placet* vote. When the sense of the discussion indicated an overwhelming "Yes," I could not help suspecting that one Father especially would, time after time, mark his ballot *placet juxta modum* just to tease the Secretary General, who first tried careful explanation, then entreaty, then exasperation, then wise cracks and finally surrender and resignation. The *juxta modum* vote would then disappear for a while, only to pop up again unexpectedly at another moment nicely calculated to amuse the assembly and exasperate the Secretary General.

There is no doubt that when Bishop John J. Wright of Pittsburgh told the press that the overwhelming vote in favor of the five propositions was a turning point in the history of Vatican Council II, he was correct. There remained a certain amount of refusal to accept the verdict, but Archbishop D'Sousa of India voiced the feeling of the Fathers generally, I think, when he called it a "mockery" to disregard so clear an expression of consensus of Council feeling.

Collegiality continued to be a problem in the course of the debate on "Bishops and the Government of Dioceses." The collegiality notion, although clearly favored by the Fathers in the straw vote, was still not a promulgated position. At this point, our limerick-writing friend was inspired to recognize the problem:

> Some Fathers say "collegiality"
> Would give the Church much more vitality.
> But Ruffini of Palermo
> In a powerful sermo
> Said it didn't have any reality!

Cardinal Browne went so far as to say that, in his opinion, collegiality could not even be reconciled with the notion of the full and supreme authority of the Pope already defined by the Church. "So, Venerable Brothers, we had better watch out— *Caveamus!*" This was hardly a way to win friends and influence people, and the Cardinal's warning to the Fathers was received with something less than delight.

The celebrated verbal exchange between Cardinal Frings of Cologne and Cardinal Ottaviani of the Holy Office took place on the floor of the Council on November 8, 1963. Cardinal Frings had severely criticized the Holy Office for continuing practices which were "out-of-date and a scandal to the world." Later, Cardinal Ottaviani, departing from a prepared script, not only defended the Holy Office but lashed out in personal counter-attack on Frings, terming his remarks as "stemming from igno-rance, if not worse." One of my friends, sitting nearby, at this point got up and started to leave. He whispered to me as he went by: "I'm going to the coffee stand. I've got to get out of here—I can't stand the sight of blood!" I went to the coffee stand myself a few minutes later and what was my surprise to see the two dis-tinguished antagonists, Frings and Ottaviani, chatting and smiling and embracing each other at the entrance to the bar.

One of the defects of Council procedure was that it provided too little opportunity for toe-to-toe exchanges. When Frings and Ottaviani squared off that day, the Council really came to life. More spirited debate like that would have enlivened the proceed-ings enormously.

The debate on the "Bishops" revolved about a number of cen-tral considerations, as follows:

1. The Bishops and the government of the Universal Church.
2. The Bishops and the government of their own dioceses.
3. The Bishops and their aides in the government of their dioceses; auxiliary bishops, the diocesan curia, and commissions, the diocesan clergy and the religious in the diocese.
4. Diocesan Synods Councils and Episcopal Conferences.
5. The boundaries of dioceses and ecclesiastical provinces.

The tenor of the remarks on the schema on "Bishops" was largely critical, mainly because the text insisted on ignoring col-legiality. However, in the end the Fathers voted to accept the text as a basis for discussion by a vote of 1,610 to 477.

Some of the more interesting developments in the course of the long and often tiresome debate were these:

The opinion was expressed that the Church should discontinue the custom of appointing bishops to "titular sees," that is, to dioceses which once were renowned in church history but which were now inactive due to an extremely reduced Catholic population. The area once called "Asia Minor" and currently a part of Turkey is a good example. Asia Minor was the scene of St. Paul's labors and the churches he established there were celebrated for many centuries. The Church keeps their memory green by giving their "titles" to auxiliary bishops under present custom. For example, in 1959 I was appointed titular bishop of "Sergentza," now the Turkish city of Istranca. Sergentza was once at the crossroads of the Christian world, and all but one of the first seven ecumenical councils of the Church were held within 100 miles of the city. But in 1453 the whole area was overrun by Moslems, and the minarets of Islam replaced the church towers of Christianity. Bishop Gerard McDevitt, Auxiliary of Philadelphia, said, in a speech on the floor of the Council, that after reading a pamphlet about his titular see, sent to him by the Vatican, he had no desire to go there, since the place seemed to have only a couple of palm trees and a few goats. With such oddities in mind, there was the suggestion that auxiliary bishops hereafter be given the title of the see they were serving as auxiliaries; and that, when a bishop retired, he simply should keep the title of his see with the added note "emeritus."

The question of the retirement age and resignation of bishops was understandably treated with kid gloves. First of all, retiring a bishop is not like retiring an employee. It's more like retiring a grandfather: he naturally remains in the household even though he can no longer actively govern the family. Our limerick writer took up this thought with spirit:

> To demand older bishops resign
> At the Council is not thought benign
> Only secular planners
> Without Christian manners
> Would churchmen to oblivion consign.

For more than a week the bishops had been giving little ten-minute sermons to each other on the qualities a bishop ought to have. However, most bishops, on this as on many another question, remained silent. But when the subject of resignation and retirement was broached, many an elderly bishop, hitherto quiet on all other topics, rose to speak on this one. One of the views expressed by one of the older Fathers was that bishops should simply be compelled, by Canon Law, to retire—at the age of 80!

Another consideration operated to restrain any serious move to set a retirement age for bishops. Undeniably the Church had been actively renewed by an energetic and effective Pope who came to the Chair of Peter at the age of 76! And so the Council skirted the whole question, contenting itself with a general observation that adequate provisions should be made for the resignation and retirement of elderly or incapacitated bishops.

Episcopal conferences came in for much discussion. Here was a most important innovation, the introduction of a new legislative body into the structure of the Church, a body close to the local situation and well informed about her problems and character.

It seemed to me that episcopal conferences would be especially equipped to frame realistic legislation on such matters as fasting and abstinence and marriage regulations.

All legislation stemming from such conferences would of course have to be approved by the Holy See. The point is that it would not *originate* with the Holy See but rather at the grass roots.

Another striking consideration was the insistence, over and over again, that the bishop's role of government of his diocese should be regarded, by himself and by others, principally in terms of *service* to his flock. Thus he would enact regulations with service only in mind, without thought of simply having his *will* prevail.

The Council decree on "Bishops and the Government of Dioceses" is a document worth careful study throughout the Church.

Appropriately, just as the subject of ecumenism was coming up for discussion at the Council, the annual reception for the U.S. non-Catholic observers was held at the Grand Hotel on November 8, tendered by the Paulist Fathers and attended almost to a man by the U.S. hierarchy, clergy and laity in Rome.

Dr. Albert Outler of Southern Methodist University was chosen to speak for the observers, and he made, as usual, a delightful presentation:

I speak as a member of a new and hitherto unapproved order which has sprung up in the Council, The Separated Brotherhood of St. Longinus—for, you know, the tribune of the Observers is placed directly under Bernini's great statue in St. Peter's!

Far deeper than mere courtesy are the inner impulses of the Holy Spirit, within your hearts and ours, where He has begun to break down the old encrusted barriers of ignorance, prejudice, and enmity that have so long divided us. He has awakened a new disposition in us all of mutual recognition, interest in dialogue, and the new experience of fellowship and affection. It is no light thing for us that we are enabled to join with you daily in the Mass and the Angelus, to follow your debates with ears cocked for their ecumenical import, to be jostled in the disorderly camaraderie of Bar-Jonah and Barabbas, to get to know you as men of grace and wisdom, and rare good humor!

What has impressed us most, I think, is your willingness to be observed; to expose yourselves to the inquiring eyes of friendly but not at all uncritical observers; your willingness to engage in the baffling enterprise of self-understanding, self-explanation, self-inspection; your willingness to risk the hazards of what Pope John called "aggiornamento".

In our audience with Pope Paul, he was wonderfully explicit about this. He said: "Our intention is to hide nothing from you, nor to conceal in any way the difficulties that obstruct complete understanding. We do not fear the tension of discussion nor the pain of waiting. Good faith and true charity are the basis for the relation we propose to you."

We are all aware of what this Council has accomplished: in the span of five short years, a wholly unprecedented change of climate in the Christian world has occurred.

Still none of us presumes that *"communio in sacris"* (worship in common) is within sight or even early prospect. Indeed, it would not be worth having at the price of compromise on your part or abjuration on ours.

It is painfully clear that yet another miracle will be required before the whole Pilgrim People of God are fully united as one people, one household of faith.

In the interim, however, there is a formidable budget of work that can be undertaken by us—together and separately.

For us, "the separated brethren," there is the task of discovering, appraising the richness of the treasures of the deposit of faith which you have conserved and served in the course of the tragic centuries of our separation.

You must realize—and not be offended by it—that the burden of our reservations toward you has not been that Rome is too catholic but rather not catholic enough. It is as we discovered your real catholicity and also as you actually manifest it that we shall be moved toward eventual reunion.

Meanwhile you are putting real pressure on us, your separated brethren, to also risk similar experiments in self-examination and reform. And it is most remarkable that one of the most effective stimuli to church reform in modern Christendom is coming from the Church that was once thought to be unreformed and irreformable!

Pope Paul, speaking last August to the monks of St. Nilus' Abbey at Grottaferrata, uttered words that we would both do well to apply to ourselves:

> We are all a little hard of hearing; we are all a little slow of speech. May the Lord enable us to hear each other's voices, the voices of history, the voices of the Saints, His own voice which is still our Law and our Power.

Please be assured that these days there is no group in the aula of St. Peter's—or anywhere else in the world—more attentive, more concerned, or more hopeful than the one in the tribune beneath St. Longinus' spear.

The debate on "Ecumenism" was preceded, as usual, by the initial presentation of the text with its *relatio* or explanation of how the commission came to write the text the way it did. In this case surprisingly, but agreeably so to the more liberal-minded Fathers, the first chapters to be presented were the more interesting and disputed sections, namely, Chapter IV (on the Jews) presented by Cardinal Bea and Chapter V (on Religious Liberty) presented by Bishop De Smedt of Belgium. However, after the general debate whether or not to accept the text as a basis for full discussion had gone on for three days (November 19–21) the Moderators suddenly announced that a vote would be taken on

Chapters I, II and III, but that a vote on whether to use Chapter IV and Chapter V, as they stood, as a basis for further discussion would be taken a few days later. The impression given was that the last two chapters needed a little more tinkering with—but not very much—to make them acceptable for debate.

As I have already said, these two chapter-subjects never did reappear for voting at the second session. I think it can be stated quite frankly that what happened was that immense pressures against the two chapters, or, for that matter, against any statement at all favoring Religious Freedom or the Jews, had built up. It was therefore deemed advisable to delay consideration of these matters until a more favorable climate had developed—not in the Council—but in the outside world from which the pressure was coming.

The basis of the pressure was fear: Religious Liberty was feared by some as likely to upset Church-State relations in certain countries where there were agreements which safeguarded the Church's rights. Also it might give Catholics the notion that they could now vote Communist with impunity. The statement on the Jews was feared because it might provoke persecution of Catholic minorities in countries whose governments chose to interpret the statement as a political one, seeming to favor the State of Israel and thereby to take sides against the Arab nations.

At first there was a bit of yielding to such pressures—not only from political sources, but also from Catholic sources—that is, from Catholics who felt that the entire schema's tone was not sufficiently harmonious with Holy Scripture. In the case of "The Jews," the explicit absolution of the Jews from the charge of "deicide" was dropped; the pressure had served only to produce counter-pressure. The moment was not at all propitious for a calm and sober statement on either question, and it was well that the two matters were held over not only to the third but finally to the fourth session when acceptable statements on "Religious Liberty" and on "The Non-Christian Religions, including the Jews" were issued as separate documents.

Meanwhile, the Fathers accepted the first three chapters on "Ecumenism" as a basis for discussion by a vote of 1,996 to 86, a tremendous victory for Cardinal Bea and his Secretariat on Christian Unity.

The debate on Ecumenism brought forth several important and striking thoughts, as follows:

> This text on Ecumenism marks the end of the Catholic Counter-Reformation. It makes us undertake a good examination of conscience regarding our past attitudes toward separated brethren.
>
> The Orthodox and the Protestants should not be treated in the same chapter because of our fundamentally different relationship with the former than with the latter. The Orthodox are not so doctrinally or sacramentally separated from us as are the Protestants and are also geared to the same system of authority.
>
> "Ecumenism" as used here is not employed in its authentic meaning as when you speak of an ecumenical (i.e., general) council. As used here, to refer to the Christian *unity* movement, the word is given a meaning first introduced by Protestants in connection with unity conferences. The word should be kept in its authentic sense.

On the Black Friday evening of November 22, I came down to the lobby of the Residence Palace Hotel to meet Father Ott at 7:40 to drive together to the Hilton Hotel on business. He greeted me with the tragic news that someone had shot President Kennedy. In vain I tried to obtain more information at our hotel, so we drove at once to the Hilton. Fifteen minutes later we could see the hotel's array of flags already hanging at half-mast.

But there was hardly any more news available at the Hilton than we already possessed. Soon we had a radio going and were surprised to find that, even in the United States, the radio stations had no more definite information than we possessed. We ate simply with Archbishop Cody and remained for about an hour afterwards discussing the tragedy. Then we returned to our own hotel, still stunned and wondering under what circumstances so terrible an act could have been performed. All we could do was to offer a "De Profundis" for the President and retire.

The Italian people were deeply affected. Saturday morning Rome broke out huge expressions of condolence on posters fixed to walls all over town. The posters bore a portrait of President

Kennedy and a statement from the Italian government. Then there was immediate closure of all places of entertainment and a proclamation by the mayor of Rome of three days of mourning.

Saturday I said my own Mass for the President and attended Cardinal Spellman's low Mass at the "American Church" of Santa Susanna which we had difficulty even getting into, so great were the crowds. On Monday Cardinal Spellman celebrated a Solemn Pontifical Mass at St. John Lateran Church. This was what is known as a "diplomatic Mass," that is, it was attended by some sixty cardinals and every possible Italian and American dignitary. The papers estimated the crowd at 10,000.

Solemnly we witnessed the funeral of President Kennedy on television by telstar. The fortitude of Mrs. Kennedy and the touching bewilderment of her two children struck us all very forcibly, overshadowing in our minds even the impressive assemblage of heads of governments who had come to the funeral.

I have always felt that President Kennedy was a providential figure destined to become the nation's first Catholic President. In the difficult task of proving to all that none need fear a conflict of religion with presidential duty, he performed superbly, without making a false step.

John F. Kennedy was a man of great qualities and a true leader, especially in the cause of peace. Pope Paul VI, in receiving the President at Vatican City on July 2, had said to him:

> (Your) untiring efforts to obtain world peace are to be commended highly, and we are confident that these labors will find a ready response in all men of good will.

Let us pray that God may give eternal rest to the soul of John Kennedy.

The last two days of the second session were marked by appropriately solemn and important acts and ceremonies:

On December 3 the 400th Anniversary of the Council of Trent was observed with an address by Cardinal Urbani. Then there were expressions from the lay auditors, Jean Guitton and Vittorino Veronese. And finally, there was the reading of the papal directive entitled "Pastorale Munus" in which wide new faculties were granted to the bishops of the world by the Holy Father.

On December 4, the Solemn Closing of the second session was held with a low Mass celebrated by Cardinal Tisserant, Dean of the Sacred College of Cardinals; also the solemn voting on the Constitution on the Sacred Liturgy and the Decree on Communications and the promulgation of these documents by the Pope; and, finally, the address by Pope Paul, closing the session.

Although the second session of the Council did enact two documents, nevertheless there was widespread feeling, after the session ended, that something was missing. What was missing was a sense of accomplishment. The high hopes with which the Fathers had set to work in September 1963, after hearing Pope Paul's challenging opening address, had somehow drooped and withered. Too much time had been simply wasted, especially in commission meetings where, it was felt, there was too much debate and too little action. Some commission members did not seem to understand their role, which was not to re-debate the issues but to revise the texts of the schemas in the light of the debate the Fathers had already completed.

As a result, the Fathers had not been able to vote on many questions which they were eager to settle. The Fathers had practically completed debate on the Church, the bishops and ecumenism. Moreover, they had been anxious to discuss Religious Liberty and the Jews. But they never had an opportunity at the second session to vote on the former or to discuss the latter, although sentiment in favor of doing so was general. If we were to complete Council documents at the rate of only one every year, we would be coming back to Rome each year for 34 years— longer than the 18 years of the Council of Trent!

When we returned to the United States, the newsmen had just one big question to put to us: "Has the Council lost its steam?"

I felt this to be so appropriate and important a question that I decided to make it the title of a special article which I wrote and which appeared in *America* on February 1, 1964:

In answer, I must reply as follows: Yes, in spite of the public proclamation of two conciliar texts, I am still frankly disappointed at

the rather meager tangible results of this session after a most promising beginning. But I am not pessimistic. I do not think there has
been a breakdown; and the steam has not gone out of the Council.

I am disappointed mainly that we did not get to vote on much
material that I believe the Fathers were anxious to vote on. I am
irritated also at the manner in which certain votes were put to us
in a way which prevented direct action on the questions at hand.
And I feel that, within the commissions, procedures which should
have served to carry out the will of the Fathers were used repeatedly to block that will, at least temporarily. . . .

Following the active involvement of the United States bishops at
the Council in the effort to get action, for example, on religious
liberty, it is good for us to take a little time out now to cool off
and reconsider matters more calmly. Such reconsideration reveals
how inevitable it was that matters so deeply affecting the Church,
and even the secular world, could not be decided too hastily and
without considerable give and take. It is true that the Fathers were
ready to vote on all the matters on which they had completed debate, and on accepting the chapters on the Jews and religious liberty
as a basis for discussion. It is also true that failure to get a chance
to express themselves directly on these questions was frankly disappointing. Particularly disappointing, moreover, was the fact that
time and again, antiquated procedure became the ready instrument
for effectively blocking votes on these matters in commission meetings and in the aula.

Nevertheless, I believe that the delay, in the end, will probably do
a certain amount of good. The Fathers, I think, must accept in their
hearts the truth and the wisdom of Cardinal Bea's pacifying words:
"These matters have not been removed from consideration; they
have only been postponed." Nor were they so naïve as to fail to
sense the serious problems intrinsic to the proposed pronouncements,
problems that transcend the internal concern of the Church herself
and affect world society.

Such considerations did indeed call for a prudent pause which will
provide the needed time to calm ruffled feelings before the next
session of the Council. So, while the delays have been irritating, this
time they were practically unavoidable and even productive of some
benefit. But there will be occasion for fewer such delays, I feel, in
the future.

But we shall fail to see the Council in proper perspective unless we continue to remind ourselves that it is not just another parliament, even though it be composed of human beings with human failings. Here at the Council, the Holy Spirit of God works, in the end, through these very human beings. There is a supernatural quality here which is lacking in merely earthly congresses. This is a key consideration of which, humbly, we must not lose sight!

Chapter 11

Religious Liberty · Revelation Again · The Jews

Once more, summer was the time for reading Council schemas, but this time there was a marked difference. Revised texts suddenly began flowing to us so fast that it was difficult to keep up with the rush of them. The one encouraging and significant aspect was that Pope Paul (the only authority who could have done so) had given the word to Council commissions to quit stalling and get the revised texts to the Fathers without delay.

Our frustration at the end of the second session stemmed from the contrast between the challenge put forth by Pope Paul in his opening address of the second session and the log jams that had developed in several commissions.

Now the Pope seemed to have things in hand again. I was not pessimistic at the end of session two; I was simply disappointed and irritated by all the delay. Nevertheless I was also convinced that we must avoid any strong-arming of the minority, or railroading renewal measures through the Council. Though the majority had the votes to spare, and though at times it took the patience of Job to put up with antiquated Council procedure, nevertheless it was important to give the minority every opportunity afforded by debate and procedure to present their case. Only when patience was finally exhausted, only when the clear will of the Council had become manifest without the shadow of a

doubt, could the supreme authority of the Holy Father gracefully intervene to require action as a last step. Apparently the
time had now arrived for papal authority to require more action
from the commissions which, in turn, would mean more action
on the Council floor.

The third session opened on September 14, 1964, with the usual
solemn ceremony, in a climate of vigilance and determination.
The majority of the Fathers were wary of Council procedure
which they suspected to be at the bottom of the frustrating delays experienced at session two. And there was among them a
determination to get more voting done at the session about to
open.

The Pope's opening address was again awaited with considerable expectation and carefully analyzed on all sides. Many found it
the least impressive of the four opening addresses at the Council
sessions. This estimate may be a carryover of the barrage of criticism directed at Pope Paul after the unimpressive end of session
two. Still, there was unquestionably a marked difference between
Pope Paul's forthright address at the start of session two and the
guarded remarks with which he opened session three. Many
voiced the impression that someone had "gotten to him." I myself
did not feel that way: a leader of so vast an assembly as an Ecumenical Council simply had to be given latitude to work out the
best possible solution to many difficulties. I felt certain of Pope
Paul's liberal and progressive intent, and it did not seem important by what oblique moves he chose to reach his goal. Clearly—
to me at least—the Pope could not tip his hand by explaining his
each and every decision to the press; and yet that is exactly what
many a newshawk expected him to do. Hence, the unfavorable
publicity.

The address was long, and it came to this: The Pope was
clearly opening the way to acceptance of collegiality, but with
much more emphasis than formerly on the theme that papal authority should in no way be compromised. Many were "under-
whelmed" by this insistence. They cited Cardinal Lercaro, who
had already pointed out that there was no trace of any separatist

movement at this Council, such as there had been after the definition of infallibility at Vatican I. Indeed, they said, never before had the papacy had such unswerving loyalty to its primacy and infallibility. Therefore, why all the emphasis and stress by the Pope, which seemed to reflect the interventions of die-hard antagonists of collegiality? I thought the question valid but minor, one which could have been foregone. Pope Paul was clearly on the side of collegiality, so why not give him some elbow-room to marshal his forces?

On the first day of business, there came the announcement of a set of new rules: The four Moderators were going to control Council activity on the floor much more than they had formerly—a move that made for highly stepped-up procedure; a speaker had to have 70 names in order to speak after cloture; even cardinals must hand in summaries of their speeches five days in advance. Each morning meeting was now to run to 12:30 instead of noon, in order to accommodate four extra speakers each day. The speed-up affected even the coffee stand which was now opened at 11:00 A.M. instead of 10:00—an unpopular move to force the Fathers to remain in their seats for the votes which began coming thick and fast.

The Moderators even blew the whistle on each other if they exceeded their ten-minute limit by as much as half a second.

Cardinal Doepfner of Munich seemed to be both the Moderator most often in the chair and the most jealous guardian of the stop-watch. One day he interrupted a fellow-Moderator, Cardinal Lercaro, with the verdict: *"Eminentissime Pater. Tempus tuum exhaustum est!"* Cardinal Doepfner, although not yet fifty years of age, was a formidable looking figure with a jutting jaw, piercing black eyes and blue-black shaven cheeks—beloved by his countrymen who affectionately call him *Unser Julius* (Our Julius). Still one bishop was so awed by his handling of procedure that he said to me: "You know, if I ever got the courage to get up and speak in that Council hall, you can be sure of one thing: it would not be on a day when *Unser Julius* is wielding the gavel!"

After a while, it seemed to me that the business of the Council was moving along perhaps a little too fast. Many a time a speech marked by sparkling originality of thought would provoke counter-thought of equal value; yet, because a speaker had to submit his request five days in advance it was often too late to make any reply or rebuttal. Thus many good ideas were lost and the element of real debate reduced. I mentioned my misgivings to Cardinal Doepfner one night. The Cardinal, however, felt that the material on the Church had been discussed so thoroughly among the Fathers and *periti* that it was unlikely that any major position would go unheard, even under the stepped-up procedures.

The topics scheduled for treatment were announced as coming up in the following order:

Religious Liberty
The Jews
Revelation
Apostolate of the Laity
The Priesthood
Missions
Seminaries
Religious Orders
The Church in the Modern World

On September 23 a number of items or events began popping all at once.

Crammed into about four hours were the following: (1) The Holy Father walking into the aula, bearing the reliquary containing St. Andrew's head, ready to be returned to the Orthodox Metropolitan of Patras, Greece; (2) The taking of six votes on the crucial issue of the Collegiality of Bishops; (3) Opening of the great debate on Religious Freedom with a star-studded cast: Cardinal Ruffini (Italy), Cardinal Cushing (Boston), Cardinal Léger (Montreal), Cardinal Meyer (Chicago), Cardinal Ritter (St. Louis), Cardinal Da Silva (Brazil), and—last but not least—Cardinal Ottaviani (head of the Holy Office).

What a batting order! I tell you nobody—but nobody—left

their seats that day for the two coffee shops. Everyone was wait-
ing, with bated breath (I think that's the term), for Cardinal
Cushing's debut (in Latin!) at the Council and for Cardinal
Ottaviani's rebuttal.

They were not disappointed.

Cardinal Cushing gave a hard-hitting, twelve-minute presentation. (Out of deference to the Cardinal he was not cut off at 10
minutes; it was his maiden speech and, after all, other cardinals
earlier had been permitted a few extra minutes.) He urged that
the Church show herself the champion of religious liberty. His
talk was spiked with English quotations: "Decent respect for the
opinion of mankind" and "Freedom is the highest political end"
(Lord Acton). But it must have irked the Cardinal to be held to a
measly twelve minutes; he usually talks for at least an hour! The
Cardinal's maiden talk made a good impression, and he sat down
with general applause ringing in his ears.

Finally, Cardinal Ottaviani. By this time I had left my regular
place and had wandered down near the cardinals' dugout where I
could see and hear everything to best advantage. I was directly in
front of the observers' stand and thus could get both Ottaviani's
remarks and the observers' reactions. Every observer had his interpreter ready for action as the Cardinal began. Ottaviani
launched into a denunciation of the Decree on Religious Liberty
which could only be described as "the last gasp" of the old thesis-
hypothesis position: namely, the position which holds that we, as
Catholics, merely "tolerate" those in our society who differ with
us, even in good faith, on religious matters, without granting that
they have anything like a "right" to follow their consciences and
live out, in worship and expression, their honest religious convictions in society. The schema under debate was far removed from
Ottaviani's position.

During this exchange, *cappuccinos* went untasted and tired
joints went unlimbered as most of the Fathers kept to their seats
to hear the great debate. It ranks with the most dramatic moments of the Council along with the first-day motion of Cardinal
Liénart to delay voting for commission members and the toe-to-
toe exchange between Cardinals Frings and Ottaviani in 1963.

Strong addresses on behalf of religious freedom were also made by Cardinals Ritter, Meyer, Léger and Da Silva of Brazil.

On the opposing side were Cardinals Ruffini (Italy), Quiroga (Spain), and Bueno (Spain), all speaking for civil restraint on religious activities when necessary, on the plea that a "Catholic" government could not give the same recognition to a false religion that it gives to the true religion.

The position of those who favored religious liberty as set forth in the schema was this: If a man has a "duty" to follow an honest conscience, he also has a "right" to do so; no one may bring force to bear upon him to make him believe, worship or express himself contrary to his honest conscience as long as he does not disturb the common good. Further, the state has no competence to judge which religion is true; hence the state cannot use its power to interfere with religious freedom, although in certain historical circumstances it may have a special relationship with a religion to which the vast majority of its people belong. Religious freedom includes the right to public expression, in a peaceful way, of one's religious views, otherwise religious freedom would mean little or nothing. Finally, the religious freedom vindicated for the individual must also be vindicated for groups, that is, denominations or churches.

Cardinal Ruffini, I think, summed up the position of those who opposed the schema with his intervention on the first day of the debate, in which he stated that the declaration should be entitled "On Religious Tolerance" not "On Religious Liberty." Cardinal Ottaviani later spoke again in similar vein. I heard the latter declare on the floor with the utmost fervor: *"Veritatem religiosam: hanc intelligo. Sed Libertatem religiosam: hanc non intelligo!"* ("Religious *truth*, this I can understand; but religious *liberty*, this I cannot understand at all.") And with this pronouncement there came a great shaking of jowls to emphasize the utmost seriousness of his contention.

At one point seven conservative speakers rose, in succession, to talk on the subject. I noted that not a single speaker from the Curia looked favorably on religious liberty.

As the debate continued, Americans were proud of Father Joseph Buckley, Superior General of the Marist Fathers and Bishop Ernest Primeau of Manchester, New Hampshire, both of whom made really brilliant addresses on behalf of religious freedom.

Bishop Colombo of the Archdiocese of Milan was heard with the utmost attention, for the present Holy Father, as Cardinal Montini, from Milan, had spoken at the first session on the same topic, on December 5, 1962. Now Bishop Colombo, apparently echoing Montini's position, was saying that "unless we pass this schema in principle there can be no dialogue with men of good will."

Bishop Colombo's intervention had a powerful influence in motivating the Fathers in favor of religious liberty. But being so motivated and actually voting yes on the question were two different things. The religious liberty issue was so "hot" at the Council that it was not voted on until the last possible moment in the final session.

September 25 was the last day of debate on Religious Liberty at the third session. Cardinal Suenens, as Moderator, asked for a cloture vote on that day and got it.

On September 23, the Holy Father took steps to return a greatly revered relic, the skull of the Apostle, St. Andrew, to the Orthodox (separated) Metropolitan of Patras in Greece, whence it came originally, as a gesture of good will to the Orientals. Briefly the story is this: On April 21, 1462, the Metropolitan of Patras sent the head of St. Andrew to Rome for protection, for Patras was in military danger. Pope Pius II solemnly received the relic at the Milvian Bridge in Rome (still in existence) and spoke of St. Andrew's head as "coming into exile," giving assurance that the relic would be returned when the time came. The time came on September 23, 1964, some 500 years later! On that evening it was placed aboard a plane and flown, accompanied by an appointed commission, to Patras, thus fulfilling the 500-year promise given by Pope Pius II.

On reflection, an even greater moment of Vatican Council had come on the previous day, September 22, the day on which the bishops voted on Collegiality. The vote was just as historic as the vote on the Infallibility of the Pope, taken on July 18, 1870. There was not the same tension, perhaps. In 1870, 55 bishops were opposed to the definition of Papal Infallibility and they left the Council—all, that is, except Bishop Fitzgerald of Little Rock, Arkansas, who remained and voted *non placet* to the bitter end, with the support of only one other Father. (Later, the "Old Catholics," a separatist group, left the Church over the issue.)

In my view the favorable vote on No. 8 did it. This was the vote that approved "Episcopal consecration, together with the office of sanctifying, also confers the office of *teaching and governing*, which, however, can be exercised only in conjunction with the Head and the members of the College."

All the other premises followed from this one. And once this was passed overwhelmingly (1,917 to 328), there was no doubt in my mind that all the rest of the votes would also, logically, follow suit. And that is the way it actually worked out.

Shortly afterward I wrote home to Baton Rouge:

> The practical consequences of the doctrine can be far-reaching. There are those who feel that a "Senate" of Bishops to act with the Pope and under him, of course, in forming high-level policy in the Church of the future is almost a foregone conclusion.
>
> My own opinion is that such a "Senate" might act as does the board of governors of a university, that is, meet two or three times a year and set very high level policy with the Holy Father presiding. This policy would then be "executed" by the Roman Curia. The feeling is that, at present, the Curia sets too much policy, in addition to executing it. This is unhealthy, like the president of a university following a self-made policy governing the lives of faculty and students. I find it hard to conceive of a full-time "Senate" nor can I see the need for one. It would be like a Bishop camping on a pastor's doorstep for the duration. It just wouldn't work!

At one point during the third session I was given a scare: it was reliably reported that seven subjects, originally slated for debate, would not be discussed at all but merely subjected to a *placet*, *non-placet* vote. The seven subjects thus to be voted on only and not discussed were:

1. The Oriental Churches
2. The Missions
3. The Religious
4. The Diocesan Priests
5. Matrimony
6. Seminaries
7. Catholic Schools

The reason given rumor was that this procedure might speed up the Council so that it could be concluded without a further session.

The adoption of such a procedure would, I felt, be disastrous to the image of the Council and to its influence both inside and outside the Church. I could see no reason why the Council had to actually issue declarations on each and every topic originally announced; but I felt that when the Council *did* issue a document, it should be one of proper importance and dignity. It was my opinion that such pronouncements could not be achieved without full debate, and that it would be better simply to drop any subjects on which there had been no discussion. In addition I saw no reason why, once embarked on the Council undertaking, the work should not be done as perfectly as possible, even if it took five years.

I was grateful, therefore, to learn that the proposal to issue undiscussed statements from the Council had finally been abandoned.

Later, it was decided by the Central Commission that all the Council texts would be discussed and processed in the usual manner, that is: (1) Brief discussion of the text in general and then a vote as to whether it could be accepted as a basis for debate or not; (2) if the vote were *unfavorable*, then the text would go back to a "commission" or to a "mixed commission" for revision in the light of the views expressed and for re-presentation; if the vote were *favorable*, then there would be (3) debate on it, first, in general again, and then chapter by chapter; (4) there would then follow revision according to the tenor of the debate with a view to winning a two-thirds vote for the revised text; (5) then would follow voting, paragraph by paragraph, or section by section of each chapter; and afterward a vote on the entire chapter. Eventually, there would be a vote on the schema as a whole, and finally promulgation by the Pope.

In practice all the steps of this procedure did not take place successively. A step in the procedure was sandwiched in between other business, announcements, and debates on other questions. Whenever a section failed to win approval, it had to go back to the commission for more revision. And then there were times when either the debate or an action by the Central Commission indicated that *new material* had to be added to the schema; new material required further debate. This was a rule which was not generally understood. (This is the very misunderstanding which was at the bottom of the emotional crisis on the fate of the Religious Liberty document at the end of session three.)

Archbishop Hallinan of Atlanta, unfortunately, missed the third session of the Council, laid low by a bout with hepatitis. I did my best to keep him adequately informed by frequent mailings. I was, myself, at low ebb in Rome during this session without his imaginative and vigorous leadership, and I was apprehensive about his health. At length, however, considerable improvement took place and Archbishop Hallinan returned to the Council to take a vigorous role in session four.

On September 30, 1964, the second debate on Revelation began. The earlier, first-session debate had found so large a number of Council Fathers opposed to the schema as presented that Pope John had ordered the text withdrawn and rewritten. The Fathers then had judged that the schema, starting with its very title, had throughout prejudged a question which was under lively study and debate in theological and biblical circles and on which the bishops themselves were sharply divided: the nature of Holy Scripture and Sacred Tradition, and their relationship to each other. A summary of the second debate, giving the positions taken by exponents of the two opposed schools of thought, will serve perhaps to further clarify the issue at stake:

First of all, the commission which had been appointed to revise the schema was itself divided. The revised version, leaving open the disputed question, was supported by seventeen members of the commission whose spokesman was Archbishop Florit of Florence. But there was a minority on the commission, seven members, who insisted on being heard on the Council floor; their spokesman, Bishop Francic of Yugoslavia, was permitted to give a minority report for them.

The minority wanted the Council to take a clear stand, particularly on this question: Are there certain doctrines which can be held by the Church, on ground of tradition alone, even though these doctrines are not based on the Bible?

The majority wanted this question, because it was disputed, left open for further study and discussion.

Some of the speakers who were on the majority side, and the positions they took in their spoken interventions, were as follows:

The late Cardinal Meyer of Chicago made a particularly brilliant address. His main points were: it is not good to speak of Revelation in overly intellectual terms because the Word of God provides us not only with definitions but also with means of making contact with God and reflecting on Him as He presents Himself to us in Revelation. Regarding tradition, two facts are central: first, tradition extends beyond the formal teaching of the Church and embraces the total experience of the People of God in receiving and reacting to God's Revelation; second, this reaction is not always without failings, such as neglect of Scripture, non-liturgical piety, and overly casuistic moralism, since the Church is a pilgrim on earth. The Cardinal suggested that the Bible should serve as a corrective norm according to which tradition can be judged.

In another important intervention Archbishop Shehan of Baltimore called for a clearer statement in the schema of the part played by the human author in the process of Revelation. He also asked for a "more balanced" notion of Revelation, one which would include both experience and interpretation and thus avoid the tendency of current manuals to emphasize only the formal communication of words.

A number of speakers for the majority complained that there

had been too extensive and too exaggerated a preoccupation with the inerrancy of the Bible to the neglect of other more important pastoral and ecumenical considerations. Cardinal Koenig of Vienna, speaking in this same vein, in one of the more interesting addresses of the entire debate, stated that increased scientific knowledge had indeed done much to establish the historic truth of Scripture, especially of the Old Testament, and to dispel many of the nineteenth-century objections against the reliability of Scripture. But, he pointed out, the same scientific affirmations contained in Scripture are simply not true. He then cited a few examples: Mark (2:22) says that Abiathar was the high priest at the time of David; actually it was Abimelech. Matthew (27:6) speaks about the fulfillment of the prophecy of Jeremias; but he really meant the prophecy of Zacharias (11:12). Daniel (1:1) says that Nabuchodonosor laid siege to Jerusalem in the year 607; but the authentic chronology, established by Wisemann, clearly places the siege in the year 610. Then the Cardinal went on to make this point: Lest the authority of Scripture suffer, we must say, sincerely and without fear, that the sacred writer's knowledge of historical matters was limited according to the conditions of his time; nevertheless, God moved him *as such* (with all his human limitations) to write under His inspiration about the things of salvation. The authority of Holy Scripture, he said, is much better defended in this way.

Cardinal Meyer returned to the debate on Revelation, October 5, with more excellent observations: Any word, he said, including the Divine Word, performs three functions: (1) It represents *something*—a fact, object or thought; (2) It reveals the *person speaking:* his intimate feelings, desires, etc.; (3) It addresses *another person* from whom a reaction and a response are expected. Now, if we construct a definition of the Word of God, embracing these three ideas which have always permeated the life of the Church, the definition will have the following effects: (1) It will show that revealed truth in Scripture consists not in separate propositions, but in the central revelation of the heart of God; (2) Inspiration will be seen not negatively simply as "inerrancy," but as positively useful; (3) Inspiration and inerrancy will be more easily reconciled since we will be prepared to show how inspiration can be in harmony with human weakness and limitations, as Cardinal Koenig pointed out.

Cardinal Bea, once head of the Biblicum, the graduate school for Bible study in Rome, stated in his talk that the schema needed some improvement, but that it nevertheless had these basic good qualities: the fundamental doctrines on Revelation and on Scripture and Tradition are well explained in the text; it has a positive tone rather than a condemnatory one—which Pope John had asked for; biblical language is used throughout; and questions still disputed among Catholic scholars are avoided.

It is my impression that there were fewer Fathers who spoke for the majority and that their presentations, however good, were not nearly as impassioned as were those made by speakers for the minority who were greatly disturbed over a supposed dangerous departure from what they considered to be the teachings of Trent. No doubt they had hoped the present Council would condemn any such trend, only to find on the contrary a majority at the Council supporting it. This made the minority desperate, which perhaps accounts for the emotion with which their case was pleaded.

The minority speakers clearly wanted a number of questions closed and settled by the Council once and for all.

Cardinal Ruffini wanted it stated that public Revelation definitely was closed with the death of St. John, and that it does not in any way continue on in the Church's reaction to Revelation or in her life which is the record of tradition. The doctrines of Trent and Vatican I, he said, have been mutilated in the schema. These Councils should be quoted in full. The reference in the present text to "the intimate experience of spiritual things" as an aspect of Revelation cannot be distinguished from "the internal religious sense" which was condemned by Pope Pius X. The Cardinal also wanted it made clear "that God could not inspire error" and that individual scholars must not be permitted to work up their own private notions about the use of literary forms by ancient writers and then apply these notions to Sacred Scripture.

It was in this strain that the speakers for the minority generally spoke. Bishop Carli of Segni, Italy, secretary for the national body of Italian bishops and often their spokesman at the Council, wound up the minority presentation with a vehement speech in which he demanded that the Council should explicitly reject the errors flowing from "form criticism." (Form criticism, in general, is the position that a better knowledge, in our day of advanced science, of the "forms" or linguistic patterns in which ancient authors wrote, provides us with a wider, more accurate and more profound understanding of the meaning of their communication now than formerly. This position applies not only to secular writers but also to the sacred authors as well.) Bishop Carli also wanted the historicity of the Scriptures emphasized, namely, the position that they are reliable historical documents. Finally the Bishop wanted the role of tradition to receive special emphasis in the text lest it seem that Scripture is thought to be the only norm and authority for religion. Tradition embraces more than Scripture and has a fundamental role in the Church. The whole text should be completely revised and a proper balance restored between Scripture and tradition based on the teachings of Trent and Vatican I, which teachings must, in no way, be compromised.

After Bishop Carli had concluded his wrap-up of the minority position, a forceful talk was made by Dom Christopher Butler, O.S.B., the Abbot of Downside in England. The notion of literary types, he said, is clearly as applicable to inspired books as to others. We must never let it appear, for the sake of some supposed polemic advantage, that our biblical scholars are not free —that they must serve the ends of apologetics first and the ends of biblical truth second. In general, let us not be afraid of scholarly and historical truth for fear that our scholars may be lacking in loyalty to the Church and to traditional doctrine. Their aim is to reach the full, objective and real truth of the Gospel tradition; they are both loyal Catholics and scientific scholars whose first presupposition is honesty of investigation. We must risk mistakes, for trial and error will eventually lead to truth. We do not want the childish comfort which comes from averting our gaze from the truth, but rather a truly critical scholarship which will enable us to enter into dialogue with non-Catholic scholars.

On October 29, 1964, the Moderators still had a number of amendments to the text of Revelation which normally would be voted on before a vote was taken on the text itself. However, a ten-day recess, needed to prepare a number of documents for promulgation on November 18, was to begin the next day, and the Moderators, sensing strong sentiment in favor of the schema as it stood, took a chance and asked the Fathers to simply approve the text at once, chapter by chapter. The chance paid off. At no time were there more than 55 votes against the text, while the *placet* vote never dropped below 2,100. At the solemn public congregation at which the constitution on Revelation was promulgated, along with the decree on the Lay Apostolate, the final solemn vote on the revised schema on Revelation was taken with 2,344 Fathers in favor of it and only 6 opposed.

A careful study of the text of the Dogmatic Constitution on Divine Revelation should be undertaken by every Catholic who seeks to keep himself informed on the renewal of religious expression in the Church. Moreover, the constitution contains a wealth of rewarding spiritual ideas and thoughts for the everyday Catholic, regarding the place of the Word of God in the Church and in his personal life. It seems clearly destined to have a vast and lasting influence on the life of the Church and on our individual lives as well.

The principal effects of the constitution, I feel, will be as follows: It will leave a number of important doors open to progress in biblical study since it defines "tradition" in a wide sense and explicitly endorses the study of literary forms in biblical research; it will make defense of biblical truth more consistent by the wider concept of "authorship" which it employs; it explicitly encourages ecumenical cooperation in Bible study; it urges greater use of the Bible in the Sacred Liturgy and in teaching and preaching; it will result in having Scripture play a much greater role in the life of the individual Catholic, who will henceforth become far more familiar with Holy Writ.

The document on Divine Revelation was well worth fighting for!

Although Religious Liberty and the Jews were both held over for final voting and proclamation in the fourth session, I think it is better to conclude treatment of them here for the sake of continuous rather than disjointed comment.

The text on Religious Liberty had very rough sailing in the third session. Unquestionably the most emotional moment of the Council came on what has been described by some authors as "Black Thursday," November 19, 1964. This was the day when a great majority of the Fathers entered the aula for 9 A.M. Mass fully and confidently expecting that a vote to accept the two documents would be taken and would pass overwhelmingly. Originally these two had comprised Chapters four and five of the Decree on Ecumenism, but had become separated from Chapters 1–3 and from each other. (Chapters 1–3 had been processed through the Council and were being readied for promulgation at the end of the third session.) Upon their separation from Ecumenism, Religious Liberty and the Jews had been sent back to commissions for reworking. At length, the revised texts were ready, after much unexplained delay. Now the Fathers thought that progression toward final discussion and voting would take place, setting the stage for passage and proclamation.

But a determined body of some 200 Fathers who bitterly opposed the Religious Liberty schema (indeed, any statement at all on religious liberty) signed a petition to the Presidency of the Council, urging that, under the rules, so much new matter had been added to the text that it was virtually a new document and therefore should be re-debated as such. Cardinal Tisserant announced, supposedly in the name of the Presidency, that this petition had been considered and granted. This announcement stunned the friends of the schema. Caught now by surprise, at 11 A.M. on Thursday, with only one other working day remaining in session three, the proponents hastily drafted a petition to the Pope to reverse the decision of the Presidency as announced by Cardinal Tisserant. Although this counter-petition carried, by report, more than 1,000 names, the Pope apparently felt that he could not graciously accede to it. However, he did guarantee that Religious Liberty would be placed first on the agenda at session four.

I was not present at the Council on that celebrated Thursday. I had returned to Louisiana for the funeral of Archbishop Rummel of New Orleans on November 9 and had not found it convenient to return for the last few days of the third session. Newspaper accounts and verbal reports later from friends who were present testified that the climate that day at the Council was most explosive. Still, on thinking it over, I found it difficult to understand what the furore was all about. I wrote out my thoughts on the matter in an article which was published in *America*, the issue of February 27, 1965, the gist of which was as follows:

First, I do not see how it matters very much whether a vote on religious freedom be taken at the third or at the fourth session of the Council. Granted, there is some danger that the force of the statement may be weakened and watered down during the delay; but in my view, this danger is remote. It is balanced by the fact that the temper of the Council is clearly to demand a full and uncompromising statement on this question of religious freedom. This temper will not be dulled, I feel, by any delay—of one session, of one year.

Next, from afar, I can even see the benefits accruing from delay.

There is the benefit of avoiding any accusation that the decree was rushed or "railroaded" through the Council, without providing sufficient time for all the Fathers to study and argue against it. After all, there were many amendments proposed and a certain amount of new matter included in the revised text. By waiting until the fourth session, all accusations of undue haste could be avoided and the image of the decree emerge untarnished. So, frankly, I feel that the Pope did the friends of religious freedom a favor by going along with the postponement.

There is also the benefit of avoiding the possible criticism that the decree on religious freedom was brought to a vote in the closing hours of session three just because the Fathers were tired and anxious to wind things up and get home.

Again—but this is pure conjecture—it would seem plausible that consideration had to be given to those Fathers who were terrified that the decree on religious liberty would upset the whole way of life they had always known—the life under concordats that guaranteed priestly salaries, religious instruction, a free Catholic press and so on. After all, some of them had known the rigors of other systems. We had heard the earnest pleas of these men on the floor of the aula, during the debate on religious freedom, and one had to take account of their apprehensions.

What it came to, perhaps, is this: The friends of religious freedom actually had carried the day in all quarters that really counted. They had achieved a statement on it; they had managed to have the statement say exactly what they wanted it to say; and they had had it speak in exactly the language they had hoped for. There was some difference of opinion about details, on the theoretical level, among the friends of religious freedom; but they were in general agreement, otherwise, on the text as it stood.

But it would not do to have the friends of religious freedom carry the day, only to leave behind fears and bitterness in the hearts of those who had opposed the decree and lost. Moreover, on a subject capable of arousing such powerful emotions, the healing qualities of time must not be underestimated. In such straits, every month counts.

The issue of Religious Liberty was, true to promise, put first on the agenda at session four, debated once more, bringing out the same old arguments, pro and con, which was pretty dull business. Still, a certain amount of drama was still in store for us.

There were 55 speakers on the subject during the five days—22 "con" and 33 "pro." All were deadly serious, impassioned pleaders; still they kept repeating themselves until everyone was more than ready to entertain a vote to invoke cloture and end the speaking.

As the United States speakers rose, one after another, a bishop beside me observed: "The voices are the voices of United States bishops; but the thoughts are the thoughts of John Courtney Murray!" Indeed, the declaration itself sounded strikingly like J.C.M.

As the likelihood of cloture drew near, the opponents of the

declaration dug in for a couple of last-ditch, hand-to-hand de-
fenses.

First, they sprayed the Council Fathers with the rumor that the
declaration had no place in the Council at all—that it was not a
theological statement. They pointed out that even its proponents
admitted that all the declaration wanted to say was that the State
had no competence in judging the value of various religions.
This, they contended, was a purely civil consideration, making of
the declaration a mere American political document aimed at
easing pressures from a pluralistic community back home, no
matter the cost to Catholics in other countries.

Leaders among the United States bishops, at this point, played
it cool. They made no concerted effort to induce cloture lest
such an effort give substance to the above charge. Next, the
opposition hit upon what seemed like a good idea: Let us have no
voting on the declaration until after the Holy Father's return
from his visit to the United Nations on October 5. After all, a
vote would only display to the world the sadly divided state of
the Council Fathers on this issue and disclose to the nations a
brutta figura of the Church which could only be embarrassing to
the Pope as he stepped up to the podium to speak at the United
Nations.

The newspapers said that at a meeting of the Council Presidency, Moderators and Coordinating Commission held jointly on
Monday evening, September 20, a decision was reached to allow
the debate on Religious Liberty to continue and to further post-
pone cloture and a vote.

Then, lo and behold, out of the clear, blue sky on Tuesday
morning, shortly after the Council Mass had concluded, Archbishop Felici, the Secretary General, mounted his pulpit to ask
for the Fathers' attention. He wanted to know how many Fathers
wished to close the debate on Religious Liberty. Those who
favored cloture could indicate their wish by standing. The entire
aula seemed to rise as one—at first sight. On second sight, one
could spot a surprising number of the Fathers sitting on their
hands. Still, the vote to close debate was overwhelming.

Here, at last, was a breakthrough. But the sitting Fathers had to be taken into account. What was desired was not only a favorable vote on Religious Liberty but a landslide, if possible; and many a sitting Father was favorable to the document but had misgivings about the appearance of indifferentism it seemed to project. These Fathers had to be assured in some way that the declaration did no violence to the concept of "the one, true Church."

When Archbishop Felici went to his pulpit the second time, you could literally hear a pin drop in the vast reaches of St. Peter's.

Then he began to read a "proposition" on which the Moderators wished the Fathers to express themselves *placet* or *non placet*.

Does the twice-amended text of the declaration on Religious Liberty (which you have before you) seem to be acceptable to the Fathers as the basis for a definitive declaration on Religious Liberty, as long as this declaration is ultimately refined so as to reflect clearly the Catholic doctrine that there is only one, true Church; and as long as it also clearly reflects the changes in the text which have been proposed by the Fathers and approved, according to the rules of regular Council procedure?

The above is not an exact translation. It is a paraphrase of technical, conciliar language which, I think, helps to clarify the exact meaning of the proposition. (The proposition used the Latin phrases *"ulterius perficiendae juxta doctrinam catholicam de vera religione"* and *"ad normam ordinis Concilii."*)

These two phrases were interesting: what one might call two jokers in the deck which had the effect of cancelling each other out. The first gave assurance that the rights of the "one, true faith" would not be infringed; the second gave assurance that the document would remain substantially unchanged in meaning and favorable to religious freedom. This was calculated to satisfy everybody except the real die-hard members of the opposition.

And so the historic vote was taken—a clear victory for Religious Liberty: 2,222 Fathers voting; 1,997 in favor; 224 opposed; and one vote spoiled.

What did this mean? It meant that the document was now "in

possession," namely, that it could no longer be *debated* or essentially *changed*. Moreover, it also meant that the document was in the possession of the Secretariat for Christian Unity, its proper Commission of the Council, and would no longer be sent officially for reworking to mixed commissions. The Secretariat would, of course, ask theological advice, privately, as the document took final shape. But substantial change in the text was now precluded.

One hundred four Fathers had asked to speak on Religious Liberty (that is the actual count) and there were "x" number of written interventions besides—perhaps 300. It was no easy task for commission members to comb that many expressions and refine them into a single acceptable text.

We went to the press conference sponsored by the United States bishops that afternoon, ordinarily held at the USO on the Via della Conciliazione; but on September 20, 1965, the crowd was so big that a larger auditorium had to be commandeered around the corner.

There were our American experts on the stage ready to face the press: Father Shea (Theology); Father Connell, C.Ss.R. (Theology); Father Trisco (History); Father Maley (Scripture); Father Hurley (NCWC); Father McCool (Scripture); and the star of today's performance, the man so often spoken of as the architect of the declaration on Religious Liberty, Father John Courtney Murray, Professor of Theology at Woodstock College, Maryland. Father Crowley of *Our Sunday Visitor* acted as chairman.

Ben Bolt of the AP, Doty of the *New York Times*, Shenker of *Time*, Sullivan of *Newsweek*, Wallace of the *Baltimore Sun* and all the other newshawks and newshens were there, despite all the talent, as well as Tracy of *America* magazine.

Despite an expectant air, the press conference was not up to par, I felt. The panel was superb, but the reporters hesitated to ask the one question that was on everyone's mind: Did the morning's vote come about because of direct Papal intervention? At last, at long last, the question was asked, and the answer was this: "If you think that there was direct Papal intervention you may very well be right. One thing is certain: The Holy Father went over the declaration, liked it and publicly declared, as Cardinal Shehan quoted him in the aula, that not only Catholics but all mankind was looking forward to a Council statement on Religious Liberty."

Some final observations and we are through with Religious Liberty:

1. The adoption of the text does not end theological debate on the subject, although it will have the effect of limiting it within a new context.

2. There is a reservation contained in the text that is causing many Fathers a lot of misgiving. The reservation is that "in certain historical circumstances" a State may have a special relationship with a Church to which the vast majority of its people belong (e.g., Eire, Sweden, Italy, Spain, many Moslem countries), as long as there is no coercion and full religious liberty for minority churches.

3. The question of taxing the entire nation and giving material support to only one Church is also a matter of concern.

4. Some (e.g., Cardinal Browne of Ireland and the Curia) continued to talk of the "Catholic State" in the language of Pius XII's "*Ci Riesche*"; but this is now a vanishing concept which will hardly be revived again.

5. Cardinal Urbani, Pope John's successor as Patriarch of Venice, surprisingly to many, made one of the most enlightened interventions on the floor on the development of theology on Religious Liberty. He said: "The documents written by Popes of the past, from Gregory XVI to John XXIII, show unquestionably how the doctrine of religious freedom and of church-state relations has been *progressively enriched;* and the teaching on religious freedom which we are now discussing is a part of that progress."

The Declaration on Religious Liberty was promulgated on December 8, 1965.

It is very difficult to put into proper focus the Decree on the Relationship of the Church to Non-Christian Religions and especially the Jews, for a number of false starts were made which received world-wide attention and even stirred up pressure from a number of powerful quarters. The false starts were these:

1. Only the Jews were considered at first; later it became evident that other non-Christian religions also had to be treated: the Hindus, the Buddhists and the Mohammedans.

2. Treatment of the Jews was, at first, part of the Decree on Ecumenism; later it was admitted that it had no place there and should be set forth in a separate declaration.

3. The contents of the original text became known and were debated by national and political groups even before they became known or were debated by the Council Fathers themselves. Later the Council debate was removed from this atmosphere and the text was discussed on its merits.

4. The document was charged, from the beginning, by persons in powerful positions as having political overtones, namely, as favoring the State of Israel in its disputes with the Arab nations. Eventually the Council stood its ground, that the statement was purely religious in the best sense; but at first there was some yielding to political pressure in making certain changes in the original text which unfortunately helped to substantiate the charge.

5. At first, the Jews were absolved from the charge of "deicide" in the text; later this passage was removed.

6. At one time there was a movement to include in the document a request for forgiveness for any harm to non-Christians that may have resulted from the attitudes of certain Catholics in the past; later, it was decided to be more positive, to look to the future with a declaration of the brotherhood of all men.

7. In the beginning crimes against the Jews were "condemned"; later, they were only "deplored."

These false starts hampered the statement and still do. Those who favor the original positions are still distressed that these were not retained. Nevertheless, to understand the decree, as it stands today, it is necessary to take a number of things into consideration:

1. The original positions taken were not taken by the Fathers as a whole. These were only suggestions made by the Secretariat which prepared the schema and supported by certain Fathers in their interventions.

2. The changes introduced were made for the very good reasons cited by Cardinal Bea in making his *"relatio"* or introduction of the revised text and were eventually approved overwhelmingly by the

Fathers as a whole. As such, these changes represent the fruit of the mature thinking of the Council. Moreover, the changes were made for purely religious reasons or the reasons of consistency and cannot be judged properly in the light of political or national considerations.

3. It must be taken into account that the passionate feelings on both sides engendered by the original text have served to greatly obscure the true nature of the statement; namely, the fact that it does present *an historic achievement*—the first such clear declaration on the part of the Catholic Church of its true relationship to the people of the Old Testament, excluding all discrimination; and the first statement, world-wide in scope, of an open and loving approach to men of other great faiths of the world.

It must be admitted that it would be difficult to find anyone who, even today, pretends that the statement is perfect in every respect. Indeed, the same could be said of any of the Council documents, since nearly every document had some votes cast against it even at the time of its final passage. But the perspective indicated above and the historic character of the document will, in time, undoubtedly cause it to be seen in a more favorable light by many persons.

The final declaration was approved in October 1965 by the following vote: Yes—2,064; No—58; Null—6.

The reasons for some of the changes were as follows and they make a great deal of sense: (1) Ecumenism, strictly speaking, is primarily a matter of relationship between Christians; only in the very broadest sense is it applied to relations with those outside the Church. (2) It was only logical and *à propos* to extend to other non-Christian bodies the same hand of brotherhood that was being extended to the Jews. (3) It was not necessary to make reference to the awkward and negative matter of absolving anyone from the charge of "deicide"; the positive statement of the true relationship between the Church and the Jewish people is fully sufficient to cover the matter. (4) Some advanced the idea that, if another Hitler came along, the Church had better be prepared to do more than simply wring her hands and "deplore" crimes against the Jews and against humanity; but it was rightly held that the word "condemns" in a Council document should only be used in connection with false doctrinal positions and that it should not be used with reference to either persons or personal actions. Besides, the Council, following Pope John's pleas, had refrained from condemnations generally, in spite of the world-wide effort for example, to have a strong condemnation of Communism.

Highlights of the Declaration on the Relationship of the Church to Non-Christian Religions

Men in our times are being drawn closer together, and the Church is studying her relationship with men of non-Christian religions.

God's Providence extends to all men; and men expect the answer to life's riddles from religion. Hence a profound sense of religion, bound up with advanced cultures, is to be found among men of the great non-Christian faiths which propose rules of life and sacred rites: the Hindus, the Buddhists and the Moslems.

A spiritual bond ties the people of the New Testament in a special way to the stock of Abraham, the Jews, who cannot be blamed— either those living at the time, or today—for the death of Christ. Nor should they be presented as rejected or accursed by God as if such views followed from the Sacred Scriptures.

The Church opposes any discrimination or harassment of men because of race, color, condition of life or religion and urges all to live in peace and brotherhood.

Chapter 12

Interlude at Session Three ·
Laity · Orientals · Missions ·
The End of the Third Session

I found life at the third session different from the two earlier gatherings, partly due to the absence of Archbishop Hallinan, who somehow always happened to be where the action was; and I had usually been there, too, either at his elbow or assisting him behind the scenes. But the advanced pace of action at the Council also had much to do with the change. This called for more reading, and one's interest was so broadened by the variety of topics up for consideration that more press conferences and lectures had to be attended. The pace of business in the aula affected the pace of life all along the line.

The Moderators kept an iron hand on procedure at the third session and time after time cracked down on repetition and overtime remarks. Even Cardinal Bea one day had to beg for "just one more minute in which to make my conclusion." And, it was amusing also to hear some of the Council Fathers (who rose to speak, with axes all sharpened ready to attack a given schema) quietly begin with the disarming words: "*Hoc schema mihi valde placet; sed. . . .*" ("This schema pleases very, very much; however. . . ."). Then there would follow a succession of mighty swings of the axe calculated to send the poor schema either to the hospital or the morgue.

The tempo of accomplishments in the aula might now be termed "impressive." In the first thirteen working days at the third session, the Council completed debate on three chapters on the Church; on one decree (on Bishops); on two statements (on Religious Liberty and the Jews and Other Non-Christian Religions); and on about half the schema on Revelation. During the various debates on those thirteen days, the Council also recorded fifty votes on various subjects.

The debates on a number of topics brought forth a few striking observations: Cardinal Suenens drew first blood by calling the present procedure of the canonization of saints "too slow," "too expensive" and "too centralized." The debate on the place of the Blessed Virgin Mary in the documents of the Council provoked many sharp exchanges. The issue became "minimalism" (giving Mary honor but carefully approving each honorary title largely for reasons of ecumenism and of restraining superstition), versus "maximalism" (the tendency to give Mary extreme titles such as "mediatrix of all Graces" which have a correct meaning, if understood properly, but which are open to easy misunderstanding. Cardinal Suenens scored again by observing that Mary's maternity must be linked with the apostolate; authentic devotion to Mary requires collaboration with others in a dynamic program of action. Marian piety, therefore, cannot be isolated from life so that Mary simply becomes an example to be admired.

Another highlight was the day when Archbishop Parente, Assessor of the Holy Office, said that he was speaking merely as the "lowly titular bishop of Thebes" (that is, *not* as a Vatican official!). He felt it necessary to make this clear since, unlike most of his associates in the Holy Office and, indeed, in the Curia as a whole, he was prepared to support the collegiality of the bishops with the Pope in the government of the Church. This must have required a certain amount of courage and independence of thought on the part of "the lowly bishop of Thebes."

Midway in the third session, with Council business moving ahead rapidly, many of the Fathers began to suspect that the Moderators were actually driving for a finish at the end of session three. I felt that this might be true, but I also felt that such a goal would be unfortunate, involving a risk of half-baked material, un-subjected to proper debate and deliberation, issued in the name of an Ecumenical Council. Then, suddenly, there came an unexpected reversal which I reported as follows in my Rome Letter dated October 9, 1964:

> The question today is: do we finish up our work at this session or is there to be another? As soon as I saw the schemas that were mailed to us last summer, I was convinced that we could never complete so much matter in one last session. Nevertheless, once we arrived here and the Moderators and Coordinating Commission organized their now famous flying wedge drive down the field, ripping off fifty votes in the first thirteen days, many began to say: Surely they are pressing for a close of the Council at this session!
>
> Today, that feeling has been completely dissipated. The newspapers report that frantic meetings are being held at the highest levels among Council leaders almost every day, about the Council time-table. Commissions are screaming that they are simply swamped. It has been said that there were as many as 750 "modi" on a certain single vote and that more than 5,000 "modi" have been entered to date on various votes. By this time, I feel that most of you will remember that an affirmative vote "juxta modum" is a "yea" vote with a reservation. The qualification is then handed in, with the vote, *in writing*. When the secretary in your aisle comes to pick up your IBM card on which your vote is recorded by electronic pencil, if you have voted "juxta modum" and entered a reservation, then you also give the secretary a paper with your qualification spelled out—for example: "I vote *placet* (yea), but *juxta modum;* and the 'modus' is this: On page 15, paragraph 8, line 35, I sure wish you would insert the words, 'namely, that of the National Conference of Bishops, not just the local Bishop!'" Now just imagine getting 750 "*modi*" like that on one, single vote, and 5,000 on all votes taken to date!
>
> But, that is not all—many a Council Father, like me, often feels that it is not necessary to rise in the aula and consume time on certain questions, but also feels that the commission studying the question should be made aware of his thinking. Thus thousands of written interventions or undelivered speeches are sent to the secretaries of the Council for transmission to the appropriate commis-

sion. And the commissions do study, very carefully, each and every written intervention.

One day during the meeting I left my place and took a stretch down in the right transept of St. Peter's. It was here that Vatican Council I convened on December 8, 1869, with great pomp and splendor, and worked for 11 months until adjourned *sine die* when Rome was occupied by the troops of Victor Emmanuel II.

I could not but be drawn back to that first meeting held here almost 100 years ago. Then, there were only 700 Fathers voting compared to the 2,600 at this session. In 1869 there were only 4.5 million Catholics in the U.S.A., compared to 43 million in 1962. Then, there were only 60 U.S. bishops; now there are 240.

And the whole outlook then was different: The U.S. bishops were mainly concerned with problems of Reconstruction after the Civil War in the South, and with immigration and the memory of nativism in the North. They were far removed from the Ultramontane quarrels which were the background for Vatican Council I. Union of Church and State, which was taken for granted in Europe, was inconceivable in the U.S.A., and the American system was regarded with suspicion by European prelates.

Today, all that has been vastly changed. Modern communications have brought the world—and the bishops—much closer together!

According to my notes, it was on Wednesday, October 7, 1964, that the interesting debate on the Apostolate of the Laity began in the Council. After five full days of debate, cloture was voted on Monday, October 12. These were five days of speeches filled with erudition, brilliance, originality, humor and deep spiritual insights. Behind the sparkling addresses of the Council Fathers there was the vast talent of that great army of *periti* who made so valuable a contribution, all along the line, to the work of the Council.

Let me here pay tribute to these experts who, on the whole, seemed to have what Franklin Roosevelt once called "a passion for anonymity." These experts exhibited no trace of "triumphalism" as far as I observe, although positions which they had been advocating, at considerable risk, for many years were not being given honorable acceptance and endorsement at the Council. It irritated me a good deal that pioneers in many a matter before the Council such as Father Godfrey Diekmann (Liturgy), Father John Courtney Murray (Religious Liberty) and Monsignor John Tracy Ellis (general *aggiornamento*) were not even present at the first session. Father Diekmann and Father Murray were present at the second session and at times thereafter. I myself finally succeeded in having the distinguished historian of the Church in the U.S.A., the biographer of Cardinal Gibbons and fighter for higher educational standards, Monsignor Ellis, honor me by attending the Council as my personal *peritus* at session four.

Now a most forthright and vigorous assertion of the dynamic role of the laity in the Church of our times began. Poor Cardinal Cento, who had presided over the composition of a lifeless, traditionally-worded and traditionally-conceived schema, and who certainly expected routine endorsement of it, was shocked to find his schema running for its life with the whole pack in full cry behind it.

My recollection is that there was little repetition and few boring addresses during the debate on the laity at session three. My notes say that interest was high among the Fathers throughout the five days of discussion. And when one recalls the vigor and originality of the presentations and the tang of the sharp exchanges on the floor, it is easy to see why the debate on the laity was one of the best of the Council. Let us get on at once to what the Fathers had to say:

To start with, it was quickly pointed out that this was the first time, in all the history of the Church, that a Council was disposed to treat, theologically or in any other way, the divine mission of the unordained, unvowed layman. Fathers were not lacking to report this previous negative treatment of the laity in uninhibited gleeful remarks as follows: Canon Law had (rather stupidly) talked of the layman as "someone who was not a cleric!" Then there was the celebrated remark that, up to now, the function of the layman was restricted to the role of "pray, pay and obey". (Only it comes out much better in Italian *"Prega, paga e zita!"*— "Pray, pay and shut up!"). Finally, one of the Fathers dryly reminded the Council that 99 per cent of the members of the Church were laymen!

These samples serve to describe the climate in which the debate on the laity was initiated. But the subject of "Catholic Action" soon became a central issue. Did the laity have a "mission" which came, independently of the hierarchy, directly from God, by virtue of their baptism and confirmation? The exercise of this mission to project the presence of Christ into their life-situations would, of course, be subject to regulation by the hierarchy. But this was not what the question was getting at. The issue was this: Did the mission of the layman have its origin in a call or mandate or what-have-you from the hierarchy; or did it have its origin, purely and simply, in the very reception of these sacraments?

The schema upheld the hierarchical view. The speakers at the Council supported the sacramental approach.

The Fathers who distinguished themselves in the course of the debate were mainly the following: Cardinals Ritter, Suenens, Liénart and Heenan; and Archbishops and Bishops De Roo, Leven, Carter, D'Souza, Hengsbach and Soghby. However, there were many other distinguished speakers who put forward important ideas.

To get the debate in focus, it is necessary to recall that the schema was, at first, a very long and detailed document which carefully treated every phase of the apostolate of the laity. It did this, of course, in the old manner: that is, as something initiated, permitted and controlled completely, in all its aspects, by the hierarchy. However, it was soon recognized that too general a treatment would trespass on the preserves of other Council documents: the theology of the layman belonged properly in the Constitution on the Church; his interest and action in spreading the faith belonged in the document on the Missions, and so on. Fortunately, such considerations were removed from the schema on the laity and distributed elsewhere. Ultimately, the laity schema concentrated only on the practical question of the *aposto-*

late of the laity, presuming the doctrinal foundations laid in other documents.

Still, there remained the problem of a wrong approach to the laity and the thorny claims of "Catholic Action" to be dealt with. And it was around these issues that the debate soon centered.

Cardinal Ritter, first to speak, gave one of those *"schema mihi placet, sed . . ."* talks. He wanted the schema accepted as a basis for further discussion, but he wanted it completely rewritten! The Cardinal swung a mighty axe: The schema had a patronizing, clerical tone in which the highest form of the lay apostolate was said to be the aid the layman gives his priest. And, incidentally, what was all the juridical material (for example, the articles about the revision of the Code of Canon Law) doing in a *pastoral* decree? Again, the various forms of the lay apostolate should be distinguished from each other by their different ends, or different means to the same end, not by their relationship to the hierarchy. Finally, lay holiness should be set forth according to the principles already laid down in *De Ecclesia.*

Cardinal Browne took just the opposite view: the schema excessively generalized the lay apostolate, making even all charitable works apostolic. *"Numquid omnes apostoli?"* ("Is everyone to be an apostle?") he asked, quoting St. Paul (I Cor. 12:29). Browne wanted the schema to stress obedience of the layman not only to bishops but also to pastors.

As the debate continued, a number of central thoughts were evident in the speeches:

1. The shortage of priests and the needs of the Church are not the basic reason why the laity are to undertake an apostolate. The main reason is that they have been given a distinct place in the People of God and a special mission by God through their baptism.

2. The lay apostolate does not merely consist in having the laity live deep spiritual lives; rather their apostolate consists in effecting the incarnation of the Church in the structures of the world. The salvation of the world can be brought about only through the laity.

3. The words of St. Ignatius of Antioch *"nihil sine episcopo"*

("nothing without the Bishop") have been abused to mean that apostolic action must always derive from the initiative, ideas and commands of the bishop alone. The bishop's authority is necessary to keep order, but there is such a thing, too, as "the freedom of the sons of God." If given this freedom, the laity will commit many errors and there will be confusion, but there is no growth without crisis.

4. Two-thirds of the human race, including tomorrow's leaders, are younger than any bishop present here at the Council. Therefore the apostolate of the laity must emphasize the role of youth.

5. Dialogue with non-Catholics and non-Christians is an important part of the lay apostolate; and our laity not only give but also receive in the exchange.

6. The basis for the lay apostolate should be made clear: namely, lay participation in the priesthood of Christ which is evident in the fact that the laity are extraordinary ministers of baptism and even ordinary ministers of matrimony.

7. The principle of subsidiarity as cited in *"Pacem in Terris"* must govern the work of the apostolate of the laity: that is, higher authority should intervene only in time of crisis, when the good of society requires it. Thus each person would be asked to assume his own responsibilities and nothing would be done on a higher level of authority that could just as effectively be accomplished on a lower level.

8. The name "Catholic Action" should not be used to mean "the lay apostolate," since it is only one aspect of it and, even then, it is defined as participation of the laity in a mission which is not their own, namely, the mission of the hierarchy. It does not, therefore, emphasize the fact that the laity do have their own proper mission, which of course is the lay apostolate. The people of God is not a totalitarian state; but (Catholic Action) is totalitarian in concept, utterly neglecting the initiative, the freedom, and the priesthood of the laity.

9. Clericalism is the number-one evil in the Church; and this schema was conceived in the sin of clericalism! It is clearly the clergy talking to the clergy, and no layman would ever be in-

spired by reading it. As a matter of fact, the laity were brought in to give advice about it only when it was too late, in the spring of 1963. What results from a schema like this is simply the perpetuation of a clericalist civilization.

The schema and its approach were not, however, without their staunch and vocal defenders. These urged that Pope Paul himself had highly praised the concept and the work of Catholic Action, and they regretted that the schema had not quoted Pius XI and Pius XII. Pope Paul had called Catholic Action "the royal road" for the laity, and actually the laity ought to be given a mandate in conscience to serve in it. Far from being too restrictive, the schema is too loose in giving excessive latitude to local bishops to call all kinds of organizations "Catholic Action." Actually, the schema gravely wounds Catholic Action, which has been our great defense against the inroads of secularism and anti-clericalism.

The opponents of the schema, because of its emphasis on Catholic Action and its neglect of the free mission of the laity, came roaring back to attack it once more in a series of speeches highly critical of the schema as it stood. Here are summaries of two humdingers by Archbishop Heenan of England and by Archbishop Zoghby of Egypt.

Heenan: The place of laymen in the Church was completely changed. No longer are the laity unlearned. At one time "cleric" or "clerk" (Italian: *"chierico"*)—that is, one who was educated —was the word for a clergyman; while the word *"idiota"* was used to describe either a fool or a member of the laity. Today the laity have great learning in many fields; however, they still need training in the religious field from priests. With regard to Catholic Action, the term has taken on political overtones since Catholic Action groups in certain countries have at times been used for political action. It would be better to use the term "Catholic Action" only in certain countries and not universally. "Lay Apostolate" is preferable. Finally, with regard to the establishment of a world-wide Secretariat for the Lay Apostolate, let us be sure to consult the laity in setting it up! It will be an opportunity of showing our devoted laity that they enjoy our full confidence.

Zoghby: The experience of the Greek Melchite Church in

Egypt, in working with the laity, shows what can be profitably done. In every town where there is a parish, there is a "commission" of laity governed at the parish level by the pastor, at the diocesan level by the patriarch. The larger commissions are made up of 24 members: two-thirds elected by the people and one-third appointed by the patriarch. The commissions help:

1. In teaching: working with priests in all that pertains to schools.

2. Through a legal committee: which acts as a court and which also directs the Church in matters respecting the civil law.

3. Disposing of the material goods of the Church: The commission does the work but nothing is done without the consent of the ordinary, the patriarch.

4. Maintaining buildings and organizing parish feasts.

5. Carrying out the works of charity.

Experience with these lay commissions shows that the laity never try to impose their own will, but do contribute expert help and advice. Those in authority who reject this kind of lay collaboration stand to lose their authority and influence over the faithful altogether.

In the light of the debate, the document on the laity was eventually rewritten and given overwhelming approval on November 10, 1965, at the fourth session, by a vote of 2,201 to 2, with 5 ballots null. It was then promulgated by the Pope at the solemn congregation held on November 18, 1965.

What did it finally say? The statement, as might be expected, reflects the fine thoughts and sentiments expressed during the debate. It deserves careful study. My suggestion is that it be studied in translation by groups. Father Walter M. Abbott, S.J., has done all of us a favor by bringing out, as general editor, the volume entitled *The Documents of Vatican II* which places each Council text in perspective by means of an introduction by a Catholic expert followed by an appraisal by a non-Catholic authority in the field. The texts are also offered in a new and very readable translation edited by Monsignor Joseph Gallagher.

As to the impact which the decree on the laity will probably have on the Catholic world, as well as the world outside the Church, a number of points could be made.

First of all, the decree contains the potential to bring about a remarkable and profound change in the role played by the laity in the Church, in our own times as well as in the future. I may even go so far as to say that the document constitutes a "Magna Carta" of the laity and of its part in the mission of Christ. For the first time in the history of the Church, there has been drawn up a constructively fashioned statement, clearly setting forth and insisting upon the fact that the layman has a mission of his own directly from Christ, deriving from his baptism and confirmation. Further, that this mission consists in his projecting the presence of Christ into his surroundings, both in private and in public.

Again, it is a fundamentally new approach to emphasize that, by virtue of this mission (which is priestly, prophetic and kingly, even as the mission of Jesus was), the layman needs, strictly speaking, no mandate from his bishop or his pastor. The document makes it clear, of course, that the hierarchy possesses ultimate responsibility and therefore authority as far as the Christian community is concerned. However, in the past, this had come to mean that all initiative and all inspiration and indeed even the minutiae of technique had to come from higher authority. So the decrees on the laity contains the potential to "evoke" or "bring about" more creative and dynamic lay action in the Church. In this field personal responsibility and freedom are vital, for, as Leo XIII once said: "Initiative is often crushed by the rough grasp from a hand without."

Will the decree actually be implemented? This is a question which no one can answer with certainty. We know of course that many an inspired program, set forth beautifully on paper, has simply failed to materialize. Canon 711, number 2 of the present Code of Canon Law, requires that two confraternities be established in every parish in the world: The Confraternity of Christian Doctrine and the Confraternity of the Blessed Sacrament. There has been considerable effort, marked by notable success, to establish and promote the CCD in America; but who has ever seen a Confraternity of the Blessed Sacrament in action anywhere? After four hundred years, not all of the reforms of the Council of Trent have yet been put into effect!

The renewal envisioned in the Decree on the Laity of Vatican Council II may therefore also remain embalmed in a beautiful text. But in view of the interest and the great practical need for action at the level of the laity in the Church today, this does not seem likely.

Instead, this is what I think will happen: It will take time to rid ourselves of the old notion that initiative comes exclusively from the hierarchy. It will also take time, on the layman's part, to understand the new freedom. Some laymen have jumped to the unwarranted conclusion that the Decree on the Laity is the signal to scuttle altogether regulation by higher authority. Their view of obedience is that there should be no commands at all, only an open dialogue between superior and subject. Hence, a great deal of new understanding must be arrived at which will provide on the one hand room for more originality of thought and freedom of action for the subject, and, on the other hand, a clear and respectful recognition of the ultimate responsibility and the necessary function of authority in the Church.

To persuade the older generation to abandon the habits of a lifetime is, finally, going to be a difficult task. There will, of course, be open and perceptive minds and apostolic spirits who, regardless of age, will welcome the new concept of the apostolate of the laity. But to bring about any profound change, generally, among most of those who belong to the older generation is something else. The younger generation, on the other hand, are already living in a world permeated by a spirit of openness, candor and freedom. They are not at all chained to the unworkable approaches and methods of the past. If they can be properly instructed in the religious spirit of the Church of our day, as set forth in the Council documents; if their energy and idealism can be directed into the channels indicated by the decrees on the laity, there is good reason to expect that a new generation of Christians will emerge, prepared to carry out their apostolate and eager to project the presence of Christ into their life situations.

One weekend in October, 1964, I flew to Genoa and drove on with friends to Savona on behalf of the Apostleship of the Sea. At

Savona I visited the Delegazine Savonese with whom I had made friends at our International Congress held in Liverpool the previous September. The continuous string of docks from Genoa to Savona serve some 1,100 ships a *day*. There are fine seamen's clubs under Catholic auspices at each city. I brought a large portrait of Pope Paul which I blessed and hung in the main lobby of the Catholic Seamen's Club at Savona.

Bishop Parodi, Ordinary of Savona, set up my whole journey —the *"programma,"* as he called it—though he could not come with me. I stayed in his residence which, like so many things in Italy, is *"molto antico"*—dating back I do not know how many centuries. Next to my room was an apartment occupied by Pope Pius VII while he was held a prisoner of Napoleon! The apartment has been kept exactly as the Pope left it: throne room, writing room with quill pens, bedroom with the original bedding and drapes. Pius VII came back to the apartment after Napoleon's fall from power and worked out a solution to the division of Italy with Victor Emmanuel I in 1815, in the same house.

At Savona I celebrated Mass over the weekend at three different churches, each of a different character: the Seaman's Chapel, a new and extremely modern parish center, and then an old-time baroque church. In each, the participation was strong, especially the singing. I was called upon to say a few words to each congregation, and my hosts simply insisted that it be in Italian!

I record this last item because the next day, after a rather listless meeting of the U.S. bishops in Rome, my friend Bishop Casey of Lincoln asked me where I had been over the weekend. I replied: "Savona. And what do you think? I had to preach three times in Italian!" "Well," he replied, "they must have gotten about as much out of that as we got out of this meeting today!"

The debate on the Oriental Churches began on Thursday, October 15, 1964.

By "Oriental Churches" are meant those churches of the East, using the Oriental rites in Mass and Sacraments, which have remained in union with the Holy See after the great Eastern separation in the eleventh century. These ancient churches, many of them tracing their beginnings back to the Apostles, have a proud and venerable tradition, and certain time-honored privileges. Although they are now mostly small in number (only five per cent of the membership of the churches in the East), these churches still retain their dignity, and although often divided among themselves in their thinking, do indeed manage to preserve their identity as well as a rich cultural and liturgical heritage for the whole Church. However, they cannot be regulated or approached by Western methods (a tactic often tried); they require a treatment which takes into account their own special position. Against this background the debate about them and their present-day position in the Church began.

Cardinal Cicognani, Secretary of State, and former head of the Congregation for Oriental Affairs, led off the proceedings by presenting to the Council three questions to which much of the debate would be directed:

1. Were converts from the Orthodox to be compelled to remain in their original Eastern rite, with appeal to the Holy See? (There are 14 different Eastern rites: the Orthodox and the Catholic rites corresponding to each other in external form.)

2. Should the presence of a Catholic priest be necessary only for the liceity of a marriage between two Eastern Christians (not for its validity)?

3. Should Eastern Catholics be allowed to receive sacraments in Orthodox Churches, and the Orthodox in Catholic Churches, under certain specific circumstances?

Cardinal Koenig, speaking as the Ordinary for the Eastern Churches in Austria, had a number of complaints to make about the schema: It did not honor the non-Catholic Eastern churches as "churches" and talked about "converting" Easterners to the Catholic Church; further it talked about "mixed" marriages and emphasized the differences instead of the similarities between the Orthodox and the Catholic Easterners which are great.

Then came Patriarch Maximus, at 86, a year older, but no less fiery than last year, to give his first talk at session three. He zeroed in on the treatment of patriarchs in the schema. The patriarchate exists in the West as well as in the East. The trouble is, he said, that everyone in the Latin Church has forgotten that the Pope is the patriarch of the West, a position which has done no harm to his primacy whatsoever. But if we expect to have any dialogue with the Orthodox, we must get rid of our present system of considering the designation "patriarch" a merely honorary title. The patriarchate must be restored to what it once was among the Catholics and still is among the Orthodox. At one time, a newly elected bishop of Rome used to send his profession of faith to the four patriarchs of the East, and they used to return the compliment when they acceded to office. Allowing for the primacy of the Pope, the patriarch and his holy synod in practice must be the last instance for all the affairs of his patriarchate. It has not been a good thing for the Uniate churches to have become Latinized, assimilated and absorbed by the West as they have been. By permitting the Eastern Catholic churches and their patriarchates and patriarchs to regain their original Eastern character, the catholicity of the Church will become truly universal (rather than merely Latin) and dialogue with the Orthodox will become much smoother!

The debate on the Eastern Catholic Churches lasted three days. During this period, a number of interesting points of view were presented:

1. The Eastern Catholic Churches are small enough as it is, without Latin Catholics trying to make "converts" to the Roman rite from their ranks. The Popes of the past had forbidden this and the Council should do the same.

2. All patriarchs should definitely be accorded a vote in the election of a Pope; otherwise, their ancient position as co-patriarchs with the Pope—granting however all his prerogatives of primacy —is subjected to the position of the cardinals who have arrived only lately in the ecclesiastical picture.

3. The Latins have applied treatment to Easterners as though they were Protestants. The differences between Eastern and Western rites are not incompatible with a unified Church; the differences between Catholics and Protestants are.

4. To be effective, Oriental hierarchies outside the East must be established in relation to the proper line of authority in each rite— not in subjection to either the local bishop or to departments of the

Holy See, as the schema provides. (Few if any of our U.S. Oriental hierarchs had much stomach for this proposition.)

5. A distinction must be made in the case of the Orthodox: in their case, it is not fitting to speak of "conversion" but of "reconciliation." As long as the synodal rule of patriarchs is downgraded, there is little hope of unity beween East and West.

The schema on Eastern Catholic Churches was given a final vote in the Council on October 20, 1964 (*Placet*—1,911; *Non placet*—265; Invalid—5). The decree was finally promulgated on November 21, 1964.

Maximos put up a brave front and vigorously advanced the cause of the patriarchs at the Council. But even he, I think, realized that the more radical proposals which he supported were unrealistic: proposals that the patriarchs, representing now greatly reduced bodies of Catholics, nevertheless, because of their ancient dignity, be given a vote in the election of a Pope; that patriarchs be relieved of their regulation by departments of the Holy See; and so forth.

The Decree on Eastern Churches, however, did pay great honor to the Orientals and reaffirm that the Church prized their resources and traditions and would protect these with all her heart. It also laid down, as a principle, that new patriarchates should be established wherever there was a need for them, thus firmly rejecting the accusation that the Church was willing to simply let them die out or to Latinize them. Moreover, the ancient discipline of the sacraments in the Eastern Churches was formally confirmed, with an exchange of ministry between priests of Eastern and Western rites being permitted "according to their faculties." The laity are directed to follow the liturgy of their own rite, but in mixed families persons are allowed to follow one rite or the other, while persons living outside the area of their rite may follow the customs of the place where they live.

Patriarchs are to regulate the language of the liturgy with the approval of the Holy See. The Orthodox who become Catholics need only make a profession of faith; while clerics may use the orders they had on joining the Catholic Church. Participation with the Orthodox which harms unity is forbidden; however, a certain latitude is permitted: under certain conditions, persons separated in good faith, in Orthodox churches, may receive Confession and Communion and the Anointing of the Sick in the Catholic Church; furthermore, under certain conditions, Catholics are permitted to receive the same sacraments from separated ministers of the Eastern churches who have valid orders.

"Missionary Activity of the Church" was debated at both the third and the fourth sessions. After refinement, a decree was produced which received a final favorable vote of 2,394 to 5 and was promulgated at the solemn meeting on December 7, 1965.

However noncontroversial the final score sounds, the debate on the Missions began in the third session in an unauspicious manner. It seems that Pope Paul wished to demonstrate his unity with the Council, as its head, and, at the same time, his fellowship with his brother bishops by doing away with the usage that the Pope does not attend a council, in person, during debate. The Pope decided not only to attend one of the daily meetings, but personally to introduce one of the schemas. The schema he chose, unfortunately, was that on the Missions. Hence on Friday, November 6, 1964, Pope Paul entered the Council hall on foot and unpretentiously sat down in the center of the presidents after presiding at the daily Mass. When the time came, he duly presented the schema himself.

Perhaps it was thought by his advisers that this was the safest schema for him to present; furthermore, few bishops would probably dare to find fault with it. There was, indeed, a certain delicacy involved in criticizing the schema without seeming to criticize the Pope himself: The Vatican department for regulating the Missions is primarily that of the Propagation of the Faith, one of the Pope's own departments. While there was no intention of calling into question the Pontiff's handling of this Congregation, nevertheless on other grounds there was powerful opposition to the schema. This opposition made itself felt to such a degree that, although the Pope himself had introduced the schema with the hope that it would be approved, perhaps with "improvements in some parts," the schema was eventually rejected and sent back for rewriting.

What was wrong with it? Apparently two principal things: The Fathers wanted a wider definition of what constitutes "a missionary territory," a definition which, when one reflects on the matter, is not at all easy to achieve. Often countries which are overwhelmingly Catholic may well be classed as greatly in need of missionary aid. Next, the Fathers wanted wider representation by the missionaries themselves on Vatican Mission Boards, especially boards which distribute funds to the missions. The commission handling the schema rather nicely worked out this delicate problem by entering certain forthright suggestions and then gracefully leaving everything up to the Holy Father for implementation.

After three complete sessions, the Council adjourned temporarily, on November 21, 1964, to allow the bishops to get back to the work of their dioceses. A respectable record of achievement had been set at last, and moreover, there seemed to be solid prospect of winding up all its work at a fourth session in the fall of 1965. Its achievements were greatly obscured, however, by the wide attention given to the failure of the Council to entertain an expected vote on Religious Liberty at the close of the third session as we have reported elsewhere. Still the record at the end of session three speaks for itself. At this point, one could classify the Council documents as follows:

I. PROMULGATED:
    1. Liturgy 2. Communications 3. The Church 4. Orientals 5. Ecumenism

II. UN-PROMULGATED:
    Most Advanced: 6. Bishops 7. Religious 8. Seminaries 9. Education 10. Non-Christians (Jews)
    More Advanced: 11. Revelation 12. Laity
    Least Advanced: 13. Religious Liberty 14. Modern World 15. Missions 16. Priests

And with matters at this stage, the Fathers left Rome with the justified feeling that one more session would be sufficient to bring the Council to a close.

Chapter 13

The Opening of Session Four ·
Priests · Religious · Seminaries ·
Interlude at Session Four

For my last trip to Rome, in connection with the Council, I decided to invite a delegation of my flock and of my friends to accompany me. Calling it "A Voyage to the Council," I arranged in advance an audience with the Pope and tickets for everyone to the solemn opening ceremonies of the Council. Forty-nine persons responded, including seven priests.

Since I was perhaps the first bishop from the United States to reach Rome for the Council, the press made a bee-line for my quarters at the Hilton to get advance impressions. Jane Sullivan (*Newsweek*) and Wilton Winn (*Time* and *Life*) were interested in the following angles: *Length of the Session* (I said: positively will close before Christmas); *State of Agenda* (I said: good—commissions have discovered a pattern of consensus among the Fathers, I feel; and the Moderators are going to step up the pace of action on the floor even more than they did last year); *Main Concern* (I said: all eleven documents to be processed have status and quality worthy of an Ecumenical Council. It is not necessary to treat every question under the sun. But what we do treat we must treat in an adequate manner); *Religious Liberty* (I said: a consensus exists and a favorable vote is inevitable on the schema as it stands; however, for some reasons, the opponents must be heard out, and they will be); *Birth Control* (I said: the Church is sensitive and sympathetic to both the problems of modern couples and the problems of world population in many countries. However, theological judgment has not clearly matured on this question, and the Council can hardly speak on specifics until this maturity develops. The Council will not attempt to by-pass general theological judgment. That is why the Holy Father has committed a study of the matter to a competent group of experts from many fields of knowledge which will report, or which perhaps has already reported, to him on their assignment); *Reform of the Curia* (I said: the Pope has himself called for it and that it would consist in having the formation of high policy in Church government placed more than formerly in the hands of the bishops working with and under the Pope. I visualize a Senate of Bishops as roughly comparable to a board of governors of a university, a policy-making body, with members of the Curia roughly like the president and deans who are executives and who carry out the policy). I was as surprised as anyone when the Holy Father suddenly issued a directive setting up just such a Senate, after proclaiming that he would do so in his opening address.

Archbishop Hallinan of Atlanta was back at the Council at session four (rooming next door to me), looking a little thin but feeling great. We had a wonderful evening with Father John Courtney Murray, S.J., Father William Leahy, Monsignor John Tracy Ellis and others, talking over the intervention the Archbishop planned to make on Religious Liberty. His theme: "The true religion flourishes best in an atmosphere of religious freedom."

The day of my embarrassment was Friday, September 17. I had decided to remain at the hotel and do some correspondence instead of going to the regular daily meeting in St. Peter's. I had listened to the interventions of the past several days and I had found the Fathers endlessly repeating arguments which had been fully presented already at the past two sessions. One hundred seventy-five bishops had asked to talk, and I expected them to say nothing much new.

At any rate, I stayed home and it was just as well, for my absence provided Archbishop Hallinan with an opportunity to give his address on Religious Liberty. With so many speakers asking to talk, it looked for a while as though Archbishop Hallinan, far down the list, would not get to the mike at all. Debate would almost certainly be terminated (so repetitious was it) before his turn came.

I, too, had prepared an intervention, but it was on a technical point which I did not judge to be of general interest; and so I sent it in to the General Secretariat as a written intervention. However, I did begin it with the salutation *"Venerabiles Fratres"* ("Venerable Brethren") which the Secretariat took to indicate an intention on my part to present a *spoken* intervention!

Well, you guessed it—they called on me in St. Peter's, over the public-address system, to come up and give my talk, and I wasn't there! I was back at the hotel writing a letter home to Baton Rouge.

All I had wanted to say was that I was in full agreement with the schema on Religious Liberty as it stood, but that I felt it would be helped by making one change, namely this: Instead of saying that Religious Liberty pertains to communities (denominations) as well as to individuals, because the social nature of man *requires* such communities, I wanted the schema to say that such communities *have their origin* in the social nature of man. Monsignor Gillespie first called this passage to my attention at home, and Father John Courtney Murray agreed that the point was well taken. So I sent in the intervention but I did not expect to be asked to give it as an address!

When they called my name to speak, Archbishop Hallinan did some quick thinking. He knew I wasn't there and that I did not expect to speak, so he asked the Secretariat to let him take my place. And they did! He made a truly fine speech and I am glad he had the chance to do so, especially after the work that went into it. It would have been ironic if my little intervention had made the cut and his not!

I took quite a ribbing from the other bishops at our hotel for playing hookey from the Council and getting caught at it. But I told them, "That's just why I stayed home today—to keep from having to listen to people like myself!"

Debate at session four began on the day following its solemn opening. True to promise, the first subject up for discussion was Religious Liberty, already treated elsewhere. It concluded, after six-and-a-half additional days of debate.

The next subject to be debated "The Church and the Modern World" I will discuss in our final chapter.

A third subject to absorb attention was "The Missionary Activity of the Church" which we have already reported in Chapter 12.

In this chapter I will discuss the Council debate and documents on the following three subjects: "The Priestly Life and Ministry"; "The Religious Life"; and "The Priestly Formation."

These were not all debated, necessarily, in the fourth session alone, for Council debate did not always keep in step with Council chronology; subjects like Religious Liberty were debated at three different sessions. Discussion of the various schemas cannot therefore be linked very well with the chronology of the Council in a report such as this, so no harmonizing of the topical and session chronologies has been attempted.

The preparatory schema on Priests was debated on October 13–15, 1964. Archbishop Marty of Rheims introduced a new and revised schema, "The Priestly Life and Ministry," on October 13, 1965. There then took place a renewed debate on the subject which was carried on for another five days. Among the more enlightened remarks addressed to the Fathers was as follows:

1. The Eastern bishops did not hesitate to point out that the schema on "Priests" reflected a Western mentality and offered little of value to Eastern priests, especially those who were married. They went on to say that it was infected with juridicism and failed to indicate sufficiently that the soul of the priestly life was the Holy Spirit. Easterners, they said, found it strange that so much attention should be given to exterior organization of the

priestly ministry instead of to the transformation of men's lives in Christ through that ministry. Moreover, the schema did not seem to be aware of the fact that the priestly ministry extended not only to Christians but to all mankind; and that priestly studies were urgently needed today to produce ministers of the Gospel who understand the modern world in which they live.

2. The schema on Priests ought to express clearly that union with Christ, for a priest, is not merely a matter of his own personal piety and devotion (meditation, prayer, etc.); it is fundamentally a matter of his *ministry*. The priest is essentially "a minister"; and it is, above all, in his ministry, his service, that he finds union with Christ. Priestly holiness cannot be based on the concept of an opposition between the interior and the exterior life of the priest.

3. The Son of God shows Himself as always worshipping the Father in love. Out of this love flows the love that saves souls. This idea should be placed at the very head of the schema on "Priests" so that the gift of self in personal love for Christ will be seen as directing the whole life and ministry of priests. Thus there will be less need to fear their negligence or defection, and thus will they better see the importance of prayer and spiritual exercises.

4. The questions raised in the schema are too conceptual and remote from the questions asked by the priests of today. Characteristic of today's situation is the difficulty priests have of finding their place in a world which regards them as alien; and their place among the laity who must look to them for animation and coordination of their work.

5. The poverty of priests in many countries is a serious problem today. These priests are poor themselves and thus unable to help the poor. The Council should act to see to it that all priests, everywhere, are given the means to carry out their ministry properly.

6. The schema says nothing of the role of assistant pastors. In larger dioceses, far more than half of the active priests are assistants and they do more than half the work. Yet the assistant has no

juridical status and almost no rights. The assistant is often spoken of and treated as a child. But he is actually a mature man with precious qualities and charisms and should not be isolated. Too often, in large dioceses, a priest becomes a pastor only when his years of vigor have passed. Indeed, a pastorate, in Canon Law, is referred to as "a benefice"—something to be enjoyed instead of a task demanding all one's energies. Would modern technology and industry spend so much time and money to train men and then use them so poorly?

Archbishop Marty, who introduced the schema, also closed the discussion on "Priests" by assuring the Fathers that the commission would do its best to revise the schema in the light of their recommendations. The commission did so, and as a result the decree on Priests was approved on December 4, 1965 by a vote of: *Placet*—2,243; *Non Placet*—11; Null—3. It was promulgated at the Solemn Congregation on December 7, 1965.

I looked forward to the arrival of *Time's* cover story on Pope Paul, for I had been interviewed in connection with the development of the story. But I was disappointed in the treatment given the Pope. I feel (and had said to *Time*) that the Holy Father is like the manager of a team who must avoid crude, sudden displays of power and authority in the interest of keeping his team working together smoothly. He may at times seem to be taking two steps forward and then one step back, but when you examine his record of achievement in retrospect (which provides perspective) you discover that his accomplishments are truly impressive and progressive, all brought about without dramatic demonstrations of power except at key and crucial points at which only Papal authority could break the impasse. That is what the Pontifical Office is for—to break log-jams and keep the material flowing and the action moving. And who can deny that Pope Paul had done exactly that in the Council?

I will never forget how he got the Council commissions working and issuing documents; how he stepped up the pace of procedure in the aula with his four Moderators; and how—by report, at least—he has been instrumental in cracking the road-blocks to Religious Liberty. No one can blame him if he wisely chooses the exact and proper moment to make his moves. In addition, why try to downgrade the powerful impact for brotherhood and peace which was the fruit of his peregrinations to the Holy Land, to India and now the United States and the United Nations? Many of the Protestant observers with whom I have spoken share my feeling that the reporting on Pope Paul has often been both inaccurate and unfair.

One Protestant observer I heard, commenting on *Time's* cover story (September 24, 1965) complained that *Time* was too naïve in judging the Pope's actions. "You've got to understand," he said, "that the Pope is a place-hitter, sometimes working the count to 3-and-2, and then dumping a neat little Texas leaguer right over the infield to bring in a needed run. He doesn't swing for the fences as Pope John did; and, consequently, he doesn't get the cheering either. But he wins the games."

Archbishop Felici dazzled the Fathers with his ability to handle Latin in his post of Secretary General. But the Archbishop admitted one day that the names of dioceses in Latin are difficult to handle. Who could ever get "Fall River," for example, out of *"Riveromanensis"*? or, "New Orleans" out of *"Neoaurelianensis"*? But I pride myself that the great Latinist seems to find most difficult of all—even to pronounce—the name *"Rubribaculensis."* That's "Baton Rouge"! Felici approached it with respect, like this: *"Rooo—breee—"* (then real fast) *"baculensis!"* His Latin name for coffee bar was *"thermopolium."* He got a lot of mileage out of that one, during his announcements, asking the Fathers to remain in their places rather than wander away to the *"thermopolium."*

Latin traffic signs inside the Vatican were the goal of Monsignor Tondini, a Vatican official. That would certainly do it! Imagine the pile-ups created by signs saying: *"Ne Praetergrediaris!"* (No passing), or *"Ne sistas"* (No parking), or especially *"Ne flectas dextrorsum"* (No right turn)!

To us in Rome the Holy Father's visit to the U.N. was a re-sounding success. And the text of his address revealed a deeply hu-man appeal of the highest quality and dignity. Many newspapers said that an address on so high a level had never before been heard in the U.N. We gave him a warm and vociferous greeting on his return to Rome. He came straight from his plane into the Council and spoke to the bishops of the world and the other Fathers of the Council immediately. I had my field glasses on him; he looked rested and brimming with joy over the results of his peace voy-age. And well he might, for this lightning journey of his to New York was one of the greatest acts in the interest of peace ever made by any single individual in our experience.

Accompanying the Holy Father to New York was Cardinal Rugambwa of Africa (there was a cardinal for every continent in the world in the Pope's entourage). Rugambwa was mistaken by many people for the new negro Auxiliary Bishop of New Or-leans, Bishop Perry, and the cardinal was almost mobbed by well-wishers!

Bishop Perry brings immense dignity, humility and compe-tence, as well as excellent judgment, to his perhaps delicate assign-ment in New Orleans. He is a highly cultivated person and a man with a winning personality—but above all, he is a Bishop of the Holy Church, a successor of the Apostles, a representative of Christ in our midst of high responsibility. And this is what all truly Catholic people will see in him.

In a moment of exuberance I wrote a letter to Bud Montet, sports editor of *The Morning Advocate*, a Baton Rouge news-paper, and Bud incorporated it in his column:

> It is 9:15 P.M. and I am sitting out on the little balcony off my room at the Rome Hilton, high up on Monte Mario, the highest spot from which to overlook the Eternal City.
>
> Far below, the buildings of the town of Romulus and Remus are shrouded in shades of evening, but the streets are picked out in a glowing piping of tiny lights.
>
> As one's eyes become accustomed to the darkness, the big black

bulk of St. Peter's dome can be recognized directly below; and, somewhat farther out in the city, one begins to make out the jagged form of that granddaddy of all the stadiums of the world—the Roman Coliseum.

On the edge of my balcony (for the sake of good reception) is a tiny transistor radio which emits surprising volume. However, what I am listening to is not the ordinary radio fare of Rome at all —the usual machine-gun-style newscast or the threadbare strains of "Domani." I am listening to words and music from the other side of the world, from a stadium many miles away from the ancient Coliseum, namely, the Gator Bowl Stadium at Gainesville where LSU is battling Florida.

And the transistor is shouting this: "Dougie Moreau has just gathered in a pass, eluded one defender and worked his way to the 4-yard line. Another play—and Stokeley takes it over for the score! Moreau boots, and it is good! Florida 7, LSU 7."

The little transistor is framed in a lovely setting: the soft, star-studded Italian sky above and the silhouettes of Rome's ancient ruins below. But the names sounding loud and clear through the light night air are not the names of Caesar or of Pompey or of Augustus; they are not even the names of Michaelangelo, Raphael or Julius II. They are names very famous these days along the Mississippi, and now along the Tiber: Screen, Schwab, DiBetta, Masters, and all the rest. The Tigers are taking on the Gators tonight even as the Romans took on the Gauls in another age and in another league. And the clash of their battle is being heard across the world!

Later I was jolted to find myself depicted in a cartoon in *Sports Illustrated*. Here I was, in the cartoon, crossing what was supposed to be St. Peter's Square, with a transistor radio and projecting aerial up against my ear, while on my cassock I sported a big LSU badge.

Bishop John B. Franz of Peoria, Illinois, who was serving as a sub-commission chairman at the Council, made a statement which helps us all, I think, to understand the work of the Council better. He said: "One must be prepared to find some imperfections in almost every Council document. Council commissions try for the greatest possible consensus—and for that necessary two-thirds favorable vote. Hence, they must carefully avoid any wording which might be open to misunderstanding. But the consequence of this approach is at times a weaker expression than one would otherwise wish. Nevertheless, one must not be trapped into placing overdue importance on any single word in a text, because individual expressions or even sentences carry less weight than does the entire document. Therefore, the emphasis should be centered on the meaning of the document as a whole."

They say the best way to judge a painting is to first attempt to take it in as a whole, before going into its details. And perhaps the same is true of a conciliar text: what counts is the over-all text and the over-all spirit.

Debate on the subject Renewal of the Religious Life was carried on at the Council on November 10–12, 1964. The final Decree as "Religious" was approved on October 8, 1965 by a vote of: Yes—2,071; No—9; Null—1.

The basic positions reflected in the debate can be well summed up by reporting the respective position of Cardinal Spellman on the one hand and of Cardinal Doefpner and Cardinal Suenens on the other.

Cardinal Spellman: The schema is satisfactory. It calls for an updating in religious life, but in a measured way. The renewal must be carried out cautiously because many persons can be deceived by some things that have been said publicly about renewing religious life even by some prelates. Under the guise of renewal, certain ideas can be proposed which would overthrow the religious life itself. There are some writers and speakers who want *all* religious to engage in certain external works which they label "apostolic." But the whole life of a religious is already "apostolic" because it is consecrated to God for the service of men. For example, there are others who are teachers in schools— we cannot ask any other apostolate from them! Those who want religious sisters to practice some form of Catholic Action or visit homes should turn to orders founded for these purposes or found new ones. It is not proper to require that *all* religious women undertake these tasks. Indeed, many superiors of religious women have revealed to me their anxieties on this point. To demand a departure from the observance of their religious rules would not be a promotion of their religious life; on the contrary, it would be a removal from it. Also, we must foster the contemplative life lest it be drowned in the onrush of activism. In the United States institutions of this kind are growing in number and fervor.

Cardinal Doefpner: The schema on the religious does not meet today's needs. It is weak. It fails to come to grips with the basic difficulties. What are the key points which need to be developed profoundly and accurately?

1. Spiritual Renewal: Even excellent institutional reforms will be fruitless unless based on a spiritual renewal. Emphasis on such renewal, especially on the part of women religious, has centered on *the forms* of spiritual life rather than on spirituality itself. There must now be a return to the sources: to Scripture, the Liturgy, outstanding spiritual masters from the Fathers on, and spiritual theology. Unfortunately, the piety and devotions of many institutes reflect an outdated mentality.

2. Accommodation of Religious Life to the Needs of our Time: Even though separate from the world, religious must realize that they pertain to this world and its people; they must see the world in a positive light:

A. How, in the face of so many technical and economic changes, can religious poverty be made meaningful not only for religious but also for the world? Many traditional forms of poverty cannot be understood by moderns.

B. The problem of obedience is grave and complex, involving superiors even more than subjects. Mere repetition of traditional teaching is not enough; something must be said also about the form and kind of obedience which suit the mature adult of our day. Above all, those destined for apostolic work must be prepared for greater responsibility and the right use of freedom.

3. Preparation of Religious: Preparation of Religious must be more profound and broader than in the past. Theological and pastoral preparation of priests must be intensified. In lay institutes, potential superiors must be given special training. In cloistered communities, the customs must be adjusted to the customs and

mentality of modern man. Spiritual harm, even loss of vocations, has resulted from present antiquated customs.

4. Problem of Typology of Religious Institutes: In the last century, these institutes have rapidly multiplied. Often their spirit is too restricted; often many congregations are doing the same work. Often religious women especially find themselves torn between a quasi-monastic regimen and over-demanding work. In contemplative communities, there is an institutional narrowness which is psychologically unbearable; hence, of many contemplative vocations few persevere.

Conclusion: A longer schema is not necessary, but the propositions must be redone in the light of the above considerations.

Cardinal Suenens: The schema does not please me at all. With respect to women religious of the active life, it is necessary that:

I. The members obtain the full development of their human qualities and be regarded as truly adult women.

II. That they enjoy the freedom needed for apostolic action. To this end, suggestions are proposed:

A. In the Doctrinal Order:

1. Their spirituality must no longer be based on the traditions and mentality of the cloister; pastors and theologians must elaborate a spirituality of the active life for their benefit.

2. The spirituality of the vows must be shown in its apostolic dimensions: observance of the evangelical counsels adds a dynamic and apostolic value to the baptismal consecration. The apostolate itself should be defined in the sense of "evangelization" so that there will be a hierarchy of values in the sister's life and each will have some time for such apostolic work. Also, the sister should be made conscious of her role of inspiring the laity in their apostolate.

B. In the Practical Order:

1. Community regimen should be reformed so that individual sisters can cooperate actively and as adults for the good of the whole, avoiding maternalistic concentration of power on the one hand and overly passive infantile obedience on the other. Canonists and qualified sisters should elaborate rules providing for:

(a) Balanced structures of government.

(b) A changed system of naming superiors.

(c) General chapters which will more faithfully represent the whole congregation.

2. Antiquated Customs Must Be Changed:

(a) Separation from the world must not be so radically interpreted as to keep them from apostolic work.

(b) The distinctive, but ridiculous, garb of many communities must be changed.

(c) Practices based on outdated notions of the inferiority of women should be abandoned.

To such remarks a Father Superior, Joseph Buckley, S.M., added:

The traditional concept of obedience is all right for monks but not for active-apostolic religious. Some superiors are always talking about the crisis in obedience. My opinion is that the crisis is with the superiors, not their subjects. The truth is that today's young people don't swallow archaic formulas like "the will of the Superior is exactly the same as the will of God." Nothing is said in the schema about the obligations of superiors to consult their council; actually, many do not know how to conduct a council meeting effectively. I suggest that the renewal of religious life is more a matter of the formation and efficiency of superiors than of greater obedience in their subjects.

One of the most notable interventions was the written intervention on the role of women in the Church entered by Archbishop Hallinan of Atlanta. The Archbishop reflected the position of the ladies present in Rome to perfection. His intervention touched upon their active participation in liturgical functions; full education in theology with a view to consultation; a voice in the shaping of the new apostolate of the laity; representation in force in all bodies which seriously affect, by their decisions, the status and interests of women, and so on. In effect, Archbishop Hallinan suddenly alerted the Fathers to the fact that the Church, in the past, has not taken much of a lead in the emancipation of women from obvious discrimination and injustice. While no action on the Archbishop's proposals was taken at the Council, it was felt that he had, indeed, focused attention of the Church on a real problem.

Next came the Decree on Priestly Formation or what was more familiarly known as the Decree on Seminaries promulgated on October 28, 1965. From the start, it received perhaps the most favorable treatment of any Council document. Its original schema was drawn up after the commission had had time to absorb the determined spirit of the Council calling for thorough-going renewal in its documents.

Personally, I was surprised to find so many up-to-date ideas in the schema and also to find them so readily accepted by the Fathers, hardly fifty of whom balked at accepting the text as a basis for discussion.

The tone of the debate on Seminaries may be derived from a summary of the interventions made:

First of all, Cardinal Meyer of Chicago, as usual, distinguished himself with a perceptive commentary on the schema as presented:

I make two general observations which may suggest that the schema should be developed and expanded more:

The essential qualities of the priesthood are that priests are men and that their work is to be mediators between God and men (cf. Heb. 5,1); these two facts constitute the basis of all seminary training. The unity of the priesthood, because of which education is said to be necessary for all priests, consists in the mediation performed through the Mass and prayer and indicates also the unity of the apostolate of every priest, whether he be diocesan or religious, in the ordinary or extraordinary ministry. Every priest is an apostle, and the source of the apostolate should be his interior life, arising mainly from the Mass. The purpose of all seminary formation, therefore, is the apostolate, but it does not follow that all seminary formation must be the same. This distinction is not evident in the schema, which seems to impose on the universal Church norms which pertain only to the formation of the clergy in the Latin Church and in the active ministry under the guidance of the bishop. The schema should take into account the principal different way of exercising the priesthood.

Although the schema states that the norms of *Christian* education are to be observed in seminary training, it does not insist enough on the priest's obligation as a Christian to attain the same perfection as all those who belong to the People of God. A priest will not be effective in his ministry unless he cultivates truth, sincerity, courage, justice, et cetera; before one can become a good priest, he must be a good man and a good Christian. These things are not evident to all candidates for the priesthood, for some look forward to it not as a *gratia gratis data* demanding human co-operation, but rather as a medicinal grace enabling them to satisfy the demands of the Christian life more easily. The schema, therefore, should stress what is expected of the students in the ethical field and show that these things are expected not merely as preparations for the priesthood, but as pertinent to the formation of a real Christian.

Next, there was a contrast presented in the views of Cardinal Emile Léger of Canada and Archbishop Dino Staffa of the Sacred Congregation of Seminaries.

Cardinal Léger: Especially praiseworthy is the way in which regional differences, the person and mentality of the student himself, his pastoral formation and his awareness of the needs of the world are taken into consideration. But certain things should be amended with regard to intellectual formation.

1. On Philosophy: It is good that the schema does not neglect the importance of philosophical instruction, but the rule proposed with regard to teaching "the perennial philosophy" should be dropped. First of all, this word is ambiguous; if it is taken to mean "scholastic philosophy," it must be recalled that there are many widely different scholastic philosophies. Furthermore, such a rule seems contrary to the nature of philosophy itself, whose inquiry, as St. Thomas stated, regards not what authors have said but what things are in themselves. Finally, the disadvantageousness of imposing so-called scholastic philosophy simply and indiscriminately on non-Occidental students is obvious to everyone. It is not for the Council to propose a particular philosophy but to give rules in accord with the requisites of faith and the valid philosophical instruction of students.

2. On Theology:

(a) I am glad that the text does not dwell ponderously on the teaching of St. Thomas. Not that his works are to be despised, but because immoderate exclusiveness ought to be completely avoided. In place of the present reference to St. Thomas, the text should conclude by citing him as a master and model for all those studying theology. In this way, St. Thomas's doctrine will not be imposed, but rather his scientific and spiritual approach, by which he creatively utilized the knowledge of his day in the service of the Gospel, will be extolled.

(b) The schema should speak more fully and insistently on the need for dialogue with the world on the part of all theologians. They are always in danger of thinking only in an artificial world, unaware even of the language of the real world. Concrete means, such as the following, should be proposed: the presence and constant consultation of some learned laymen in the seminary, the reading of studies comparing the Church's teachings with present ideas, pastoral experience of professors and students, et cetera.

(c) Many have already mentioned in the Council the need for a renewal of moral theology. Manuals are often filled with a casuistry and legalism that do not seem primarily and fully Christian. Since these failings are so deeply rooted, a special paragraph of the schema should be devoted to moral theology and to the necessity of joining it closely with dogmatic theology and Sacred Scripture.

Archbishop Staffa, in the name of a number of bishops of both the West, and especially of the East: For the dialogue with the world today, it is necessary to be steeped in the philosophical and theological sciences, with St. Thomas as the leader. Progress in knowledge cannot be made in separation from truth, indeed such a separation is an impediment to progress. Progress does not make already detected truth the subject of inquiry, but must be integrated with this already detected truth. The Church must seek that philosophy which best fits the needs of revealed truth. Truth is not confined to the West or East, nor is it an impediment between East and West. Thus the teaching of St. Thomas should be preserved in seminaries, as papal documents have declared.

I was especially interested in the Decree on Seminaries and its contents since one of the most interesting projects attempted in our five-year-old diocese is a minor seminary that we are developing year by year. Speaking at the dedication of the new minor seminary at Jackson, Mississippi, on March 17, 1966, I had occasion to remark that we had developed fourteen points or principles in the organization and conduct of a minor seminary which we were delighted to see confirmed in many respects by the stipulations of the Council. The fourteen points are as follows:

1. *Screening*—that is the testing and the accepting only those candidates who possess a proper balance of qualities and who offer a well-founded prospect of perseverance;

2. *Counselling*—by a carefully selected staff of priests who are able to understand, communicate with and inspire their charges;

3. *The Faculty*—a highly qualified and nicely balanced group of instructors from the ranks of priests, brothers, sisters, lay men and lay women with emphasis on teaching ability and interest in youth;

4. *Normal Living*—a daily life-experience not too far removed, by artificial regulations and exercises, from that of the average high school boy;

5. *Home Contacts*—recognition of the important role that parents, home and family have to play in the formation of a future priest;

6. *Food*—not fancy but substantial and in attractive variety;

7. *Good Spirit*—which consists in a true affection and respect on the part of the student for his school and for his superiors; a healthy loyalty to them; and a quiet pride in the work his school is doing;

8. *Faculty Interest and Knowledge of Students*—this springs from supernatural motives; it is cultivated by true interest, without partiality, in each student's welfare and by hard work; and it results in an amazing consensus among faculty members as to each student's personal qualities;

9. *A Physical Education Program*—not haphazard, but directed by experts and harmonized with the high school athletic program of the community;

10. *Spiritual Guidance*—by men trained to the task:

a. Solidly based on a *personal encounter* with Christ, our Lord;

b. *Not routine:* but meaningful and carefully prepared;

c. *Providing proper information;* on the priesthood and about the priestly life;

d. *Calculated to inspire* students to make sacrifices in pursuit of so noble a calling;

e. Yet not forcing too full a commitment to the priestly vocation on students at so early an age;

11. A Meaningful *Liturgical Life;*

12. *High Standards* of Academic Achievement;

13. *Languages*—with a view to actual use and especially to conversation;

14. *Music, Art and General Culture*—opportunity for development of personal artistic and musical talents, for choral work, debate; a good library and a good atmosphere for contact with history, music and good art.

On the basis of these principles our experience in Baton Rouge has been as follows:

1. *An increase in applicants* to enter the program: this year, 80 applications representing nearly all parishes in the Diocese. (By contrast, one parish, formerly, had only one vocation in 200 years!)

2. *Conservation of vocations*—only *3 drop-outs* in 2 years; where as formerly it was not uncommon to lose half the original number of beginners over the same period.

One of the most important points of renewal called for in the Council's Decree of Seminaries was the provision that seminary programs be developed by the national body of bishops according to general guidelines of the Sacred Congregation of Seminaries and Universities. This program of priestly training, originating at the national level, would, of course, require approval from the Holy See. Nevertheless, one can anticipate a profound change in the pattern of seminary training which, under the above system, will be recognized to meet, more effectively, local conditions and needs. We have, therefore, every reason to look forward to a renewed American seminary truly adapted to the mentality and requirement of American life and yet, at the same time, truly reflecting the essentials of the Catholic way of life. The result should be the formation of future priests more in contact with the day-to-day needs of their people and more aware of the contribution they can be expected to make in a much wider field of priestly endeavor.

Chapter 14

· Education · Church and World ·
End of the Great Council

As the fourth session headed down the stretch, Education again came up for consideration. Neither Archbishop Hallinan nor I had been present for the debate on Education in 1964, hence we approached the question as a virtually new topic. The schema seemed to us too general and completely lacking in punch. Old Newman Club men, we knew that the academic world, both Catholic and non-Catholic, was watching the Council, hopefully expecting from it a vigorous declaration on Education. But somehow things were not going well. Restlessness arose also among other Fathers who wanted a fresh, virile and updated statement, a statement genuinely relevant to the problems of the educational world of our times, a Magna Carta of Catholic education.

Soon the restlessness among the few developed into a state of anxiety, stemming from two factors:

1. The oft-heard remark that the Council cannot really say very much of significance on Education because of the variety of educational systems existing in the nations of the world; that each nation will have to work out its own significant statement later.

2. A preview of the actual text on which the Fathers would soon be asked to vote—*placet* or *non-placet,* without any further discussion, or even "reservations."

In contending with the dispirited attitude, reflected in point one, some Fathers replied that Pope Pius XI had been faced with a similar situation of a variety of national education systems, and yet produced his famed encyclical *Divini Illius Magistri*, on the Christian education of youth, which proved relevant to the problems of his era.

But what would a fresh relevant document be like? The positive-minded Fathers felt it should encompass a number of vital ideas, nearly all of which, as a matter of fact, had been presented in the debate in November, 1964:

1. The important distinction between the *State and Society* in talking about education (as urged by Bishop Malone of Youngstown, and the Newman Apostolate).

2. A proper treatment of the rights of parents (urged by Cardinal Spellman of New York).

3. At the very beginning, a synthesis clearly indicating (but not fully developing) the philosophy and theology of Christian Education (Bishop Malone).

4. The concept of liberty within education: particularly the liberty of scientific investigation (urged by Cardinal Leger [Canada], Cardinal Ritter [U.S.A.], Bishop Donahoe [U.S.A.], Nwedo [Nigeria]).

5. The interlocking harmony of the various roles of the family, the State and the Church—instead of setting each one against the other by emphasizing merely the rights of each.

6. A good "tone" to the document, pastoral and apostolic, as urged by many Fathers (Cody, U.S.A.; Elchinger, France; Gouyon, France; Pohlschneider, Germany). Such a document would preclude unseeming brevity (treating the whole university question, for example, in four paragraphs), unevenness and generality.

7. In addition to vindicating the rights of the Church to teach salvation and the means to it, as a divine institution, there should be a vindication of the right of the Church to teach other (e.g., secular) subjects as a private institution (as urged by Bishop Donahoe, U.S.A.).

8. Religious and Moral Education must be vindicated for all Catholics and for others as well in so called "non-religious" institutions of learning, where such exist. The care and instruction of students in this area, moreover, to meet the needs of the times, must

no longer be treated in the old, negative, protective ("save their faith") way. Even Pius X, in *Acerbo Nimis*, as far back as 1910, did not use that approach. On the contrary, there must be a clear-cut stress put on the concept of Church action as "leaven"—the Church causing ferment at all levels in the university community, even at the level of the university as an institution as such, offering to all her truth and her theology. A Church not merely proselytizing but a Church permeating and apostolic.

9. Then there should be thorough and adequate treatment also of the many "factors" in education: The educand, the parish, the teachers . . . as well as the so-called "*authors*" (family, State, Church). It is in this area that Catholic educators are seeking signposts and guidelines from the Church today. For example, it will do little good to treat the family merely in its environmental aspect (by saying that it is the "first school," etc.). It will be vitally necessary to emphasize the dynamic role of the family in education as making its own very important contribution, in cooperation with school policy and curriculum.

10. There has been a progressive enrichment of the philosophy of education since "*Divini Illius Magistri*" of Pius XI. The schema must, therefore, breathe not only the spirit of Leo XII and Pius XI but also that of Pius XII, Cardinal Newman, and especially Pope Paul VI who in the past three years has had some very significant ideas to set forth to the world in his allocutions. All these advances must be reflected in any document issued by the Council.

11. There must also be coordination of the schema on education with the other conciliar schemata which mention education, for example, the schemas on the Church and the Church and the Modern World.

12. Finally, the schema on education must treat adequately the role of parents, of the teaching apostolate and of the missionary activity of the Church, and show how these are related to the teaching office and function of the bishops.

I wrote home in a Rome Letter at the time, September 25, 1965: "The more I think of it the more I am inclined to feel that a revision now, in order to include all these ideas, is too large an order at this late date. . . . One of two developments might be able to do justice to the importance of the subject at hand: 1. A Post-Conciliar Statement, carefully and fully treated after profound and expert discussion, or 2. A full-blown Papal Encyclical, updating '*Divini Illius Magistri.*' "

The possibility of an encyclical attracted me the more I considered it. I felt it would relieve the Council of embarrassment in its attempt to reconcile so many divergent approaches; it would give the Holy Father ample opportunity to develop his own magnificent ideas on education which he had only partly disclosed, in comparatively short allocutions, thus far; and it would have immense impact on the world of education if expressed in a document of encyclical rank.

As for the way in which the Fathers would be asked to vote, I reported further to my diocese on October 8: "The amended text on Christian Education was distributed to the Fathers this week. It will be voted on October 13—but simply *placet* or *non-placet*. There will be no more discussion on it or even 'modi.' Many of the Fathers . . . are not at all satisfied to have this document go before the world of education as a solemn statement of an Ecumenical Council."

With this feeling abroad, there was some talk that the Commission handling the matter might decide to cast a few more straws in the wind by asking for a vote on a number of "queries" before taking a final tally.

With so many divergent points of view, from men of so many different countries and educational systems, expressed in commission meetings, I felt it unlikely that we would get a really strong document out of the Council. So I could not help but continue to think in terms of an encyclical letter on education by Pope Paul—a document of the stature of *Pacem in Terris*, a document which would be quoted and become the subject of convocations throughout the world.

Pope Paul's capabilities in this field were already manifest. Consider what he wrote to Father Theodore Hesburgh, president of Notre Dame University, on September 4, 1965. The words have the ring of Newman in them:

> The great modern university is a city of the mind, a vast classroom of instruction, a laboratory of discovery and research, an infinity of small rooms containing solitary scholars and writers, a studio of

artistic production, an endless conversation, a meeting place for scholars and a home for its students. Here men are intimately involved in the search for truth. University life is a commitment to study and thought if it is to remain faithful to what it really is. It has a spiritual vocation as well as a cultural vocation which it proclaims and nurtures.

Imagine a major encyclical letter on education in that style! It would pick up where the Council document left off and supplement and complete it; and it would have the respectful attention of the entire educational world of our day.

Toward the end of the fourth session, there were a number of recesses to permit commissions to catch up on work. I took advantage of one of them to visit, for the first time, that marvelous country to the north, that wonderland of art—the ancient cities of Bologna, Modena, Verona, Vicenza, Padua, Ferrara and Ravenna.

In five days, Bishop Robert J. Dwyer (Reno, Nevada), Father Joe Schumacher (Dallas, Texas) and I, rolling along the autostrada in a tiny Lancia could do no more than get a fleeting impression of the country. But in Bishop Dwyer, a student of history, we enjoyed a guide who could put into perspective everything we saw.

Throughout our tour, the Bishop had abundant grist for his mill. For in this region of Italy there took place—mainly in the twelfth century—a flowering of artistic genius whose output is preserved, in amazing measure, in spite of the ravages of time and even of the destructive power of modern warfare. For this is the area, near the Po River, where some of the most bitter fighting of the Italian campaign in World War II occurred. The wonder is that so much beauty has survived.

Our experience, however, did put a strain on my powers of artistic digestion. For example, any first-rate museum in the world would feel that the acquisition of a single fresco by Giotto would be a priceless treasure; but at Padua one finds a whole building—the Chapel of the Scrovegni—filled with three tiers of Giotto frescoes. The frescoes are about 700 years old, still preserved today in all their glorious color and delicate expression.

Speaking of preservation and delicacy, you find at Ravenna, as every art student and world traveler knows, the unbelievable Byzantine-style mosaics, no less than 1,400 years old, which still stand there today—not in a state of ruin or decay—but in their full perfection and in all their sparkling beauty. The secret, of course, in producing mosaics is not the painstaking labor of getting all those little pieces of marble and metal and glass to somehow add up to an acceptable image, reasonably close to a painting. The secret is to get each tiny element to reflect light in such a way as to give the entire work a character of jewel-like brilliance and an aura of majesty. An ordinary mosaic-maker can produce the former; it requires a genius to achieve the latter.

Why should such genius be available, in such abundance, at a place like Ravenna at the time of Justinian? Or why should a school such as that of Giotto blossom so luxuriantly in this hill country at the turn of the twelfth century? Whatever the answer, one cannot help being struck forcefully by the shocking evidences of subsequent decline in art on every side. Even with all this cornucopia of exquisite beauty all around them the baroque decorators barged into the very precincts and sanctuaries of medieval and Renaissance art with their tremendously busy and overloaded adornments. Indeed, many of their painters and decorators must have had to spend hours working at their elaborate contrivances—with the clean, simple beauty of the older masters only a few feet away! And the decline continues even to this day. You will find—as indeed we did—some of the most empty representations of religious figures and themes in bilious colors, side by side with the glories of the finest masters. Discrimination has departed.

Here is one last impression of the glorious past of this part of Italy. We were tendered a luncheon by His Excellency, the Most Reverend Salvatore Baldassari, Archbishop of Ravenna, who is not only the successor to Cardinal Lercaro (now at Bologna and an outstanding figure at the Council) but also the successor to Maxentius who was Archbishop of Ravenna when Justinian was Emperor, more than 1,400 years ago. The present Archbishop and I compared our standing: I am the first Bishop of Baton Rouge, but he does not even know how many archbishops preceded him at Ravenna in fourteen centuries!

Toward the end of the fourth session a feeling spread abroad that the Council, in the end, would not change things very much. What is said in documents—the feeling ran—is one thing; but what actually results from this in real life is another. And, of course, this remains quite true—as far as it goes. However, when documents *are* implemented they sometimes make all the difference. And sometimes they make a difference in ways that cannot be foreseen easily at the time they are written.

The Constitution of the United States, for example, provides for a Supreme Court; but no one, at the time of its writing, could have anticipated the natural development of the court's importance or the influence of John Marshall on that development. Much less could anyone at the end of the eighteenth century have envisioned the present role played by the court in American life. Yet the Constitution contained the seeds of this fulfillment. And we may expect similar impact on Christian life to be felt, far into the future, because of the seeds of healthy development contained in the documents of Vatican II—seeds which will grow and flourish only when exposed, as the history of the Church unfolds, to certain conditions and a certain climate. Make no mistake about it: the documents of the Council possess a potential under God's Grace and Providence, capable of changing the world!

If I were asked to select the three most significant key-words for an understanding of the work of the Council, I think I would nominate these three: emphasis, understanding and balance.

Emphasis: The Council has been teaching nothing new, actually. It has only been emphasizing ideas that lacked emphasis in the past, and it has removed emphasis from concepts long overemphasized. The current emphasis is strongly on such ideas as participation in the liturgy, contact with separated brethren, collegiality of the bishops—none of which is really new. And emphasis has been removed from such concepts as the danger of indifferentism, the remote majesty of divine worship, and in-dulgences—all of which are still within our religious concern. But this Council has demonstrated the great impact on Christian life that a shift in emphasis can make, without any change at all in the content of teaching.

Understanding: It seems to me that the world has taken to the Council with so much enthusiasm that it has perhaps expected a bit too much of it. And this has led to a lack of understanding of many of the Council's aspects: its scope, its intent, its approach and its final achievement. An accurate understanding of these aspects would go a long way toward a true, over-all evaluation of the Council and its work.

Balance: This quality has been lost so often in reporting the Council that "balance" has become an important word. Very often specific happenings, short-run disappointments and the hu-man qualities of persons at the Council have been reported in a manner that produced a distorted image of what was really tak-ing place. This is not meant as an indictment of the press. On the contrary, the daily working press did an accurate, even impres-sive, job in many respects. Nevertheless, the fact remains that there was a good deal of writing about the Council which was superficial, insofar as it permitted its attention to become so ab-sorbed in spicy bits of coffee-bar rumor and gossip that many people never got to grasp the real, inner story of the truly great work of the Council.

Cracking wise was always a tension reliever at the Council, and some of the cracks were fresh and funny, like the remark of the bishop who said: "I really don't mind if they do drop celibacy; the trouble is that marriage seems to be the only alternative!"

Or again, there was the observation that the Holy Father has had such marked success with his "peregrinations" to the Holy Land, to India, and to the United States, that he may just take up governing the Church from a plane, as a permanent arrangement, and let all this outmoded protocol go by the board. Though this was an intentional exaggeration, still there is a grain of truth in it: namely, that the Pope, having so successfully gone out to the world on three notable occasions, may continue and even increase this type of papal apostolate to men of good will in many another continent and country in the future.

Now we come to the debate on the famed schema "No. 13," as it was known. The numbering of the various schemas became changed as things developed, but the old title held on to this one, more formally known as "The Church and the Modern World."

The debate went something like this:

"Naturalism" came to be the issue: the position that *natural solutions* are the answer to the world's problems.

What the schema and those who supported it were trying to assert was this:

The Church has immense resources: Revelation and Grace (supernatural); spiritual and physical endowments (natural). The people of the world, gripped in the throes of new and gigantic problems, are looking to the Church to put these resources at the disposal of mankind in harmony and cooperation with all men of good will.

The gigantic modern problems are the problems of poverty, hunger, war, industrialism, knowledge and education, colonization and independence, problems of the modern family and the population explosion, cooperation of nations, world law, the advancement of culture, the status of women, the political community, and so forth.

The Church's possession of Truth and Grace and her desire to share these with all men is clear. It has been stated many times in many documents and is, of course, of prime importance, superseding all other considerations. It hardly needs emphasis, as though it were some new approach.

But what does need emphasis in our day is this stance, which for the Catholic Church is rather new: namely, our sympathy for and involvement in the solution of the world's problems, in cooperation with all men of good will everywhere, even on the natural level—but, of course, for religious reasons.

The Church, let us admit, in the past has not expended its resources very often or universally in this manner, with other men or other groups. Such joint efforts, it was feared in the past, might run the danger of doctrinal or moral contamination, of heresy or indifferentism. Hence, there has been in the past an excessive protectiveness, a withdrawal by the Church from the arena in which the world's problems are thrashed out.

A good example is the modern university. No one can doubt that attitudes and solutions powerfully affecting the problems of the world have, for a long time, been developed in the great secular universities. Yet it is from the great secular universities that the vast majority of the world's leaders are coming. This situation cannot but have a strong impact on the kind of solutions ultimately applied to public problems by the leaders of our day. Here is an arena from which the Church at first withdrew, but which she is now beginning to enter again in force.

The schema on the Church and the Modern World simply wanted to say:

1. We recognize the problems.
2. We sympathize with those who are suffering.
3. We are interested in actively solving the problems.
4. We possess considerable resources for doing so—first of all, *supernatural* (Truth and Grace), but also *natural* too (spiritual and physical) which we wish to place at the disposal of all.
5. We wish to collaborate with others in doing so.
6. Our possession of the one, true faith is no barrier to such cooperation; on the contrary, it is a great stimulus in this direction;
7. Finally, we recognize that there are certain natural and religious values and resources possessed by our separated brethren which they, too, can contribute to the cause of human betterment and compassion.

Now, since the Church has long insisted on her possession of Truth and Grace and offered these freely to all who would be converted to the one, true religion, there is less need to emphasize this aspect of the matter.

But an offer to cooperate with all men of good will in applying even natural solutions (and an acknowledgment that others, too, may have something to contribute to the solution of the world's problems) is rather new. Therefore, it understandably has received somewhat more attention in the schema. But this does not mean any downgrading of the fundamental mission of the Church to bring the Gospel and the Grace of Christ to souls.

Nevertheless, the charge was made, almost every day during the debate in the aula, that the schema was just too "naturalistic." The main contention, repeated by speaker after speaker, was that it did not stress the fact that *sin* is at the bottom of all the world's evils and that repentance and penance and conversion are actually the big issue of this age, as of every age.

This kind of charge was hard to handle. No one, of course, wanted to give the impression that he was minimizing in any way the truly fundamental doctrines of original sin, of personal sin, or of the saving quality of the Redemption of Christ on the world.

What the schema said was that Christ not only taught resignation to God's will, He actually cured diseases; He not only forgave repentant sinners, He broke down barriers by speaking for example to separated brethren like the Samaritan woman at the well, and by citing the Good Samaritan for an award. He was interested in the problems of the world wherever He found them.

But we, on the other hand, have allowed ourselves to become absorbed mostly in our own problems, *in strictly Catholic problems*. Now the time has come to open a lot of windows and look out at the problems of humanity which we can do so much to solve.

This was the core of the argumentation, from day to day, in the aula.

The schema on the Church and the Modern World after preliminary debate in both the third and fourth sessions was eventually accepted as a basis for a declaration. Then it was debated at the last session, section by section. Since there are ten sections, the debate was lengthy.

As the Council waded into the debate, I made the following report home on the outlook and the atmosphere in which it was being debated:

"Old 13" is still in commission but reaching, we hear, a compromise draft that will bring it to the floor on time with a good chance of normal passage. This means, of course, that it is undergoing quite a bit of revision, changing it from its too specific former character to something less precise in terms of its solution for the world's ills.

No doubt this is as it should be. Nevertheless, I'm afraid there will be great anguish and gnashing of teeth among those who have come to expect the text on the Church and the Modern World to step in and solve their favorite problem. For example, here in Italy I have heard continually—from Bologna to Rome—that this document should certainly take up the question of divorce Italian-style (i.e., divorce is not permitted at all, even civilly, in accord with the Lateran Treaty between the Italian government and the Holy See).

Obviously, the schema could not deal with such a localized matter. But even on questions that have a truly worldwide bearing, the Council could never reach a consensus if it attempted a too particularized a solution to modern problems. For example, commission members find in their ranks what might be described as both "pacifists" and "realists," with the same strong feelings about war that you will find among the Fathers themselves. Hence, they could hardly ever reach a consensus on a document that attempted to be too specific on that subject. Moreover, a two-thirds vote in the aula would be a practical impossibility, even if the Commission did work out such a text.

Besides, commissions have to watch out for those *modi*, which can still be introduced in the voting. It is true that a vote *placet juxta modum* is a favorable vote, with a reservation attached that must be in substantial conformity with the spirit of the text as it stands. Still, there is also the vote *non placet*, which can reject the whole text or any section of the text put up for a vote. And if a text gets so specific that it spells out in detail a solution distasteful to any large number of Fathers, there is the real possibility that the text will be rejected lock, stock and barrel.

What is the prospect, then, for the Church and the Modern World? In my opinion, the text will now become neither a solemn decree nor constitution, nor even a less solemn declaration or position paper. I think it will wind up as a "Message to the World," that is, a letter expressing the concern of the Church in our day for every human problem, and her willingness to work these problems out in cooperation with all other men of good will, even on the natural level but without going into specifics.

Of course, this will greatly disappoint those who look to the

Council to really come to grips with what they consider the "big problem of the day," whether it be birth control, the status of women, war and peace, divorce in Italy or world poverty and hunger. Still, such a statement of concern—which is about all you could ever get a two-thirds vote on—will lay the foundation for future solutions in practical, post-conciliar discussion and action.

Here are some of the more striking thoughts which were voiced as the debate proceeded:

1. "Today the natural sciences seem to be imbued with a Cartesian spirit—that is, a mathematical spirit which seeks to acquire knowledge of the world mainly according to measurements, numbers and weight, etc. But we know that to understand nature profoundly and fully, other methods are also required which are capable of speaking to man in metaphysical terms, terms from which natural science abstracts. For example, a purely mathematical way of thinking will never discover the metaphysical depth of things, nor the causes which are proportionate to effects, nor the contingency and finality of things. But the scientist of our day is so accustomed to the Cartesian way of thinking that his faculty of reason seems to be diminished with respect to metaphysical reality (e.g., the reality of truth or the reality of faith)."

2. "The Council should assert that Science poses one of the greatest problems of our age for human liberty—namely, the problem of the right use of almost unlimited power which Science gives men today. The schema does not answer the growing anguish of modern science in the face of the smallness and fragility of man confronted by an immense and unfriendly universe and in the face of an ever-increasing number of discoveries whose direction and finality are unknown and disputed. Scientists, more than others, feel this anguish and are developing a greater sense of responsibility. They, better than others, are aware of the options now facing men which control the fate of the human species itself. This schema should say this: Reverence must be had for life, especially for human life; and scientists must acknowledge to-

gether the final goal of all their great work: To tell the glory of God!"

3. "I propose, concretely, that the Church launch a deep and long-term campaign of education, inspiration and moral influence to promote among Christians and all men of good will a live understanding and concern for world poverty and to promote world justice and the development of all peoples."

4. "I suggest that the economy of dispensation, such as that found in the 'Petrine Privilege,' be considered in attempting to aid the conscience of a spouse who is condemned to a life of marital solitude, through no personal fault, e.g., who has been unlawfully abandoned."

5. "The distinction between a just war and an unjust war no longer holds. You have to take into account today the *means* employed in making warfare. An offensive war, even for legitimate reasons, could be unjust because of the weapons used."

Some Fathers asked forcefully that the Council come right out and condemn altogether *any kind of war*, whether offensive or defensive, since total war today, given atomic weapons, simply means the total destruction of all involved.

However, Archbishop Philip M. Hannan of New Orleans, in his intervention at the third session, had defended the right of a nation to its own defense against unjust aggression and the right to choose warlike defense of liberty rather than succumb to slavery. And at the U.N., the Holy Father also seemed to take this position, namely, that defensive weapons, "unfortunately," are still needed. Archbishop Hannan, who had led the U.S. bishops in this position, had another intervention ready for the floor on this subject at the fourth session. However, he was required to leave the Council in order to go to New Orleans for his installation on October 13, 1965, and so had to hand his intervention in as a written statement only.

As the Council entered November, 1965, the morality of modern warfare was the great issue. One side emphasized this point: atomic warfare means total destruction and therefore solves nothing. Hence, it is not a reasonable, apt or even licit instrument for peace. This side would not say, in so many words, that even slavery is better than total destruction as a solution (because in slavery you at least have the possibility of somehow overthrowing or converting the tyrannical regime). It would only say that, whatever the possible solutions to unjust aggression, atomic warfare is not one of them.

An opposing side emphasized this point: a man is always entitled to resist the enslavement resulting from unjust aggression. Besides, it is not true that all atomic weapons involve total destruction of society; some atomic weapons are limited in their effects. Therefore, it should be stated *that war, indeed, in some circumstances, is a reasonable, apt and morally licit means of preserving the peace*, even if limited atomic weapons are used as a deterrent against a foe armed with and ready to use the same weapons. This side also felt it unfair for the Council to condemn implicitly nations which are actually engaged at present in resisting unjust aggression in various parts of the world (for example, the U.S.A. in Vietnam).

Schema 13, chapter 5, as revised, *omitted a passage that was in the original chapter*. The passage omitted said this: that the stockpiling of atomic weapons is not, in practice, to be condemned. The reaction to the dropping of this passage was interpreted differently by different bishops. Some bishops felt that the omission of the passage constituted, and was intended to be, a condemnation of those who stockpile atomic weapons. Other bishops felt that omission of the sentence did not constitute a condemnation; that now the schema neither condoned nor condemned. They said that the document as now written intended to *set a tone* which emphasizes peace and the positive approaches to it. They call it a "prophetic" tone which strives to say, like Pope Paul at the U.N.: "No more war!" while, at the same time, admitting that defensive weapons "unfortunately" are still needed.

Two thousand two hundred forty Council Fathers voted November 17 on the section on war (81–86): 2,081 voted *placet*, 144 *non-placet* and 17 ballots were void.

Then, later on the same day, a vote was taken on the whole of Chapter 5, the Promotion of Peace. When you vote on an entire chapter you may then put in reservations, and the vote went as follows: 2,227 Fathers voting—1,656 *placet,* 45 *non-placet* and 523 *placet juxta modum.*

Apparently there were less than 600 Fathers who disapproved of the text as it stood. Still a certain confusion remained. At a press panel one newsman asked the question whether a Catholic could cooperate any longer with stockpiling as a process. He was assured that the schema did not intend to condemn stockpiling as a practical measure, that it simply meant to urge everyone to work for peace by cultivating an interior approach, an attitude of soul, so rooted in love and justice that war would become regarded as a useless solution. The schema now states something like this: whatever may be said for or against this "strategy" (of stockpiling), the use of "scientific force" (i.e., atomic power) is of no help, in itself, as an instrument of peace.

On November 19, 1965, Pope Paul received the U.S. bishops (along with the Canadian bishops) in personal audience. We first assembled in the Consistorial Hall of the Apostolic Palace and were seated, some 180 strong, around the walls, which made it possible for the Holy Father to move along the line and greet each one of us individually. He made us keep our skullcaps on during the meeting, although Vatican protocol requires their removal in the Pope's presence. Felici, the photographer, followed the Pope around the room snapping photos of His Holiness with the various bishops. Then the Pope stood up on a platform and we all crowded around him for a group picture. After that, we moved into the adjoining Clementine Hall where chairs had been set out for us. Here the Holy Father sat down and talked to us in an informal manner.

Pope Paul is often visibly moved in public as he speaks on certain subjects, but he seems seldom to smile and he is said to be a little distant in his manner. In spite of this, he was warmth itself at our audience. Indeed, after speaking to us informally, with a few joking references here and there, his secretary brought up to him a text bound in red leather. At this point Pope Paul made a humorous gesture that we all enjoyed immensely; taking the bound manuscript in his hand, he adjusted his glasses, looked up and said in English: "And now, I make you a little spitch," and then, with almost a mischievous wink, he added: "Official, you know!" This was a gentle nudge at Vatican protocol which requires that, even after the Pope has been talking familiarly to the bishops for 15 minutes, in view of his position and their position, for the sake of good form, he is still expected to read a formal address to them!

The reworking of the text of the Church and the Modern World in accordance with the *modi* entered by the Fathers did not result in any really major changes in the basic meaning of any of the chapters. There were a number of *interesting* changes, however, as well as a number of interesting *refusals* by the Commission (and its sub-commissions) to make changes in the existing text. This was true especially of Chapter 5 in which war is considered.

1. Section 80 toned down the language somewhat in speaking of atomic war. Previously, terms like "under no consideration licit" had been used in speaking of the wide-spread destruction to be expected from atomic war. Now it was simply stated that atomic war can easily get out of hand and exceed "the legitimate limits of defense." This wording only *implies* that this is illicit. At the same time, it also implicitly admits that there is such a thing as legitimate defense; and that atomic weapons only *can* get out of hand—that it is only *possible* for them to do so. Strictly speaking, it does not flatly condemn all use of atomic weapons as immoral.

2. Section 80 also omits a passage from Pope John's *"Pacem in Terris"* which was found in the earlier text. This passage had said, in paraphrase, that it is unreasonable to regard war as an "apt" means of "redressing violated rights." Pope John's *exact* words would not have fitted into the tenor of the text, and the

Commission felt that *"Pacem in Terris,"* at this point, should be quoted as it stood or not at all. The art of paraphrasing was felt to be just too risky.

3. Section 80 drew fire from a group of American bishops, led by Archbishop Hannan, for saying that the possession of atomic weapons is a mighty big temptation to some nations which have such weapons to use them wrongfully.

4. Section 81 then goes on to say that atomic power tempts people to think that it is the *only* factor in preserving peace, whereas it is only a means of preserving, for a time, under certain circumstances, a *temporary stability.*

5. Section 81 further states that, whatever may be said (for or against) the effectiveness of atomic power in keeping such temporary stability in the world, atomic power itself cannot assure a certain and true peace and, moreover, actually tends to spread conflict among nations. The American bishops who are in opposition say: On the contrary, atomic power is the very thing that has stopped aggression in many parts of the world in our day. Injustice, not modern weapons, lead to war. Still, all had to admit that the new text in Section 81 no longer made snide references to "the wealthier and more powerful nations" which can afford nuclear arms!

The spirit of genuine freedom with which Council business was conducted is well illustrated by the outcome of one small written intervention asking for an emendation of the text of the sections on war. In Chapter 5, page 64, line 29, there appeared the words, "which under no circumstances can be morally right," referring to the *vast destruction* of mankind which *can be caused* by atomic weapons. One single bishop, out of some 2,300 present, entered a written request to have these words dropped from the text. His reason was that, although the moral condemnation was actually aimed at the "vast destruction," an ambiguity existed: the clause could easily be misunderstood to say that atomic weapons were immoral. Even though the request was made by one lone bishop, the commission accepted his point and removed the words from the text in its final draft, and the schema was promulgated that way.

One of the most important paragraphs in Chapter I of Schema 13 (the chapter on Matrimony and the Family)—one dealing with birth control—is now to be found in a footnote at the end of the chapter. This footnote first refers the reader to Pope Pius XI's encyclical on marriage, "*Casti Connubii*" (1930) and to Pope Pius XII's "Address to the Italian Midwives" (1951). Then the footnote cites Pope Paul VI's "Address to the Cardinals" (1964) at the time that he appointed his special commission to study and report on the new (or seemingly new) factors with a bearing on family limitation. The footnote goes on to state that certain questions which need further and more diligent investigation, by the order of the Pope, have been referred to a commission for the study of population, family and birth problems of our day. When they shall have completed their study and when they shall have reported to the Pope, then the Supreme Pontiff—and he alone—will decide the outcome.

Now, since the teaching authority of the Church had reached this stage, the Council had no intention of proposing concrete solutions immediately to such problems. The chapter, however, contains many wonderful things about marriage and the family. It would be a pity, then, were these riches obscured by a preoccupation with the question of birth control on which actually the Council had nothing to report.

One day toward the end of session four, the Holy Father was reminded by someone close to him that although a number of Council events had been held at other Roman basilicas, none had yet been held at the Basilica of St. Paul Outside the Walls. St. Paul's is more than a great basilica in Rome. It is the place at which Pope John took occasion to announce to the world for the first time, on January 25, 1959, his intention to convoke an Ecumenical Council.

Pope Paul not only agreed with the suggestion; he became enthusiastic over it. On his own, therefore, and to the delight of the Secretariat for Promoting Christian Unity and that of the non-Catholic observers, he worked out a plan to conduct a prayer service dedicated, like the Council, to the promotion of Christian unity.

The title and the program of the function, held on Saturday, December 4, at 5 P.M., was extremely interesting. The official title was: "A Prayer Service *(Sacra Celebratio)* for promoting Christian Unity, at which the Holy Father, Paul VI [not "The Supreme Pontiff"], assisted [not "presided over"] along with the Fathers of the Ecumenical Council as well as the observers and guests delegated to attend the Council."

The program was as follows:

1. *Entrance Chant:* Psalm 26 (in Latin), while the Pope entered the basilica, intoned by the Benedictine monks attached to the basilica. The whole congregation sang, between verses, the antiphon: "The Lord is my light and my salvation."

2. *Introductory Prayer:* This was an invitation to prayer, said in Latin, by the Abbot of St. Paul's. Then, after a moment of silent prayer, the Pope himself recited the Collect in Latin.

3. *Scripture Readings:* First, I Paralipomenon (Chronicles) 29: 10–18—read by an observer in his own language. After the reading, the canticle "Now Thank We All Our God" was sung in English. This hymn is found in a number of non-Catholic hymnals, but it is also used now by Catholics in some areas. Second, Romans 15: 1-6 —read by a Catholic, in the language of his country. Then there followed an "Alleluia" sung by the congregation (verses in Latin by the monks of St. Paul's). Third, Gospel: Matthew 5: 1–12 (Beatitudes), read by an observer in the language of his country.

4. *Address:* by the Holy Father.

5. *Litany:* An observer invited all to pray that God may be pleased to preserve the marvels of His power and mercy in His Church. Another observer alternated with a Catholic in announcing the various petitions, to which all responded "Kyrie eleison." These petitions were recited alternately in English and in French. The observer who made the initial invitation to prayer then recited the final prayer of the litany.

6. The Holy Father invited all to recite the Our Father in their own language.

7. *The Final Invocation:* recited by the Holy Father (in Latin). "The grace of Our Lord Jesus Christ and the love of God the Father and the communion with the Holy Spirit be with you all."

8. The Congregation sang the Magnificat (in Latin). As this chant neared the end, the Holy Father quietly left (presumably to avoid any demonstration toward himself).

It may be noted that the above Program of Prayer was a matter only of certain persons taking part, not a ceremony in which the various churches, as such, were in any way formally represented. It was a matter of special interest that the ceremony took place *in a church* and not in a secular hall of some kind.

It is hardly necessary to comment on the unique ecumenical character of this event. Apparently, it was so much a proposal advanced on his own initiative by the Holy Father himself that even the Secretariat for Christian Unity and the observers were completely taken by surprise—and delight!

At the solemn public plenary session of the Council (December 7, 1965) a declaration was read simultaneously in St. Peter's Basilica in Rome and in Istanbul, the See of Greek Orthodox Patriarch Athenagoras I. The declaration sought to end the psychological block existing between the Roman Catholic Church and the Orthodox churches of the East which grew out of a split between the two churches in the eleventh century.

The declaration was the result of studies conducted by Catholic and Orthodox scholars regarding the exchange of excommunications between Pope Leo IX and the Patriarch of Constantinople, Michael Cerularius, in the year 1054, an event which signified the beginning of the great rupture between the two Christian churches which has persisted to the present day.

The declaration was approved by Pope Paul VI and Patriarch Athenagoras I. Its public reading marked one of the most significant advances in centuries toward the ultimate goal of a reunited Christendom.

The reading of the declaration in St. Peter's was only one of a number of important events on December 7. The last four documents to be approved by the Council and the Pope were promulgated, thus becoming the newest and final fruits of four years of Council meetings.

The results of the formal voting on the last four documents were as follows:

Religious Liberty:	Yes, 2,308; No, 70; Null, 8.
Missions:	Yes, 2,394; No, 5; Null, 0.
The Church in the Modern World:	Yes, 2,309; No, 75; Null, 7.
Priestly Life and Ministry:	Yes, 2,390; No, 4; Null, 0.

December 8, 1965—the morning Vatican Council II was accorded a solemn, ceremonial closing—was a happy day in Rome. On all sides bishops and *periti*, auditors and observers, in smiling moods, exchanged warm greetings as they met in St. Peter's Square and hurried to their respective stations. Many of them said, over and over again as they walked along, that it was difficult to realize that the great Council was at last over; that it had come off amazingly well; and that it would be wonderful now to anticipate the good things the Holy Spirit had in mind in the way of future results.

As we climbed up the center steps, with the beautifully hung temporary altar, throne and seating on either side—all in the open air—someone remarked that "it must have taken a lot of faith or gall or something" to make such massive preparations outdoors on a December day in Rome. But the weather was nearly perfect—with a soft, brilliant sun above and a pleasant, cool breeze blowing just strong enough to send a skullcap flying every now and then.

One must give great credit to those who plan these immense Vatican functions. Some people have little taste for all the baroque trappings, but taken as a whole these massive and intricate ceremonies are brought off with a fine flair, a sense of the dramatic, and an impressive religious impact that are hard to beat. The crowd itself is one of the most important props. People cluster like moss on the top of every available building overlooking the square, particularly the great Bernini colonnades on either side which often serve as a skating rink for the boys in the Sistine Choir. And then there is that vast sea of humanity rolling out of St. Peter's Square into the Via della Conciliazione, with everyone breathlessly awaiting the entrance of the Holy Father—an entrance traditionally greeted with "Vivas" from a hundred thousand throats.

The Holy Father said a Low Mass in which there was full and joyous participation. Afterward there was a well-planned program which, given the importance of the occasion and the traditional Roman manner, naturally occupied two hours. Next day the press said, "With three short words—'Go in Peace'—Pope Paul ended the four-year Council today." To which one bishop responded: "Three short words! Yes, after three million other short words!" For first of all, there was the Holy Father's own parting message; then there was the formal reading of the decree officially closing the Council; then there was the blessing of the altar stone to be used in the new church to be built commemorating the Council, in a needy section of Rome; and then a few more appropriate ceremonies.

There were some memorable moments in the ceremony. It was impressive to watch the Holy Father, at the elevation, raising the Sacred Host and the Chalice in the sunshine and slowly turning until he had held them, with arms extended, to face each section of his vast congregation, north, south, east, and west. And it was moving to hear words spoken by various cardinals, messages to all classes of mankind, while representatives of each group approached the Holy Father to be greeted and blessed by him. There was Jacques Maritain, his white hair blown around in the breeze, representing the intellectuals; there were three ladies, including the wife of the President of Italy and Miss Monet, the first female auditor, representing the women of the world; and there was even a workman from Milan dressed symbolically in his overalls, and a man with a seeing-eye dog on leash, representing the sick and afflicted.

Finally, following the appearance of six little children from the six continents of the world, there came forward six bishops—Council Fathers from the same continents—to sing out the parting acclamations or expressions of joy over the great work completed. I could not help but note that care was taken to back up the bishops, unobtrusively, with six strong-voiced members of the Sistine Choir, so that the acclamations rang out over the square with power and excellent quality.

Then came the Holy Father's final blessing and his dismissal, "Go in Peace!" And the Second Ecumenical Council of the Vatican was gloriously launched down the runways into the sea of history.

What are my feelings, as a bishop—as a Council Father who participated in Vatican II from beginning to end—now that the great four-year gathering in Rome is closed and finished?

First of all, I think it would be unrealistic to attempt to judge the accomplishments of Vatican II, as they stand now, unless one did so against the hopes and expectations we entertained as we assembled for the first time back on October 11, 1962. From this perspective, I feel that Vatican II not only accomplished its objectives, it more than did so. These very objectives were enlarged and enriched as the days of the Council went by, and as the Fathers grew in understanding of what the world needed from them and as they began to see what is really possible at a council.

Next, I think the Council has had great success already in winning a favorable response from all sorts of persons and groups outside the Church. I find on all sides an attitude of willingness to believe that the Catholic Church has been sincere all along in her avowed intention of reforming and renewing all things within herself which called for self-examination and self-improvement. This is no small accomplishment.

Finally, I can foresee ahead certain difficulties and vast labors for all the forces within the Church in their attempt first to understand and then to carry out the proposals of the Council. On the one hand, action should keep pace with the state of men's minds in some respects: in some areas it will be necessary to educate well before moving ahead. Yet, in other respects—for example, liturgy—our people, and even our priests, will learn and come to feel natural "by doing."

One thing is certain: we have stimulating, exhilarating days ahead of us. Bishops have returned to their dioceses greatly encouraged, and with high hopes of what the Holy Spirit has in store—not just for the world at large, but for their own dioceses. These bishops have returned with sixteen documents tucked under their arms, but anxiously wondering just how to go about getting their priests and people to digest them carefully. For the problem of education now looms before them, and it is not an easy problem to solve.

The more imaginative, energetic, and articulate heads of dioceses in the U.S. have already given to the press interesting indications of how they intend to push forward. Some have announced that they will hold "Little Councils"; others have declared that advisory conferences of laymen, religious and priests will be set up without delay; still others have wondered aloud about how one goes about establishing a "Presbyterium" (or synod of priests) in the diocese, such as that referred to in *De Ecclesia.* Nearly all have something up their sleeves which will involve the enlightened action of laity, priests and religious more extensively than ever before, according to the spirit of the Council, in the planning and carrying out of a renewed apostolate in their dioceses.

For all of us bishops I plead for a little time. Pope Paul doesn't leave anything on his desk for long, and we bishops who have been "over there" won't either.

It was good to return home again after the Council closed. Nevertheless, come fall 1966 we bishops will miss the return to the now familiar haunts of Rome, the brother-bishops we got to know so well there, the *periti* who rendered us such excellent assistance, and the daily scene on the Council floor.

On our last night in Rome St. Peter's was empty; the coffee bar was closed for good; the carpenters were waiting to pull down the seats and tribunes in the aula. Vatican II had passed into history; but it will be a long time before we will ever forget the familiar accents of Archbishop Felici, the Secretary General, pleading with the Fathers to stay in their seats and not repair to the coffee bar until after the voting. And how can we forget the profound experience, the lofty inspiration, the extensive education and the fraternal bonds which, in God's goodness, we enjoyed as secondary benefits of that the Council which Pope John, in an inspired hour, was prompted to convoke for the good of the Church and of all mankind?

Now, let us join together in prayer, study and in labor to bring to realization the primary benefits of the Council which are the reform and renewal of the Church in our day!

God be with you!

Bishop of Baton Rouge